S. M. Burnham

The Roman's Story in the Time of Claudius I..

S. M. Burnham

The Roman's Story in the Time of Claudius I..

ISBN/EAN: 9783337042158

Printed in Europe, USA, Canada, Australia, Japan

Cover: Foto ©Lupo / pixelio.de

More available books at **www.hansebooks.com**

THE
ROMAN'S STORY

IN

THE TIME OF CLAUDIUS I.

BY

S. M. BURNHAM, M. A.

Author of " STRUGGLES OF THE NATIONS." "PLEASANT MEMORIES OF FOREIGN TRAVELS." "LIMESTONES AND MARBLES." "PRECIOUS STONES."

ILLUSTRATED

"Ecce Agnus Dei."

"There shall come a Star out of Judah,
A Sceptre shall rise out of Israel."

BOSTON
A. I. BRADLEY & COMPANY
1898

PREFACE.

This story treats of a subject that has awakened the attention of the world for ages, and engaged the thoughts of many writers at different periods, yet it has never been exhausted and something new may be developed at every investigation.

The sacred writers are more or less concise in their description of the events of their times, and in their biographical narratives they frequently omit details that are of great interest. In the life of Christ, only a very few incidents are related about him until he was thirty years of age, when he entered upon his public ministry, but no thoughtful person supposes the years previous to that event were without occurrences of special interest connected with his life, though no authentic record has come down to us. Traditions of various kinds there have been, but they have neither "sense nor reason."

In this story of his life, some things recorded are fancies, but they were intended to be consistent with his character and the Scripture records. The condition of the world at the time of the Saviour's advent has been described according to the accounts of contemporary, authentic historians. The introduction of the Roman is, of course, purely imaginary, yet it is what might have happened at the beginning of the Christian Era, when Palestine was under the dominion of the Roman Empire.

The method pursued of arranging the miracles, parables, and discourses of Christ in separate divisions, and describing the places where they occurred was intended to assist the memory and awaken an interest in these localities. The advantage of a special study of the earthly life of our Saviour cannot possibly be fully estimated. Daily reading may be a benefit, but it needs to be *studied* carefully, constantly and prayerfully.

The author has depended largely upon the Scriptures for thoughts on the subject, with the exception of consulting a commentary on some special text in regard to its signification, but has not read any of the biographies of our Lord that have been written by uninspired writers. The work was begun some time ago, but not completed until recently.

Repetitions sometimes occur because necessary to illustrate different subjects that are introduced in the narrative.

The author is aware that the narrative is open to criticism on various accounts, especially for the reason that some things stated are not recorded in the Scripture, and the question may arise, is it proper to introduce fancies in writing upon sacred themes? It was intended that the imaginary scenes and events should be consistent with truth and the nature of the subject, and the reader can examine the Biblical narrative and ascertain what are facts and what are fancies.

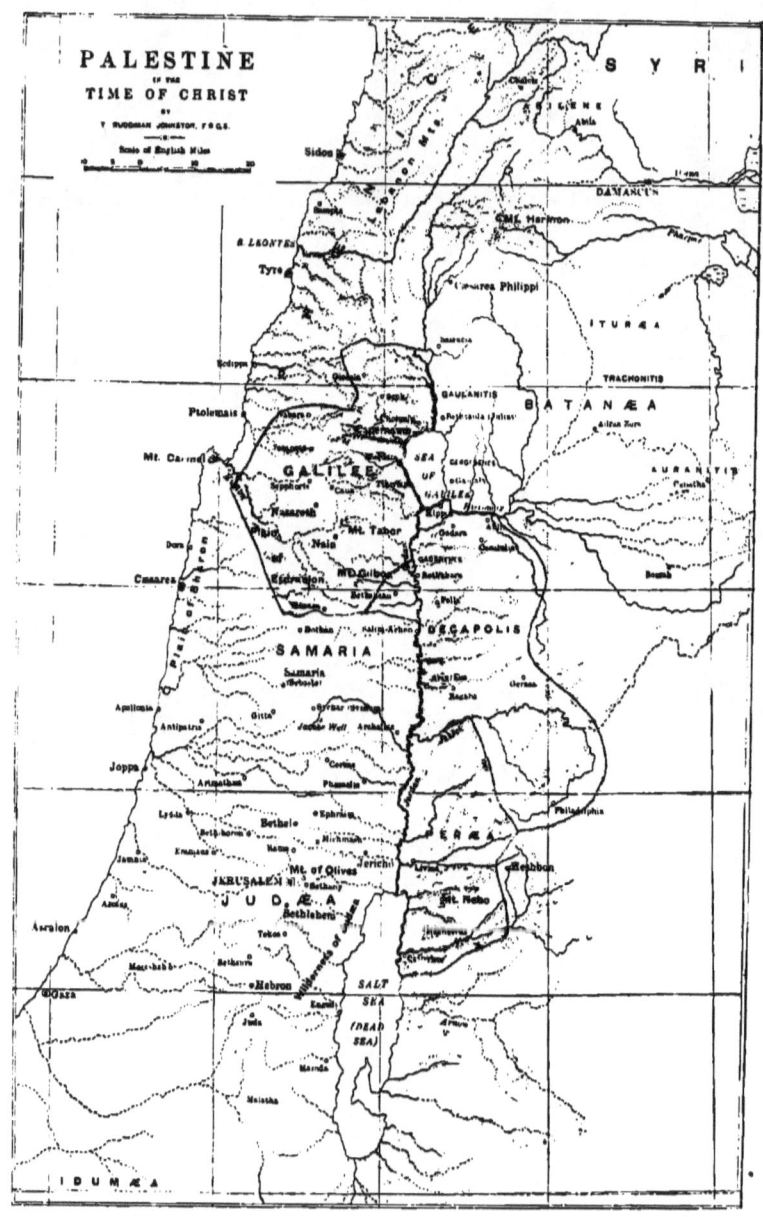

INTRODUCTION.

THE ROMAN EMPIRE AT THE BEGINNING OF THE PRESENT ERA.

POMPEY, the Roman general, having conquered Syria, Phœnicia and some adjacent countries, invaded Palestine, laid siege to Jerusalem, and after three years captured the city, 63 B. C.

The conqueror was given a triumph at Rome in which three hundred and twenty-two princes and twenty-one kings appeared as captives. During his campaign he had taken one thousand fortresses, nine hundred towns and eight hundred ships; had brought twelve million foreigners under the dominion of Rome and placed $25,000,000 in her treasury.

When Pompey, surnamed the Great, invaded Palestine, the Jews refused to submit to the Romans, and closed the gates of Jerusalem, therefore the conqueror laid siege to the city and after a prolonged contest captured it, entered the Temple and penetrated to the "Holy of Holies," a desecration the Jews regarded with horror, since no one was ever allowed to enter except the High Priest, and he was permitted to do so only once a year.

In the war between Pompey and Cæsar, the battle of Pharsalia, 48 B. C., was decisive, giving the supremacy to the latter, when he was made dictator, and was the first ruler to bear the distinguished title of Cæsar. The contest between Antony and Octavius ended in the overthrow of the former, and the establishment of the Roman Empire with Octavius as the first emperor—Augustus being his title and not his name. He was the son of Octavius and Atia, a daughter of Julia, the sister of Julius Cæsar, therefore the nephew of the great conqueror. He was born 30 B. C. and died 14 A. D. His father died when Octavius was four years old, but his education was carefully directed by his relatives.

When very young Octavius joined his uncle J. Cæsar during the campaign against the sons of Pompey in Spain; thence was sent to Illyricum to receive a practical training in military affairs, and while here news was received of the assassination of his uncle Julius at Rome, when, with a few associates, he immediately left for Italy. Arriving at Brundusium he learned that his uncle had adopted him as his heir, when he assumed the name of Cæsar, and was saluted as such by the soldiers.

Though only twenty years of age at this time, he exhibited extraordinary tact and prudence in the management of public affairs, which were in a very perplexing and dangerous condition. There was a want of union between him and Antony, but eventually they became reconciled and it was arranged that the authority should be divided among Octavius, Antony and Lepidus under the title of Triumvirate, but a war soon followed, and after the battle of Philippi there was another division of the provinces of the Roman Republic. The competition for the mastery of the world was now between two rivals, namely, Antony, who was to rule the East, and Octavius, the West. As might have been expected, friendly relations between the leaders were soon interrupted, and the battle of Actium, 31 B. C., virtually ended the Roman Republic, when the Roman Empire came into existence, though Octavius was not invested with imperial authority under the title of Augustus until 28 B. C. This honor was conferred upon him by the Roman Senate and people to express their reverence for him.

The Republic had existed four hundred and seventy-eight years, while the Empire continued to flourish until 180 A. D., when it began to decline.

The establishment of the Roman Empire has been considered a remarkable political achievement. The government of

Octavius Augustus was a monarchy in fact, but a republic in form. His dominions extended from the Atlantic to the Euphrates, and from the forests of Germany to the Arabian and African deserts, comprising in all a population of one hundred million people, including almost every variety of race and civilization. His government was tranquil; the Temple of Janus, always shut in time of peace, was, during his reign, closed three times. Such an era was eminently fitted for the advent of the Prince of Peace.

At the beginning of the Christian Era Palestine was divided as follows: On the north was Syria, or the Tetrarchy of Abilene, under the government of Lysanius; on the east of the Jordan, the most northerly region was the Tetrarchy of Philip; south of this was Decapolis, or the territory of Herod Antipas, extending to the head of the Dead Sea. Still farther south was the Arabian Desert. West of the Jordan lay Phœnicia, bordering the Great Sea, or the Mediterranean; between this territory and the river was Galilee, with Samaria on the south, and still farther below, the region was called Judea. Galilee comprised the northern or upper district, named "Galilee of the Gentiles," and southern Galilee. Samaria, nearly in the centre of Palestine, did not extend to the sea on the west, while Judea included the region from Samaria to Arabia Petrea, and from the Dead Sea to the Mediterranean. Perea, the territory beyond the Jordan, that is, east of it, comprised eight provinces or cantons, namely, Perea in a more limited sense, Gilead, Decapolis, Gaulonitis, Batanea, Auronitis or Iturea, Trachonitis and Abilene.

Galilee was the most extensive region of Palestine, and comprised the territory of Issachar, Zebulun, Naphtali, Asher, and a part of Dan in the division of the land after its conquest by the Israelites. "Galilee of the Gentiles" was so called on account of the number of immigrants from other countries, as Egypt, Arabia and Phœnicia. According to Josephus, it contained much wealth and paid high taxes. Though the natives were brave and high-spirited, they were inclined to sedition and rebellions. Their customs and dialect were different from those of Judea, and they were regarded with contempt by the inhabitants of the latter country, so that the name Galilean was given to the Saviour as a term of reproach.

Since Palestine had become a province of the Imperial Government, it is important to understand the rank and office of the Roman governors. After the conquest, certain provinces were governed by a class of magistrates called tetrarchs, meaning a fourth, an office that originated with the Gauls. The name was subsequently given to any ruler subject to a king or emperor, without reference to the fact that he governed one-fourth of a people or region. Herod Antipas and Philip were denominated tetrarchs, though they did not rule one-fourth of the country.

Proconsuls governed Judea after the reign of Herod Agrippa. They were sometimes Roman knights and sometimes freedmen. Both Felix and Festus belonged to the latter class.

Procurators were officers sent by the emperor to the provinces reserved for his special use to exact tribute, administer justice, and repress seditions. Some of the procurators were dependent upon the proconsuls, though they exercised great power, even over life and death.

The military force comprised six cohorts, five of them being stationed at Cesarea, and one at Jerusalem, but during the great national festivals at the capital, the procurators from Cesarea were present to maintain order.

A cohort comprised from five hundred to six hundred Roman soldiers, or the tenth part of a legion, a body of infantry numbering from three thousand to five thousand men. Each cohort was divided into ten companies, and each company comprised two centuries, whose commander was styled a centurian. His rank corresponded to that of captain in modern armies.

INTRODUCTION.

A tribune was a Roman officer or magistrate chosen by the people to protect them from the oppressions of the patricians or nobles, and defend their liberties against any encroachments by the Senate and consuls. Their number was gradually increased from two to ten. There were also military tribunes, from four to six in each legion, and tribunes of the treasury.

Censors were officers of the State and were first appointed by Servius Tullius, King of Rome. They exercised great and irresponsible power, and were regarded with fear and reverence. Their duties were, first, to register the citizens and take an account of their property; second, to regulate the public morals; third, to administer the finances of the State. Cyrenius, a Roman senator, sent by the Emperor Augustus to take the census of Palestine, was afterwards appointed governor of Syria.

The Jews were always restless under the yoke of Rome, and their insubordination finally led to open rebellion, when the Romans invaded the country under Vespasian and Titus, Roman emperors, 70 A. D., captured Jerusalem, destroyed the Temple, and carried a large part of the people into captivity from which they have never returned as a nation.

Judea was first invaded by Pompey, 63 B. C., and its conquest was made more thorough, 52 B. C., when Antipater was made proconsul of Judea. His son, afterwards Herod the Great, King of Judea, was then fifteen years old; he was on the throne at the beginning of the Christian Era. The family of Herod descended from an Idumean or Edomite, whose ancestor was Esau, the brother of Jacob. Herod was born 71 B. C., and was appointed king by the Roman Government, 34 B. C., and at his death, his kingdom was divided among his sons who ruled as tetrarchs. Archelaus governed Judea, Samaria and Idumea; Herod Antipas ruled Galilee and Perea, and Philip was governor of Batanea, Gaulonitis and Trachonitis; all were subject to Rome. Archelaus was deposed by the Emperor Augustus 7 A. D., when Judea was placed under a

Roman procurator. About 31 A. D., Philip died, when his province was added to Syria, but 37 A. D., it was given to Herod Agrippa with the title of king. The territory of Abilene and that of Damascus were also added to his dominions. In 39 A. D., Herod Antipas was banished to Gaul, and his tetrarchy was added to the kingdom of Herod Agrippa, who two years later received from the Emperor Claudius the government of Judea and Samaria, thus uniting Palestine under one nominal king. On the death of Herod Agrippa, 44 A. D., the country again became a part of Syria with the name of Judea, and was governed by a procurator.

Nearly all the nations had been brought under the sway of Rome; at the beginning of the present era, intercourse between different countries was safe and easy; one language, the Greek, was very generally spoken, and the condition of the world seemed favorable for the introduction of Christianity.

The Aramæan language was the vernacular tongue of the Jews of Palestine in the time of our Saviour, and was the one he used. This language originally prevailed in Syria, Babylonia, and Mesopotamia, and has sometimes been called Syro-Chaldaic, especially in Palestine. As long as the Jewish nation maintained a political independence, the Hebrew was the language of the country, but after the conquest by Assyria and Babylonia, the Jews lost the use of their native tongue together with their national liberty. The Babylonish-Aramæan dialect supplanted the Hebrew, by degrees, and became the common language of the people, though it was partly supplanted by the Greek. The proper names of persons in the New Testament are largely Aramæan, for example, the word *bar*, meaning son, used as a prefix, and also the significant surnames to distinguish some characteristic of the person who bore them; as Boanerges, Barabbas, Cephas, and others. Some geographical names are of this kind, as Beth and En, Cephron and others, used as prefixes.

CONTENTS.

CHAPTER I.
Jerusalem 15

CHAPTER II.
Letters of Claudius 25

CHAPTER III.
The Messenger or Forerunner 32

CHAPTER IV.
The Emperor's Edict 44

CHAPTER V.
The Babe of Bethlehem 53

CHAPTER VI.
The Childhood, Youth and Manhood of Jesus . . 66

CHAPTER VII.
The Public Ministry of Christ 75

CHAPTER VIII.
Preaching in Galilee. The Apostles 84

CHAPTER IX.
The Miracles of Christ 102

CHAPTER X.
The Miracles of Christ — Continued . . . 115

CHAPTER XI
The Miracles of Christ — Continued . . . 128

CHAPTER XII.
THE MIRACLES OF CHRIST — CONCLUDED 138

CHAPTER XIII.
THE PARABLES OF CHRIST 153

CHAPTER XIV.
THE PARABLES OF CHRIST — CONTINUED 164

CHAPTER XV.
THE PARABLES OF CHRIST — CONTINUED 178

CHAPTER XVI.
THE PARABLES OF CHRIST — CONCLUDED 191

CHAPTER XVII.
DISCOURSES OF CHRIST 204

CHAPTER XVIII.
DISCOURSES OF CHRIST — CONTINUED 224

CHAPTER XIX.
DISCOURSES OF CHRIST — CONTINUED 241

CHAPTER XX.
DISCOURSES OF CHRIST — CONCLUDED 254

CHAPTER XXI.
CLOSING SCENES 263

CHAPTER XXII.
CLOSING SCENES — CONCLUDED 274

CHAPTER XXIII.
AT THE CROSS 286

CHAPTER XXIV.
THE RESURRECTION AND ASCENSION 298

ILLUSTRATIONS

1. THE GOOD SHEPHERD
2. THE NATIVITY
3. LA MADONNA DEL SILENZIO
4. THE MADONNA DI S. SISTO
5. FLIGHT INTO EGYPT
6. FLIGHT INTO EGYPT
7. THE INFANT SAVIOUR
8. CHRIST AT THE AGE OF TWELVE YEARS
9. CHRIST REASONING WITH THE SCRIBES
10. CHRIST DISPUTING WITH THE DOCTORS.
11. JOHN THE BAPTIST IN THE WILDERNESS
12. CHRIST. By Carlo Dolce
13. CHRIST AND HIS MOTHER
14. JESUS, MARTHA AND MARY
15. CHRIST WITH LITTLE CHILDREN
16. LITTLE CHILDREN BROUGHT TO CHRIST
17. CHRIST PREACHING FROM THE BOAT
18. STILLING THE TEMPEST
19. THE CRY OF PETER
20. FEEDING THE MULTITUDE
21. THE TRANSFIGURATION
22. CHRIST LAMENTING OVER JERUSALEM

23. THE WOMAN OF SAMARIA
24. THE DAUGHTER OF JAIRUS
25. CHRIST ENTERS JERUSALEM AS A CONQUEROR
26. THE LAST SUPPER
27. PETER DENYING CHRIST
28. CHRIST LEAVING THE PRÆTORIUM
29. THE CROWN OF THORNS
30. CHRIST ON CALVARY
31. THE CRUCIFIXION
32. DESCENT FROM THE CROSS
33. DESCENT FROM THE CROSS
34. THE WOMEN AND THEIR DEPARTED LORD
35. A SHEPHERD AT THE CROSS
36. THE RESURRECTION
37. EASTER MORNING
38. SUPPER AT EMMAUS
39. THE ASCENSION OF CHRIST

MAP OF PALESTINE. In the time of Christ
PLAN OF JERUSALEM. In the time of Christ

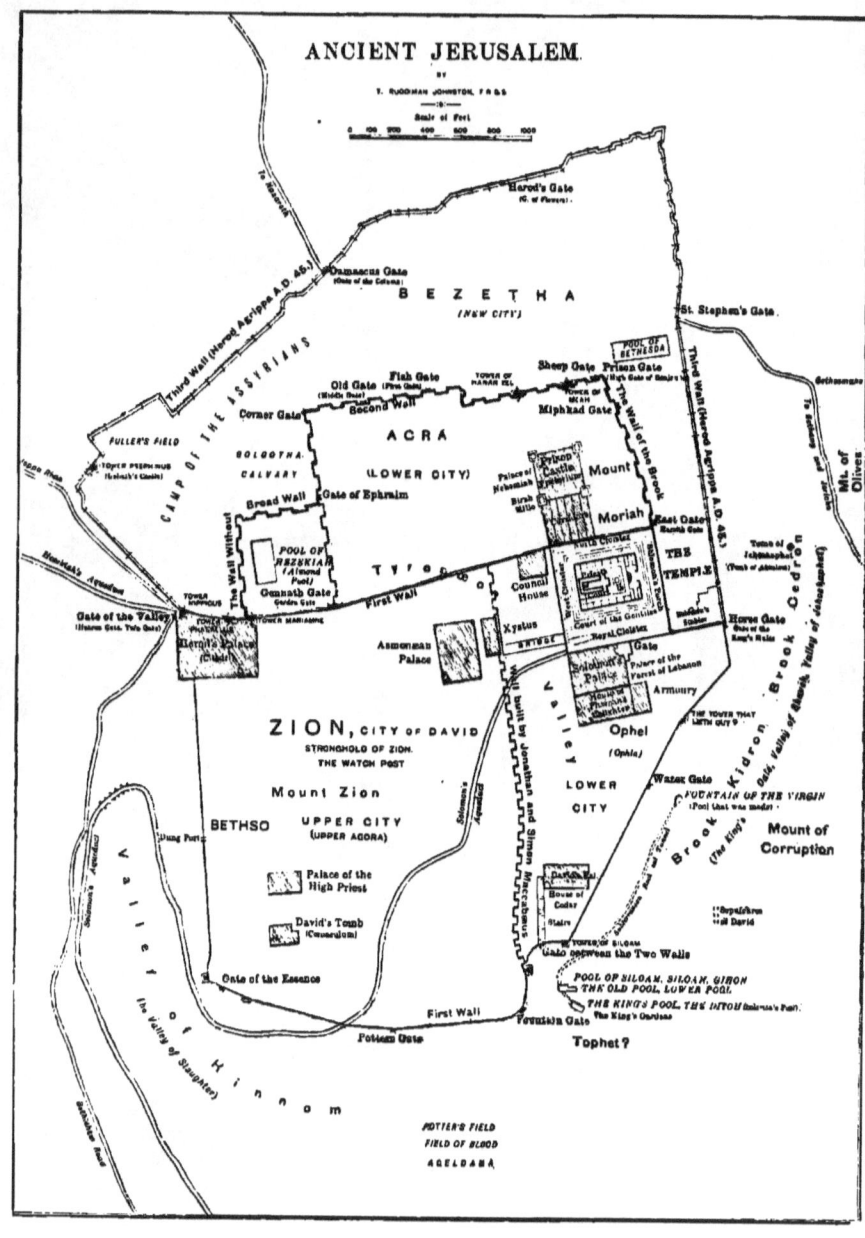

CHAPTER I.

JERUSALEM.

A GENERAL description of the capital of Palestine, the most interesting and celebrated city of the ancient world, where the most important and remarkable events have occurred, is necessary in order to understand the history of the Jewish nation and the scenes connected with the life of Christ.

Jerusalem, or Salem, as it was sometimes called, is a very ancient city, and was the home of Melchizedec, who is styled "King of Salem," in the Scriptures. It was in the possession of the Jebusites until captured by David, when it eventually became the sacred city of the Hebrews, the capital of their country, and the centre of Jewish worship where the temple was built. The ancient city called Jebus, taken by David, was small compared with the later one named Jerusalem, meaning "the abode of peace." The older town occupied an elevation opposite Mount Sion or Zion, where David built a new one called the "City of David," containing a royal palace.

The region about the city was barren, but well-watered by the brook Cedron and the fountains of Gihon and Siloam. The Temple of Solomon was built on

Mount Moriah, one of the small hills belonging to Mount Zion.

Until the close of Solomon's reign, Jerusalem was the metropolis of the whole Jewish nation, and became noted for its wealth and splendor. As an evidence of its riches David left an immense sum of gold comprising 21,600,000 pounds sterling, and 3,150,000 pounds of silver, for religious purposes, and Solomon acquired 3,240,000 pounds of gold during a single voyage of his ships to Ophir. Silver was so abundant in Jerusalem at that period, it was not considered of much account. During the reign of this prince the capital was distinguished above all other cities of the period for wealth and commercial importance, but later, on account of its civil and foreign wars, its wicked rulers, and its idolatrous practices, it was subjected to a series of calamities for more than nine centuries, that no other city can afford a parallel.

During the reign of Rehoboam, the son and successor of Solomon, ten tribes revolted and established a separate kingdom, leaving only the tribes of Judah and Benjamin that formed the Kingdom of Judah. Four years later Jerusalem was taken and plundered by Shishak, King of Egypt, and in less than a century and a half after this event the city suffered from an invasion by Joash, King of Israel.

The next peril was from the East. Sargon or Esarhaddan had become master both of the Assyrians and the Chaldeans, when he sent Tartan, that means his commander-in-chief, to Palestine, who captured Manassah, the son of Hezekiah, the fifteenth king of Judah, put him in chains, and took him a prisoner to Babylon. To this time Manasseh's life had been fearfully wicked, but while in Babylon he was led to repent of his sins, and after returning to Jerusalem, he effected great reforms in religion, and fortified the capital, which was called the "Second City."

Jerusalem was captured by Pharaoh, King of Egypt, during the reign of Josiah, less than seventy years after the last invasion. At one time it was attacked by Ptolemy of Egypt during the Sabbath, when the Jews would offer no resistance, on account of the day, and 100,000 prisoners were captured. This city was besieged three times by Nebuchadnezzar, King of Babylon, and the inhabitants were carried into captivity, when for seventy years it lay in ruins, but after Babylon was taken by the Medes and Persians the Jews were permitted to return to their own country and rebuild the capital and the Temple, when Cyrus the Persian restored all the vessels of gold and silver, plundered from the Jews by the Babylonians. The enemies of the Jews, however, succeeded in hindering the work, but Darius ordered it to be resumed, when it went forward until the sixth year of his reign, though the city with its walls remained unfinished until it was completed under the direction of Nehemiah, who encountered great difficulties in the work. The Samaritans attacked the workmen with weapons, in order to interrupt their labors, but they persevered, working with a tool in one hand, a defensive weapon in the other, until in fifty-two days the wall was completed, 445 B. C. After this achievement the city was gradually restored and remained under the protection of the Persian Empire until this power was overthrown by Alexander the

Great, some years later. After his death, Judea, with its capital, came under the dominion of the rulers of other nations, called by Daniel the prophet the kings of the North and of the South, first to one and then to the other. Discord and corruption prevailed, the office of High Priest was sold to the highest bidder, while some of the Jews forsook the religion of their fathers and adopted that of the Greeks.

Antiochus Epiphanes, King of Syria, 170 B. C., plundered Jerusalem and killed, it has been estimated, 80,000 Jews, and two years after he sent Apollonius with an army, who threw down the walls, erected fortifications, and cruelly oppressed the people. He then attempted to abolish the Jewish religion by an edict commanding all the inhabitants to conform to the Greek mode of worship, and at the same time he placed a statue of Jupiter Olympus on the Jewish altar. These stringent laws aroused the spirit of opposition, when Judas Maccabæus with some followers arose in arms against the Syrians and defeated the generals of Antiochus, recovered Jerusalem, purified the Temple and the sacred places that had been defiled three years by pagan idolatry. Several members of the family of Maccabæus held the position of sovereign and High Priest at the same time Jerusalem was free from Syrian control though it was twice besieged, first by Antiochus Epiphanes, and afterwards by Antiochus Sidetes. Hyrcanus threw off the Syrian yoke 130 B. C. and reigned twenty-one years. Judas, who succeeded him, made important changes, and assumed the title of King, which was adopted by *his* successors, but after a period of little less than fifty years a dispute arose between

Hyrcanus II and his brother Aristobulus, which resulted in the success of the latter, and he occupied the throne until the Roman conquest under Pompey, when Jerusalem was captured and Judea was made a Roman province, 63 B. C.

The Kingdom of Israel established after the revolt during the reign of Rehoboam continued about two hundred and fifty years, or from 975 B. C. to 721 B. C., when it was conquered by the Assyrians. The Kingdom of Judea, under eighteen different sovereigns, maintained its existence one hundred and thirty-three years longer, when it was overthrown by the Babylonians 588 B. C.

Julius Cæsar, having defeated Pompey his rival, appointed Antipater governor of the country, an Idumean by birth but a Jewish proselyte. He was the father of Herod the Great who reigned at the beginning of the Christian era. After the siege and capture of Jerusalem by Pompey, it remained in ruins about forty-seven years, when the Emperor Hadrian began to rebuild it. He erected a heathen temple and dedicated it to Jupiter Capitolinus and named the city Ælius after himself. The population comprised a larger number of pagans than Jews, until the time of Constantine the Great, about 323 A. D., who, having made Christianity the religion of the Roman Empire, restored the ancient name of Jerusalem to the city, and constructed many Christian churches and other edifices. About thirty-five years later, Julian the Apostate, who had abjured the Christian religion, attempted to rebuild the Temple, to prove that the prophecy affirming it should never be restored was false. He engaged a large number of workmen to lay the foundation, but was checked in his attempt by the interposition of Divine Providence, witnessed both by pagans and Jews. It is said flames of fire issued from subterranean caverns and killed many of the workmen, so the plan was abandoned.

Jerusalem continued in nearly the same condition until the seventh century A. D., when it was taken and plundered by Chosroes, King of Persia, and many Christians were killed or sold as slaves. The Persians were soon after defeated by the Emperor Heraclius, who recovered the city and restored it to the Christians, but the Jews were not allowed to come within three miles of it. The Mahommedan sect arose about this time, or the first of the seventh century, and conquered the greater part of the East. Caliph Omar, the third leader after Mahomet, besieged Jerusalem, and by prolonging the siege, the city, on account of great suffering and fearful crimes within its walls, capitulated, 637 A. D., and has been in possession of the Moslems ever since, except during a short period under the Crusaders.

The time when the pre-historic city was founded is very remote, for during the wars of Joshua it had a king named Adoni-Zedeck, who originated the league to conquer the Gibeonites. The first allusion to its site was under the name of "The Land of Moriah," to which Abraham was directed to go and offer his son Isaac as a burnt sacrifice. The city is situated among a central chain of mountains, thirty-three miles from the Great Sea and twenty-four from the River Jordan. As early as the Hebrew invasion, it was styled "a royal city," and it is referred to as the "city of strangers," meaning those not Israelites.

Jerusalem, in its prosperous condition, occupied the summits of four hills, namely, Zion on the south, Moriah on the east, Acra in the centre, and Berzetha on the northwest. The whole city was surrounded by deep, perpendicular ravines, where it was not protected by walls. The hills of Zion and Acra faced each other and were separated by a valley. The hill on which the "Upper City" was built being higher than the other, was called a fortress by David, on account of its strength. The natural supply of water for the city was augmented by a reservoir in the ancient part, perhaps the same as the Pool of Gihon where Solomon was annointed king. The only perennial spring is that of Siloam, and the only stream near, called the Brook of Cedron or Kedron, is in a deep and rugged ravine through which a torrent descends to the Dead Sea after heavy rains. A reservoir, northeast of the site of the Temple, is supposed to have been the Pool of Bethesda, meaning "House of Mercy."

This remarkable city has been captured and plundered *seventeen* times at least, and according to some writers, twenty-four times, and millions have been slaughtered within its walls, yet it still remains. During the time of Christ, it seemed to be at the height of its glory, and was the pride of the nation. It has been estimated there were as many as 2,000,000 persons who attended the festivals at Jerusalem at this time, so that the city and surrounding villages were thronged with visitors on such occasions. It is not surprising that Jesus, who knew what terrible calamities were about to come upon the city, wept over it. The Temple at this period was called the " Second Temple " and was enclosed by courts. That of the Gentiles covered about fourteen acres, and around this court were marble colonnades supported by four rows of pillars, and covered by a roof of cedar. These colonnades were known as Solomon's Porch and sometimes were called Herod's Porch, which afforded shelter for traders and their merchandise. Here the money-changers sat by their small, portable tables, with platters or trays to hold the money, and it was such as these Jesus upset when he said, "Make not my Father's House a house of merchandise." The yearly tax for the Temple was half a shekel, a coin of uncertain value as now understood, and it was necessary to pay it in the national currency, therefore strangers from different countries were obliged to exchange their foreign coin for Jewish money. The Temple of Christ's day was the one rebuilt by the Herods; the work begun in 20 B. C. was completed by Herod Agrippa 64 A. D.

The city of Jerusalem has furnished metaphors for an exalted spiritual state, and it sometimes denotes the union of all God's people in one church. The command of Jesus to his disciples was to go into all the world and preach the gospel, beginning at Jerusalem. Heaven is considered the seat of the New Jerusalem, as the author of the Book of Revelation describes a new city by that name, after the destruction of the earthly one. He speaks of the city of God, the New Jerusalem, the celestial city that had no temple or any other peculiarity of the Jewish service. The New or Heavenly Jerusalem has been the theme of

THE NATIVITY.

Christian poets in all ages and among different nations, while their hymns on the subject are used in the churches. John the Evangelist describes a wonderful city shown him in his vision by the angel, while he was an exile in the Island of Patmos. It occupied a square of 12,000 furlongs or 1,500 miles and was enclosed by a wall equal in height to its length and breadth. It had twelve gates each formed of a single pearl, three gates on every side guarded by angels, one stationed at each, and on these gates were the names of the twelve tribes of Israel. The walls had twelve foundations with the names of the apostles inscribed on them. They resembled the jasper stone in lustrous beauty, and were decorated by twelve species of gems of different colors in the following order, beginning with the lowest, namely, jasper, sapphire, chalcedony, emerald, sardonyx, sardius, chrysolite, beryl, topaz, chrysoprase, jacinth and amethyst. The streets of the city were paved with gold.

There was no temple in the city described by the evangelist, as in the earthly Jerusalem, neither was it lighted by the sun, moon, or any other of the celestial bodies, but it was illuminated by the glory of God and the Lamb; neither were the gates ever closed as there was no night there, nor was anything permitted to enter that would do any harm, for all evil spirits and all wicked human beings were excluded, and only those were admitted whose names were written in the Book of Life. A gentle river of pure water clear as crystal flowed from between the throne of God and the throne of his Son, while there grew on both sides of this river a "tree of life" yielding twelve different kinds of fruit every month, and the leaves of the tree possessed medicinal qualities adapted to heal all human maladies. The inhabitants of this remarkable city were permitted to see God "face to face," a privilege no earthly being had ever been allowed, while His name was inscribed upon their foreheads. This wonderful city was called the *New* Jerusalem in distinction from the *Old* city by that name, and it contained the mansions Christ went to prepare for his disciples, who will be crowned, to begin a reign that will be eternal.

CHAPTER II.

LETTERS OF CLAUDIUS.

ONE of the officers in the Roman army whose name was Aurelius Pompilius, remained in Palestine after the conquest, and was appointed to a civil office by the Roman Government. His son Claudius was a native of the country, born 20 B. C., or sixteen years before the birth of Christ, whose advent occurred four years before the beginning of the present era. Though young Claudius had been trained in the pagan religion of his countrymen, yet by coming in contact with the Jewish people, and learning something of their religious belief and mode of worship, he began to question the heathen system, and after much thought on the subject, came to the conclusion that there was only one God, the Creator of all things, hence idolatry, which enjoined the worship of many gods, must be offensive to Him. As the result of his reflections he renounced the religion of his ancestors and became a Jewish proselyte.

Having succeeded his father as an officer of the Roman Government, he had an opportunity of visiting all the different regions of Palestine and becoming familiar with their natural features, the character of the inhabitants, their customs and occupations. These advantages were of great importance to him in recording the events of the thirty-three years of the life of Christ, whose remarkable history was recorded by this Jewish proselyte, who himself became a disciple of Jesus, in a series of letters written to his friend and kinsman, Justinian, living at Rome. These records were made during the reign of the Emperor Tiberius, and in the Greek language, the common mode of communication at that period, though the author had become familiar with the Aramean, which was generally spoken in Palestine by the common people. Some of his ideas he acquired from the Jews or other nations living in that country, but to most of the scenes described he was an eye-witness.

The letters of Claudius, written upon vellum, were found in Rome many years after, and translated into English with explanations and additions illustrating the subject. These records treated of the natural features of Palestine, its political condition, with a sketch of its rulers, the religious sects of the Jews, the history of John the Baptist, the prophecies concerning the Messiah, the life of Mary and Joseph, the decree of Augustus and the registration; the journey to Bethlehem with a description of the town, the birth of Jesus; the shepherds and the Wise Men, Herod's policy and what followed, the escape into Egypt, the bloody decree and the great lamentation, the recall and journey to Nazareth with a description of the city; Christ's first visit to Jerusalem, his life until thirty years of age, his public ministry, his sufferings, death, resurrection and ascension.

The description of Nazareth, the home of the parents of Jesus, is briefly as follows. It was a small town in the southern part of Galilee, lying about half-way between the Jordan and the Great Sea with Mount Tabor on the east and the snow-covered mountains of Hermon and Carmel on the west. It was situated on an elevated site with a precipice on one side and was enclosed by hills and mountains. The position of the town afforded a magnificent prospect to a thoughtful admirer of nature, and here, amid these grand and beautiful scenes, Jesus spent the first thirty years of his life, and after he entered upon his public labors he preached in the synagogue at Nazareth where the citizens, notorious for their wickedness, would not listen to him, and on one occasion, they attempted to throw him over the precipice in order to kill him, but he escaped out of their hands. Such was the home of Mary, the young Jewess, whose history is blended with the most remarkable events that ever occurred on earth. There was another individual of the tribe of Judah, the same as that of Mary, whose history is connected with that of her Son, — Joseph the son of Jacob and grandson of Matthan, to whom this Hebrew maiden was affianced. Both descended from the royal house of David and both were natives of Bethlehem, a town of Judea, about seventy-five miles south of Nazareth.

There lived in this southern town, according to the Roman's story, a man of the tribe of Judah, named Levi, whose wife was called Anna. Their family included several children, the youngest being named Mary. She was a remarkable child, attractive both in personal appearance and character, while her loving, confiding and obedient disposition won the affections of all her acquaintances. Her parents, being devout worshippers of the God of Israel, had trained their children in all the observances of the Mosaic law. Mary from her early childhood manifested a devout spirit and an aversion for the pleasures that so often prove a snare to the young, while her gentleness, obedience and affection made her an example for the other members of the family. Her pious mother faithfully instructed her in social and domestic duties, and her father taught her the history of her nation and the writings of the prophets, especially those relating to the coming Messiah. whom his countrymen were expecting would soon appear.

When Mary reached the age of womanhood, her family left Bethlehem of Judea and went to Nazareth, perhaps with the expectation of improving their financial condition. The Jews, at this period, had been subject to Rome for a considerable time and, though they had been deprived of their national independence, their capital had been taken and their beautiful Temple profaned, yet they could not forget their former glory and prosperity, and were expecting a prince and conqueror to appear who should free them from their enemies, and restore their eminent position among nations.

While Mary was at Nazareth she become affianced to Joseph according to Jewish forms. The father of the family selected companions for his children, both sons and daughters, but if a son had a preference for any one, he asked *his* father to obtain the consent of the maiden's father to the marriage, but a father could not

LA MADONNA DEL SILENZIO.

dispose of his daughters without the consent of their brothers. If there were no brothers, the daughters who became heiresses to an estate were compelled to marry some kinsman of their own tribe. The marriage vow was a covenant between the father and brothers of the bride and the father of the bridegroom, made in the presence of witnesses; sometimes the covenant was committed to writing and confirmed by an oath.

The marriage presents were given to the brothers, while the dowry went to the father of the bride. There was usually a period of ten or twelve months between the contract of marriage and the celebration of the nuptials, and though there was no communication between the affianced parties, yet they were considered and spoken of as husband and wife. At the close of the probation, if the intended bridegroom was unwilling to fulfil his engagement, he was obliged to give the intended bride a bill of divorce, the same as if she had been his wife. The punishment of a woman for infidelity to her vows was death by stoning, though she might be only engaged to her intended husband.

Before the period of her engagement had expired the Angel Gabriel appeared to Mary at Nazareth to announce the birth of the Saviour. According to the custom among the Jews, the apartments of the female members of the family were in the rear chambers of the house, usually in the upper story, and sometimes they were in separate buildings kept closed to every one except the master and a trusted servant. Behind these rooms were gardens into which the inmates could look and obtain a limited view of the world outside.

Mary had retired to her apartments and was engaged

in reading the Scriptures, a duty she had faithfully observed from her early childhood. She unrolled the parchment until she came to the prophecy of Isaiah, saying that a virgin shall bear a son who shall be called Immanuel. She paused in her reading and thought, what could the prophet mean? The prediction originally applied to an event in the history of Judah, when the nation was threatened with an invasion by the combined armies of Syria and Israel under Rezin and Pekah during the reign of Ahaz. It was a critical time, and the king was in great distress, but when told by the prophet that he should be delivered, he required a sign that the Lord would fulfil his promise. It was that a virgin would become the mother of a son, and before the child was old enough to discern between good and evil the deliverance would come.

While Mary was engaged in deep thought there appeared a strange phenomenon. Though the sun had disappeared behind the mountains surrounding Nazareth, the room was filled with a bright light surpassing that of midday, and while the door was closed, there appeared a glorious being who saluted her in the language of her country, saying, "Hail! thou art highly favored: the Lord is with thee, blessed art thou among women." The quiet, gentle and humble maiden was astonished, and greatly troubled at the sudden appearance of this mysterious visitor, and wondered what could be the meaning of his extraordinary salutation. When the angel saw that she was alarmed he said, "Fear not, Mary, thou hast found favor with God; thou shalt bear a son and he shall be called the Son of the Highest." The maiden was again perplexed, inasmuch as the time of her espousals had not come. The angel then announced that her child would have no earthly father, but would be called the Son of God.

After the messenger had explained the miraculous event, Mary acquiesced in the divine will, even at the peril of being disgraced and considered deserving to suffer an ignominious death; at least she would awaken suspicions of her virtue in the mind of her affianced. This did occur, and he had the right, according to law, to make her an example by a public divorce, but being an honorable man, he intended to annul their marriage contract privately.

While thinking on the painful subject he was relieved by a communication from heaven in a dream, revealing the truth, when his confidence in his affianced was completely restored. Joseph in this instance, as in his future conduct towards Mary and her child, was gentle, tender and unselfish to a remarkable degree.

But little is known of the life of Mary's husband, but it is quite probable he died before Jesus entered upon his public ministry. When on the cross, our Lord commended his mother to the care of one of his disciples, an act implying that Joseph was not then living.

CHAPTER III.

THE MESSENGER OR FORERUNNER.

BEFORE proceeding with the story of Jesus, it is proper that the history of another individual should be given, the one who was sent as a forerunner or messenger to prepare the way of the Lord. The metaphor alluded to the custom of commanders of armies to send "forerunners" to prepare roads and remove obstacles in the way of the approaching army on its march. This messenger of the coming Messiah was John the Baptist, son of Zacharias and Elisabeth, both of the tribe of Levi, the father was a priest, and a descendant of Aaron the first High Priest. It is said of the parents of John that "they were righteous before God, walking in all the commandments and ordinances of the Lord blameless." There was, however, one blessing wanting in their family life, and one they would have highly esteemed, a child to enliven their home and perpetuate their family names. This want of descendants was considered by the Hebrews a great misfortune.

Zacharias was a priest of the course of Abia or Abijah, the eighth in the order of the twenty-four classes, of which each one officiated at the religious ceremonies one week at a time. When the priest was engaged in the ceremony of burning incense in the Temple the people were offering prayers in the court outside. The incense used was composed of valuable substances, largely of frankincense, and was burned morning and evening in the Holy Place. The altar for this purpose stood near the veil which divided the Holy Place from the Most Holy. On the north side stood the table of shew-bread, and on the south the golden candlestick. The altar of incense was eighteen inches square and three feet high, the top, sides and horns were overlaid with gold, and a crown of gold was on the lid. It was carried by rods passing through four gold rings on each side.

When Zacharias was standing by the altar at the evening sacrifice, there appeared a celestial being on the right side of it. The priest was alarmed, but the angel said, "be not afraid," and then told him his prayers were answered, and that he should be blessed with a son whose name should be called John. Gabriel, for it was he, described the character of the promised child, his mission, and the success of his labors. He was to prepare the way for the coming of the Messiah who it was expected would soon appear.

As such an event seemed improbable the priest doubted, and required a sign that the prediction would come to pass, when the angel announced the startling intelligence that he was Gabriel, sent to bring the glad tidings, and as a sign that his words were true, he, the priest, would be dumb until the prediction was fulfilled. Zacharias was chastised for his unbelief, for he should not have doubted the heavenly messenger.

The officiating priest was not accustomed to remain

in the Temple longer than half an hour when performing his duties, but on this occasion he tarried so long, the people outside became anxious and wondered why he did not come out. Their amazement was great when on his appearance, he could not speak and was compelled to communicate with them by a motion of his hand. He continued his duties at the Temple, however, until the time for his customary service had expired, when he left for his own home. It was a proof of his fidelity in the performance of his duties, that he remained after his loss of speech. The home of this aged couple was in one of the towns of Judea, probably a Levitical city. After the promised child was born the friends come to congratulate Elisabeth on the joyful occasion, and when the babe was eight days old, they named him for his father, but his mother said he should be called John. Her friends were surprised since none of his kindred were called by this name, and they made signs to the father to know his wishes about it. As he could not speak he motioned for writing material, that is, a small tablet covered with wax, and an iron pen or stile, and wrote, "his name is John," when he immediately recovered his voice and praised God. He had been dumb so long his friends supposed he had been smitten with paralysis and would never recover his speech, therefore, when his voice was restored, they were filled with awe, and the remarkable event was proclaimed throughout all the hill country of Judea, and those who heard the wonderful story exclaimed, "What manner of child will he be?"

The father was moved by the Holy Spirit to utter a prophecy concerning this child, and also on other subjects. In this poem Zacharias said, "The Lord God of Israel has visited and redeemed his people; He has raised up a horn of salvation as he had promised." The horn was the symbol of strength, and this horn was the Messiah of the house of David as predicted by the prophets. Zacharias continued, "God promised Abraham and confirmed it with an oath that he would bless his posterity." He then addressed the infant, saying, "Thou shalt be called the Prophet of the Highest, and shalt go before the face of the Lord to prepare his ways." This prophet would give salvation and forgiveness of sin, and would be a light in darkness, and a guide in the way of peace. In his prophecy, Zacharias intimates the work of John and the plan of redemption in elegant and forcible language.

John was consecrated from his birth to the sacred office of preaching the glad tidings of salvation, but as he belonged to the priestly order, he would not begin his public ministry before the age of thirty, and until then, he remained with his friends in the hill country of Hebron. Little is said by the sacred historians of his life previous to that time, though doubtless, it was spent in preparation for his divine mission; he may have assisted in the religious services of the law. As his parents were aged when he was born, they probably died while he was young. It is said of him in the Scriptures that "he waxed strong in the Spirit, and was in the deserts," that is, regions sparsely inhabited, "till the day of his showing unto Israel." After years spent in solitude, self-denial and communion with God, he acquired the discipline which prepared him for his important mission.

The prophecies concerning John the Baptist are various and striking. He was represented under the name of Elijah or Elias who, the Saviour declared, was John. His appearance and manners excited general attention; his garment was made of camel's hair and was confined about his waist by a leather girdle, a dress indicating a hermit life, and his food consisted of locusts and wild honey.

The camel yielded a fine hair from which a beautiful cloth was manufactured but he also afforded a long, shaggy hair of which a coarser and cheaper cloth was made for the poorer classes. A robe of the latter, confined by a leather girdle, was the usual dress of John. Locusts, to a great extent, supplied food for the common people. They were from two to three inches in length and resembled the grasshopper in form. Sometimes they appear in such numbers as to darken the sky and in a short time they will devour every vegetable in the region they visit. The Jews were allowed to use them for food, and some species are eaten in Oriental countries at the present day, and are considered a delicacy.

Wild honey may have been that found in the rocks of the deserts of Palestine, a land said "to flow with milk and honey." There was also a kind called wild honey or wood honey deposited by a small insect on the leaves of trees, and which dropped from them to the ground. This may have been the kind that supplied food for John. Both his raiment and food indicated his poverty.

Though he belonged to the tribe of Levi and was the son of a priest, yet he is called a prophet, or at

THE MESSENGER OR FORERUNNER. 37

least he assumed that office, but his most important mission was that of a pioneer of the coming Messiah. His preaching was decisive and very impressive; he faithfully reproved, warned and exhorted his hearers, urging them to repent, giving as a reason "the kingdom of heaven is at hand." A large number of the followers of Jesus had been first awakened by the preaching of John. His first mission station was at Betharbara beyond the Jordan, that is, on the east side, but he afterwards moved up the river to Enon, on the west side. The reason given for the change was "because there was much water there" therefore better adapted for the baptism of his disciples.

John became so popular and so eminent, that many of the Jews thought he might be the Messiah, but he decidedly affirmed he was not. He always manifested an unambitious and humble spirit, and when Jesus came to him to be baptized he declared that he was unworthy to perform the rite for one so exalted in character. His fame spread throughout the country and he was followed by persons of all ranks, sects and parties, so that the question was generally discussed whether he was not the Christ.

It is said that John came preaching in the wilderness of Judea, a region east of the Jordan and the Dead Sea. The word translated wilderness means a region covered with rocks, forests and mountains better adapted to pasture land than tillage, though it contained inhabitants and scattered villages. In the time of Joshua, there were six cities in what was called a wilderness. Had the word implied what it does at the present day, it would have been absurd to preach in such a place.

When John saw that many of the Pharisees and Sadducees came to be baptized, he addressed them in language so severe though true, it is surprising they listened to him. He called them a generation of vipers, the most poisonous of serpents and used as a figure of speech to denote cunning and malignity. The serpent was also a symbol of prudence, and was so used by Christ when he said to his disciples sent to preach the gospel, "Be wise as serpents." John said to those who came to hear him, "Who hath warned you to flee from the wrath to come?" He was surprised that sinners so hardened and hypocritical should have been awakened to their danger and induced to flee from it. "If you are sincere," said he, "bring forth the fruits of repentance, and reform your lives."

The Jews believed that because they were the descendants of Abraham they were entitled to special favors, but the preacher told them that God was able to raise up children to Abraham from stones, that is, such a thing would be easier than to make those who are proud and hypocritical, subjects of the kingdom of the Messiah, implying that the privilege of birth was of no avail without a righteous life. It has been supposed by some persons that "these stones" meant the Roman soldiers some of whom attended upon John's ministry.

The preacher, employing another figure, said, "The axe is laid at the root of the tree," indicating that the tree was to be cut down, not merely trimmed to make it bear good fruit, but to be cast into the fire. By these metaphors the idea was taught that a kingdom of righteousness was to be established; that persons would be judged by their lives, and not by birth or

THE MADONNA DI SAN SISTO.

profession. "I baptize you with water upon repentance," declared the preacher, "but He that cometh after me is mightier than I, whose shoes I am not worthy to bear or unloose." By shoes are meant sandals then used for the protection for the feet. They were made at first of wood for the soles, but later they consisted of leather, and were bound on the foot by thongs, hence the expression, "loose them." The upper part of the feet was left uncovered. Upon entering a house, the sandals were removed and left outside and in departing from it they were resumed. To loose and bind on sandals and carry them for his master was the duty of the lowest servant, therefore, when John said he was not worthy to perform this act for the Saviour, he expressed the greatest humility. The prophet continued, "He," meaning Christ, "shall baptize you with the Holy Spirit and with fire, whose fan is in his hand, and he will thoroughly purge his floor, and the wheat will be gathered into the garner, but the chaff will be burned with unquenchable fire." There has been a difference of opinion about the meaning of some of these passages. The baptism of the Holy Ghost represented a heavenly influence pervading the mind and heart, but the "baptism of fire" is not so clear. Some have supposed that it meant the afflictions and persecutions that would try men under the gospel dispensation; others, that it signified wrath and judgment, as fire is a symbol of vengeance, and again, it may have reference to the doctrines Christ would teach, as a powerful and purifying influence. Whatever John may have intended by his language, it is a fact that the truths uttered by the Saviour were very searching and opposed to the natural inclinations of the unregenerate heart, though multitudes did accept them.

When the people asked John the question, "What shall we do?" he replied, "let him that hath two coats give one to him that hath none, and do the same in regard to your food." When the publicans made the same inquiry the answer was, "exact no more than is your due," and to the soldiers, he gave three rules: "first, do no violence to any one; second, accuse no one falsely; third, be content with your wages." It is probable these offences were common among the soldiers, but it is not certain whether they were Romans or Jews in the Roman army, as Judea was a province of the Empire. The Baptist required of all his converts proof that their repentance was genuine.

Although John was only six months older than Jesus, yet they had never met until the Saviour came to him to be baptized, when it was revealed to the Baptist that the one on whom the Holy Spirit, in the form of a dove, rested was the Christ; he then bore witness that Jesus was the Messiah. Other prophets had predicted his coming, but John affirmed he had already come, and pointed him out as "the Lamb of God who taketh away the sins of the world."

The career of Christ's forerunner ended suddenly and tragically. Herod Antipas, son of Herod the Great, had repudiated his wife and married Herodias, the wife of his brother Philip, while the latter was still living. This caused a great public scandal, and John reproved the king for it, telling him the marriage was not lawful, which aroused the anger of Herod who sent him to prison. When the king celebrated his birthday with his courtiers and prominent men, the daughter of Herodias, named Salome, danced for the entertainment of the guests. This pleased the king exceedingly, when he rashly promised with an oath to give her whatever she asked, even to the half of his kingdom. The damsel consulted her mother who directed her to ask for the head of John the Baptist. The king regretted his rash vow, yet on account of the guests, by whom he did not wish to be considered a perjurer, he sent a soldier to execute the bloody deed and the head was given to the damsel who carried it to her mother. The headless body was buried by his disciples. This tragical event, one of the most startling recorded in history, when all the circumstances are considered, occurred 32 A. D., when the martyr was in the prime of life, and at the height of his success during his brief mission.

The scene as the imagination pictures it is thus described by one writer: "Here are two brothers, Herod Antipas, the ruler of Galilee and Perea, and Philip, the governor of another part of the dominions of their father, Herod the Great. Herod Antipas had discarded his lawful wife for the sake of marrying Herodias, the companion of his brother Philip, in direct violation of the law. She was the mother of Salome, and the granddaughter of Herod the Great, therefore a relative of Herod Antipas. Both the husband and wife were guilty of violating the seventh commandment and to this crime they added that of murder.

"It was for reproving Herod on account of his shameless conduct, that John lost his life. Herodias had been wishing for an opportunity to kill him, and now it was offered on the occasion of a birthday festival. While the king and his wife were seated upon their thrones, surrounded by their courtiers, witnessing the wanton dance of the young damsel amid the cheers of a sensual audience, there was another individual praying in the dark gloomy dungeon of the fortress into which he had been placed for his fidelity to the cause of morality, not knowing what his fate might be. At length he hears the sound of footsteps, and sees the gleam of a lighted torch, when presently a soldier appears with a drawn sword, attended by one bearing a light. The prisoner, who is John the Baptist, knows his hour has come, and he offers a silent prayer, when he is rudely seized by the soldier who, by one stroke of his sword, severs the head which, dripping with blood, he passes to the torch-bearer, and then throws the headless body back into the dungeon. This ghastly head, still bleeding, is brought to Herod who, having it deposited on a platter taken from the table, gave it to Salome and she carried it to her mother." What was finally done with it is not known, but there is no doubt the greatest indignities were offered to it. The headless body was recovered from the dungeon by his disciples and buried.

John the Baptist was one of the most eminent characters of the Sacred Scriptures, and perhaps nearer perfection than any other merely human being, Christ being divine as well as human.

Before closing the history of this remarkable man, it may be in place to refer to an interesting incident connected with the mother of Jesus. When Mary was informed by the Angel Gabriel, at Nazareth, of the advent of the expected Messenger, she decided to make a visit to her cousin Elisabeth. It is not certain that she was accompanied by Joseph, and as her visit was prolonged, it is probable she was not. She was doubtless escorted by friends, and as the distance was considerable, she would be likely to ride on a camel, attended by a driver.

Having arrived at the home of Elisabeth, Mary saluted her, expressing great joy at the meeting. The Spirit of the Lord inspired her cousin, when she uttered a blessing upon her guest, to which Mary responded in a beautiful poem expressed in the language of an humble devout heart, in which she praised God, first, for his mercy to her; second, for his mercy to all mankind; third, for his special goodness to his people. She continued her visit about three months and then returned to her home. The occasion had been one of joy and gratitude for both these pious women. Doubtless they conversed about the distinguished honor conferred upon them as prospective mothers of the remarkable children that were to be committed to their charge; about the wonderful revelations that had been made of events that had no precedents, and were surprised why they, above all other women, were selected to fulfil the remarkable prophecies and sustain the honorable positions to which they had been divinely appointed. Hitherto they had lived only humble and obscure lives, unknown beyond a narrow circle of friends. Mary having completed her visit of several weeks, returned to Nazareth, quietly waiting the accomplishment of the prediction of the Angel Gabriel, as related in a previous chapter.

CHAPTER IV.

THE EMPEROR'S EDICT.

Augustus Cæsar, the Roman Emperor, issued a decree that all the inhabitants of Palestine should be taxed, that is, a census or enrolment should be made, or a list of the citizens, their employments, their property, etc., to ascertain the number of Jews in the country, and the amount of their wealth. In taking a census of the Jews, families were kept distinct, therefore each one went to the home of his kindred to be enrolled. The sect called Galileans arose under the leadership of one named Judas a few years after the birth of Christ, on account of this enrolment ordered by Augustus. They claimed that God alone should be recognized as Master and Lord, therefore they withdrew from the other Jews, and offered their sacrifices apart from them. As Jesus and his apostles were from Galilee, they were suspected of belonging to the sect of Galileans, and the name was given to them as a term of reproach, as before stated.

Both Joseph and Mary were members of the tribe of Judah, though of different branches, consequently they went from the city of Nazareth in Galilee, where they resided, to Bethlehem, their native place, to be enrolled,

FLIGHT INTO EGYPT.

since both descended from the royal line of David, a native of this southern city; the distance from Nazareth to Bethlehem being not far from seventy-five miles. The animals used for travel were the camel, ass and mule. Camels were employed for carrying heavy burdens and also for riding. They required but little food or drink, hence were very useful in long journeys, when they followed one another in a line comprising seven, tied together by a cord. A servant led the first one in the line, while the last camel wore a bell to notify the leader that the procession was unbroken. A cloth or blanket was thrown over the back of the animal, and sometimes a kind of saddle like a basket was used, especially when two persons rode together. A covered vehicle divided into two compartments protected by curtains, except in front, was used chiefly for women. When the rider wished to dismount he took hold of the servant's staff and by his aid descended. The camels of wealthy owners were sometimes adorned with chains and rich ornaments. The long journey from Nazareth to Bethlehem required some preparation, especially under the circumstances existing in the family of Joseph.

A camel, it is presumed, was provided for Mary and her handmaid, with the conveniences for women, while Joseph rode by her side on a mule, and a man-servant accompanied them to guide and care for the animals. There was a large number of travellers from different parts of the country going to Bethlehem and other places in the vicinity for the purpose of being registered, many of them accompanied by women and children whose parents did not wish to leave them at home.

Some of these people travelled faster than others, so that they were separated and arrived at Bethlehem, some earlier and some later than others. The first to reach the town were the most fortunate in securing a lodging-place at the public inn, while those obliged to travel more slowly were compelled to occupy such places as could be found.

Joseph, the tender, loving companion, guarded and cared for Mary with the most thoughtful vigilance. He was constantly by her side, assisting her to alight when necessary and remount her camel when starting again, neither would he allow the animals to move too rapidly lest she might become greatly fatigued. They travelled only a few miles a day and stopped for the night at the inns by the way. Leaving Nazareth early in the morning they journeyed south and crossing the River Kishon, entered the Valley of Esdraelon which is called the Great Plain, also the Valley of Jezreel, the largest plain in the country, extending from Mt. Carmel to the sea, and is about thirty miles in length, and twenty miles in width. Being a fertile region, it has been the camping-ground for nearly all the armies that have traversed the Holy Land. Here Barak with ten thousand men defeated Sisera with his nine hundred iron chariots; here Josiah, King of Judah, was killed while fighting the army of Necho, King of Egypt. When the Amalekites were encamped in the Valley of Esdraelon, they were attacked and defeated by Gideon, and in this region the Assyrians had their headquarters during their invasion of Palestine. Since those days nearly all nations of the East have at different periods pitched their tents here, including Jews and Gentiles, Saracens and Christians,

Persians, Druses, Turks, Arabs and even the French of a later date.

Continuing their journey Joseph and his companion came to Shechem, where they passed the night. This was another place of great interest in the history of the Jews. Shechem, called also Sychar, was near the grounds Jacob bought of Hamar and gave to his son Joseph, and where his remains were buried after they were brought from Egypt by the Israelites according to his request. Resuming their journey in the morning, they came in sight of Mt. Ebal and Mt. Gerazim, memorable in the history of their nation, one for the blessings proclaimed from its summit on the obedient, and the other for the curses uttered against transgressors. These mountains were near each other with a deep valley between, in which reposed the town of Shechem. Moses commanded the Israelites, after they had crossed the Jordan, to separate into two companies, when six tribes were to occupy Mt. Gerazim and pronounce the blessings, and the other six tribes were to declare the curses from Mt. Ebal.

As the travellers continued their journey, they came to Bethel where Jacob had his remarkable dream when fleeing from his brother Esau. It was twelve miles north of Jerusalem, and on the east was Ai where the Israelites were defeated in a battle, on account of the sin of Achan. Joseph and his company spent the night at Bethel, and in the morning, crossing the small stream of Kedron or Cedron, they came to the village of Bethany two miles east of Jerusalem. The Kedron has an historical interest as David, when fleeing from Absalom, crossed it barefoot and weeping, and Asa, Hezekiah and

Josiah, kings loyal to the God of their fathers, manifested their hatred of idolatry by casting into the stream the ashes of the offerings made to heathen divinities. At length the party came in sight of Jerusalem, which they had not forgotten. Mary remembered the beloved city she had seen in her childhood, and Joseph had been accustomed to attend its yearly festivals. They were now approaching Bethlehem, only a few miles south of the capital, when the perplexing question was suggested, would they find suitable accommodations, as there was so large a company going to this small town? Their fears were not groundless, for when they arrived the inn was overflowing with travellers, therefore they were compelled to occupy a place used for the beasts. In a caravansary, it was common for the people and the animals to lodge in the same place. There is a difference of inns among Oriental nations where travellers are accommodated, some being merely a place of rest situated near a fountain, if possible, and consisting merely of naked walls. Another kind has an attendant to care for them, while a third class is occupied by families who supply provisions for those on a journey and has a storehouse for goods, and conveniences for stables. Travellers usually furnish themselves with blankets or other suitable coverings for sleeping, and with provisions, and the means of cooking them.

During a journey which required several days, as they travelled slowly, Joseph and Mary would naturally employ the time conversing about the interesting places they passed, and in admiring the fresh verdure of the fields, the time being April, and the ripening of the early fruits which were being gathered. At length they arrived at Bethlehem, without danger or delay, though travelling under peculiar circumstances, but as they could not be accommodated at the public inn, they were obliged to occupy rooms in a stable, or the place appropriated to the use of domestic animals.

Bethlehem, one of the smallest towns in Judea, is one of the most interesting on account of the important event connected with it, one that affects the whole human race. The meaning of the word is "House of God." It is one of the oldest places in Palestine, and before the advent of the Messiah, it had become famous in the Jewish history on account of several notable events connected with it, and as the home of some distinguished persons. It was the birthplace of Ibzan, one of the judges of Israel, and near it, Rachel, the favorite wife of Jacob, died and was buried, and here was the home of Boaz and Ruth. It was situated in the territory of Judah, and is called in the Book of Genesis, Ephrath, and by the prophet Micah, Ephratah, who says, "And thou Bethlehem Ephratah, though thou be little among the thousands of Judah, yet out of thee shall he come forth unto me, that is to be ruler in Israel." Bethlehem was the home of the Levite who lived with an idolator, and to this town Naomi came with her daughter-in-law. The place was fortified by King Rehoboam, therefore it was a walled town. It has been called the "City of David," since it was his native place, and where he spent the earlier period of his life as a shepherd, and it is probable that he composed some of his immortal poems in this vicinity, including the 23d Psalm, beginning, "The Lord is my shepherd, I shall not want." The town is situated on the ridge of a hill bordering a deep valley and from a certain point the Dead Sea can be seen.

The inn of Chimham named for the son of Barzillai of Gilead, who accompanied David to Jerusalem after the rebellion of Absalom, was a halting-place for those going to and coming from Egypt, and it may have been the inn mentioned in the account of the birth of Christ. Some writers have supposed that Jesus was born in a cave near the town of Bethlehem, as ancient caverns were sometimes used as places of shelter, but the Sacred Scriptures give no intimation that Mary occupied a cave; on the contrary, it was a manger belonging to an inn or khan, where her child was born.

The Emperor Hadrian, 117–138 A. D., planted a grove on the place tradition ascribes as the birthplace of the Saviour, in honor of Adonis who, in mythology, was the youth favored by Venus, which remained one hundred and eighty years, until the Empress Helena, the mother of Constantine the Great, 316 A. D., had the grove removed and a Christian church erected on the site. At the present day, a monastery stands over the supposed "Cave of the Nativity," with walls and battlements giving it the appearance of a fortress. The monastery was destroyed by the Moslems, but it was rebuilt and occupied by Greek, Roman and American Christians, each nationality having separate apartments. It is said that Jerome, 331–420 A. D., who founded a convent at Bethlehem, occupied a cell in it where he wrote his Commentaries and completed the Latin Vulgate of the Scriptures.

During the wars of David with the Philistines, who had a garrison at this place, an incident occurred at the well of Bethlehem, mentioned in the account of his campaigns. His troops, together with their commander, became exhausted from fatigue and thirst, when their leader in despair exclaimed, "O that one would give me drink from the well of Bethlehem, which is by the gate!" Some of his brave soldiers rushed forward with their water-jars, broke through the enemies' lines, hastily drew water from the well and brought it to David, but he would not drink it since it was obtained at so great a risk of life, therefore he poured the water upon the ground as an offering to the Lord.

Both Joseph and Mary were descendants of Abraham through the royal family of David, of the tribe of Judah, as previously stated, and it was important that Jesus should descend from both these ancestors, since it was so predicted by the prophets. Mary was said to be the daughter of Eli, by the Jews, and by the early Christians, the daughter of Joakim and Anna. Joakim and Eliakim are synonymous, while Eli or Heli is an abridgement of the same word. She was the cousin of Elisabeth, the mother of John the Baptist, as before mentioned, and Bethlehem was probably her native place. It is claimed that she had other children besides Jesus, because his brethren are mentioned, as James, Joses, Simon and Judas, and it is stated that he had sisters also, but their names are not recorded. That these were called his brethren does not prove they were the children of Mary, since among the Jews near relatives were called thus. That they were not the brothers of Jesus, with the same mother, seems probable, since when on the cross he commended his mother to the care of one of his disciples. It is possible that Joseph

was a widower when he espoused Mary, and that these
"brethren" were the sons of his first wife. However
that may have been, it is sad to think they did not
accept Jesus as the Messiah, and treated him with contempt, but in Acts i, 14, it is said that the brethren of
Jesus were among those who met for prayer, therefore
they may have repented and believed in him.

CHAPTER V.

THE BABE OF BETHLEHEM.

WHEN Joseph and Mary went to be registered, it is presumed they made suitable preparations for the journey by taking with them such things as would be needed for their convenience, and also servants to attend to their wants, so their quarters at the hostlery were comfortable. After the babe was born, the maid-servant attended to the infant, bathed him and then wrapped him in "swaddling clothes," as was the custom, and placed him in a little bed in the manger. It was the practice among the Jews to place around the body of the new-born infant a band called "swaddling clothes." The mother remained at home forty days after the birth of a son, and twice as long if her child was a daughter, and after the expiration of this period she went to the Temple to make an offering, which consisted of a lamb a year old, if she could afford it, but if she was poor, two turtle-doves and two young pigeons. On the eighth day after the birth of a son, he was consecrated to the service of the Lord by the rite of circumcision, and was named at the time; the name was usually significant and sometimes had a prophetic meaning. Mothers usually nursed their offspring from thirty to thirty-six months, and when the child was weaned a feast was given. The sons remained in the care of the women of the family until the age of four years, when they came under the father's control and were instructed in the Mosaic law and the business of life. For a more extensive training, they were sent to a school conducted by a priest or Levite. The daughters were kept more secluded than their brothers, and were trained in domestic affairs.

The first-born son was entitled to special favors. He received a double portion of his father's estate, and exercised authority over the younger members of the family similar to that possessed by the father, and was priest of the household until that office was transferred to the tribe of Levi. The authority of the father was exercised over his wife, children, grandchildren and servants. He was at liberty to use unlimited power and inflict extreme punishment, though there were some restrictions imposed by Moses to this dangerous authority. Jesus, being the child of a Jewish mother, was trained as was the custom of his nation.

The Hebrew year was divided into periods of two months each, namely, the harvest, extending from the first of April to the first of June, when the temperature at the beginning was agreeable, but at the close the heat became oppressive. Summer comprised June and July, when the heat was intense; this was the time of fruits. During August and September the heat was so great that the inhabitants often slept under the open sky or on the tops of the houses, but from October to December the weather was frequently cloudy and rainy. Winter succeeded, when snow, ice, cold winds,

FLIGHT INTO EGYPT.

thunder, lightning and hail were not infrequent, and the streams were filled with water.

On the first of April there were indications of spring: the trees put forth their leaves, the fields were covered with grass and grain, and the gardens began to bloom. During May, June, July and August there was seldom rain. It was the custom in Palestine to drive the flocks to the mountains and uninhabited regions for the summer, and gather them into folds the latter part of October or the first of November, when the cold weather began. While pastured in the hilly regions, it was necessary they should be watched day and night to prevent them from straying, and protect them from wild beasts. The watchers remained all night with their flocks under the open sky, as the climate, at that season, was mild.

At the time of the Saviour's birth there were shepherds tending their flocks on the hills surrounding Bethlehem, where the Shepherd King of Israel long before was engaged in the same employment, which suggested to his mind some of the beautiful metaphors contained in his poems.

While these pious shepherds of Bethlehem were watching their flocks by night they were suddenly startled by a remarkable brilliancy in the heavens, surpassing anything they had witnessed before. This supernatural appearance alarmed them, when an angel immediately appeared and calmed their fears, and at the same time announced the birth of the Redeemer in the city of David, that is, Bethlehem. He told them they would find the babe wrapped in swaddling clothes and lying in a manger. To confirm the angel's message, there suddenly appeared a multitude of the heavenly host, praising God, saying, "Glory to God in the highest, and on earth peace and good-will to men." The birth of Christ awakened the interest and called forth the songs of praise from the whole celestial choir, since it magnified the glory of God and brought salvation to the human race. Having fulfilled their mission, the angels returned to heaven.

These shepherds were devout men, and were looking for the expected Messiah, therefore they resolved to confirm the glad tidings. They said to one another, "Let us go to Bethlehem and see this wonderful child."

Leaving their flocks in the care of others, they went in haste and found Joseph and Mary with the babe cradled in the manger. They could not keep the glad tidings to themselves, but proclaimed the news to others, so that the remarkable event was made known to all the inhabitants of this region, exciting great wonder and curiosity. Satisfied that this infant was the promised Saviour, these shepherds returned to their flocks, filled with joy, which they expressed by praising God for the wonderful things they had seen and heard.

When the shepherds first saw the babe in his lowly crib, doubtless, they were disappointed, for they supposed in common with their countrymen that the expected Messiah would appear as a prince, hence would be exceedingly glorious, but as they gazed upon the lowly infant, their disappointment was changed to delight. A halo of glory appeared to surround him and the humble child seemed changed into a cherub when they prostrated themselves before him and paid him homage.

Wise Men from the East came to pay their devotion to the infant Redeemer. These men were called Magi, a term used in Oriental countries to denote philosophers and especially astronomers or astrologers. Different opinions have been entertained about these Wise Men: some have supposed they came from Arabia, on account of the nature of their gifts brought to the infant Jesus, while others have thought they were pious men who had some acquaintance with the Hebrew prophecies, and were themselves favored with divine revelations, and that they might have been the descendants of some of the patriarchal saints. According to recent discoveries by Assyrian scholars, the term Magi was given to the learned men, to philosophers and the priestly class by the Persians and Babylonians. They were regarded in Persia of the highest importance as being the servants of God, diviners, astrologers, etc. Their religion was purer than that of the heathen nations; they worshipped the invisible God whose outward symbol they believed was fire, hence they were styled "fire-worshippers." There was a tradition among the ancient Persians, that the Divinity they acknowledged would appear in human form, and that he would triumph over the power of darkness symbolized by the serpent. This belief may have originated from the accounts about the Garden of Eden and the serpent.

When Babylon was conquered by Cyrus the Persian, the Magi found a class in the captured city similar to their own, with whom they eventually united and formed one order. It may have been through Daniel the Hebrew prophet, when occupying a high position at the Persian court, that these Eastern sages learned about the Jewish expectation of a Messiah. He, perhaps, told them of the prophecy of Balaam who uttered this remarkable prediction, "There shall come a star out of Jacob, and a sceptre shall rise out of Israel." They, perhaps, associated the advent of Christ with this star. This tradition was, doubtless, familiar to the Persian and Babylonian Magi at the time of the Saviour's birth. The number of Wise Men who came to Jerusalem is not mentioned, but some have supposed there were three, whose names were Caspar, Melchior, and Balthazar, while others make the number twelve.

As previously stated, there was a general expectation among the Jews that the Messiah would soon appear. Suetonius, the Roman historian, referring to the rumor, said, "An ancient and settled opinion prevailed throughout the East, that the Fates had decreed some one to proceed from Judea who should attain universal empire." Similar declarations were made by Tacitus, a Roman historian, and also by Josephus and Philo, who were Jews. Trusting these reports, the Wise Men came to do homage to the young prince, and arriving at Jerusalem they inquired where he was to be found, "for," said they, "we have seen his star in the East," that is, we in the East have seen his star, "and are come to pay him our homage." The appearance of a new star or comet was regarded in Oriental countries as an omen of some remarkable event, therefore the Magi considered this phenomenon as a sign of the advent of the expected Prince.

There have been many conjectures about the star that guided the Wise Men. Of course, it could not have been one of the heavenly bodies known as stars, since they are established in the heavens, and are of immense size. It is probable it was some luminous appearance, such as a meteor occasionally seen at the present day. It is said in the Scriptures that "The glory of the Lord shone around them," that is, a great light appeared which may have been visible from afar. The star or luminous meteor went before them during their long journey, and conducted them first to Jerusalem and then to Bethlehem when it remained suspended over the place where the infant Saviour was cradled.

It was customary to offer gifts to royal persons, when admitted to their presence, therefore these Magi had brought costly presents comprising gold, frankincense and myrrh. Frankincense was a natural production of Arabia, but it was, doubtless, an article of commerce since it was considered highly valuable. It was a kind of gum obtained from a tree by making incisions in the bark, and when burned it emitted a fragrant odor, therefore it was used in religious ceremonies. Myrrh was also an Arabian product obtained from a tree, and was used for embalming, especially in Egypt, and for ointment in Judea. Sometimes it was mingled with wine for rendering the senses dull in case of suffering, as was done at the crucifixion of the Saviour.

Mary, though surprised at the remarkable events attending the birth of her child, kept silence, but meditated upon them, not comprehending their significance. She felt a great responsibility rested upon her and distinguished honor had been shown her, but instead of becoming proud of the dignity, she was more humble, watchful and prayerful. When the infant was eight days old the customary Jewish rite was performed, and he was named Jesus, according to the direction of the Angel Gabriel. After the usual time had expired, that is, forty days after his birth, his parents carried him to Jerusalem to present him to the Lord in the Temple, and offer the customary sacrifices, which consisted of turtle-doves and young pigeons, thus proving his parents were not wealthy. While in the Temple an aged saint named Simeon, who had been waiting for the "Consolation of Israel," came in. It had been revealed to him by the Holy Spirit that he would not depart from this life before he had seen the Christ, and when the babe was brought into the Temple, he took him in his arms and blessed God, expressing a willingness to depart, as he had seen the salvation of the Lord. He predicted that the child would be a light both to Jews and Gentiles. He blessed Joseph and Mary and then prophesied concerning the child, and gave intimations of his future sufferings and death. There was also an aged woman eighty-four years old, named Anna, a prophetess, and constant worshipper at the Temple, strictly observing all the ordinances of the Lord, who, coming into the House of the Lord, gave thanks and spoke of the child to those expecting the redemption of Israel.

When Herod the King heard of the birth of Jesus, he and his friends at Jerusalem were greatly troubled, for he supposed the young infant might become a powerful rival to his family, if not to himself. He had obtained the crown by crime and bloodshed thirty-four years before, and now the royal sceptre might pass to other hands, since the general belief was that a prince was soon to appear as a ruler of the Jews. What could

THE INFANT SAVIOUR.

be done to prevent it? After some deliberation, Herod formed a plan which revealed his cruel nature. He called together the members of the Sanhedrim or Great Council of the Jewish nation, comprising seventy-two members of priests and scribes and inquired of them where Christ would be born. They replied, "In Bethlehem of Judea, according to the predictions of the prophets," and referred to the language of Micah, "Thou Bethlehem, Ephratah," etc. The king then privately called the Wise Men, and inquired of them what time the star appeared, that he might know the exact age of the child. He told them to inquire and seek diligently for him, and then return and inform him, that he might go and worship the babe.

Herod veiled his wicked purpose by the semblance of religion and succeeded in deceiving the Wise Men, who left Jerusalem for Bethlehem, when the star went before them until they came to the place where the mother and infant were. It is spoken of as a house, which suggests the idea that Joseph had secured more comfortable quarters. The star seen by the Magi when in the east had appeared in the direction of Jerusalem or in the west, which led them to suppose the expected prince would be born at the capital of Judea.

Being warned of God in a dream they did not return to Herod, but left for their own country by a different route over which they came to avoid being overtaken by the officers of the king when he learned they did not intend to return to him. Herod was exceedingly angry at the conduct of the Wise Men, and resolved to be avenged. In the meantime the angel of the Lord appeared to Joseph in a dream and told him to take the young child and his mother and flee into Egypt, where they must remain until further directions, for Herod was planning to take the life of the babe. They would be safe in Egypt, since that country was not in the jurisdiction of the King of Judea. The distance from Bethlehem was about sixty miles, and the journey must be made in great haste. Egypt, at this time, was a Roman province, but there were many Jews living in the country who had their synagogues and religious services as in their native land, therefore the exiles found some of their own countrymen who were allowed the liberty to worship God according to their own views. This country, which had been the land of bondage to the Jews, now became a place of refuge for the child regarded as the King of that nation. As far as known, this was the only time the Saviour left Palestine, his native land.

After receiving the command of God, Joseph made immediate preparations to leave, and started in the night, so that his sudden departure might not be known. It is probable they travelled in the same manner as when they left Nazareth for Bethlehem. They were supplied with the means of living, perhaps, from the presents of the Wise Men. How long they remained in Egypt is uncertain, but it was until the death of Herod the Great in the thirty-seventh year of his reign. By the escape to Egypt the prophecy of Hosea was fulfilled, that says, "Out of Egypt have I called my Son." This originally referred to the escape of the Israelites from the country, under the lead of Moses, yet it would apply to Jesus also, as both events could be expressed in the same language.

After the death of Herod, the angel of the Lord told Joseph in a dream to return to his native land, for it would be safe to do so, since his enemy was dead. He directly obeyed the heavenly message and returned with his family to Palestine, but when he learned that Archelaus, the son of Herod, reigned in Judea, he was afraid to remain in that region, and being encouraged by another dream, he went to Nazareth in Galilee, a city familiar both to him and Mary. Thus the predictions of the prophets, that the Messiah should be called a Nazarene, were fulfilled. To be a Nazarene implied humble birth, therefore one that was despised; it was to be, as expressed by the prophet, "a root out of dry ground, having no form or comeliness."

When Herod learned the Wise Men had returned to their country without his knowledge, he committed one of the most fearful crimes on record. It was his original plan to send a court official to murder the infant Saviour, but as he was disappointed by the Magi, it could not be known which was the intended victim, therefore he commanded *all* the male children under two years of age, found in Bethlehem and vicinity, to be killed, so that the words of Jeremiah in describing a sad incident in the history of his people could be applied to this fearful tragedy. His language is, "In Rama was there a voice heard, lamentation, weeping and great mourning, Rachel weeping for her children and would not be comforted, because they are not." These pathetic words expressed the sorrows of the mothers in Bethlehem whose infants were slain by Herod. It is not known how many "Innocents" perished, but as the decree included not only those in that town but also in the adjacent region, the number must have been considerable. Since the bloody edict of Pharoah there had not been so fearful a calamity in Jewish households.

Rama was a small town belonging to the tribe of Benjamin, and about six miles from Jerusalem. It was the burial place of Rachel the wife of Jacob, therefore she is represented as weeping for her children, that is, her descendants. Here the prophet Samuel was born and died, and it was the place where Saul was anointed King of Israel. It has been identified with Aramathea, the home of Joseph who entombed the body of Jesus after his crucifixion, though some writers have thought the home of both Samuel and Joseph was thirty miles from Jerusalem. Rama was situated on an eminence commanding a view of an extensive region, diversified by hills, plains, valleys and cultivated fields, and on the west could be seen the Great Sea or the Mediterranean.

In the reigns of David and Solomon it may have been a summer resort for the royal family as some of David's beautiful poems, especially the 104th Psalm, appear to have been composed in sight of the sea. After the conquest of Jerusalem by the Babylonians, the captives were collected at Rama to hear their sentence, the prophet Jeremiah being one of them. The nobles had been slain, the king's eyes put out after witnessing the murder of his sons, and then the captives were started on their sad journey to Babylon, to be disposed of according to the will of the emperor.

Herod the Great, who occupied the throne at the birth of Christ, was appointed governor of Galilee at the age of twenty-five, and became engaged in some of the wars of that period. He went to Rome, obtained the crown of Judea, and finally got possession of the whole country by cruelty and artifice. To make himself popular with the Jews, he rebuilt the Temple and made it a magnificent edifice. He possessed distinguished talents and was prominent among the rulers of his time, but his crimes afford a fearful example of human depravity. His massacre of the Innocents is mentioned in the Sacred Scriptures, while Josephus the historian says he murdered Aristobulus, the brother of his wife, because he was popular in Jerusalem; that he ordered Hyrcanus, the grandfather of his wife, to be put to death, though on a certain occasion he saved the life of Herod; he caused Mariamne his wife and Alexandra her mother to be publicly executed, and two sons of his wife to be strangled in prison. A short time before his death, he commanded the chief men of the nation to assemble at Jericho, under penalty of death if they refused, to be held as prisoners for the purpose of being executed when he died, that there might be mourning throughout the land. This fearful order was not, however, obeyed.

Herod the Great died in the sixty-eighth year of his age, when his kingdom was divided among his sons. Archelaus, who received Judea, Idumea and Samaria, was cruel and tyrannical like his father. He caused three thousand persons in Jerusalem to be put to death, but after a reign of nine years, the Emperor Augustus banished him to Gaul on account of his crimes, where he died.

CHAPTER VI.

THE CHILDHOOD, YOUTH AND MANHOOD OF JESUS.

The life of Christ, it has been said, may be divided into three periods: First, from his birth to the age of fourteen years, which may be considered the educational period; second, from fourteen to thirty years, when he labored as a mechanic; third, from thirty to thirty-three years, or from the time he began his public ministry to his death.

The sacred historian says, "The child Jesus grew and waxed strong in spirit, filled with wisdom, and the grace of God was upon him." His early education devolved upon his parents, who doubtless faithfully instructed him in the religion of their nation, as was their duty. The Jewish laws were especially definite and imperative on that subject, no one being allowed to grow up without an education, therefore schools were established for that purpose, and when the child was of the proper age he was sent to these institutions. Jewish parents were very careful that the moral and religious training of their children should not be neglected.

Jesus in his youth must have been unlike other children, both in his moral and intellectual qualities. Since he was perfect, he never could have manifested any of the waywardness common to the young; he was never disobedient, irritable or disrespectful, never could be persuaded to do a wrong act though tempted by his associates, and for this reason he was sometimes insulted and abused by the wicked boys of Nazareth, as he was in later years by these same boys when they became men and attempted to murder him. By his parents, teachers and the priests he was regarded as a remarkable child, and many were the conjectures about his future career, yet no one except his parents knew the peculiar circumstances attending his advent into the world.

It was the custom of the Jews to train their sons for some useful employment without regard to their station, as was the case of Paul, a highly educated man, who was taught the business of tent-making. Joseph, the husband of Mary, was a carpenter, and Jesus was instructed in that branch of mechanics, for Mark, the evangelist, says, the people, surprised at his wonderful deeds during his public ministry, said, "Is not this the carpenter?" Though Joseph was not his natural father, yet he was his legal parent, and felt a deep and tender interest in Mary's child. On one occasion he relinquished his business to watch over and protect the Babe of Bethlehem and his mother during their journey. Joseph affords an illustrious example of an unselfish, devout and honorable man. His considerate treatment of his affianced when he supposed she was guilty of a scandalous offence, his love and care for her after he understood the case, his self-denial in providing for her during their long and tedious journeys in Palestine and Egypt, all prove him to have been one of the most honorable of men, as well as one of the most faithful servants of the Lord. That nothing is said of him during the public ministry of Christ seems to imply that he died before that period, and the fact that Jesus, when on the cross, commended the care of his mother to one of his disciples, is proof that her husband was not then living, as previously stated.

From the return of the family to Nazareth, after leaving Egypt, nothing *special* is said about Jesus in the Scriptures until he was twelve years old. Joseph and Mary were conscientious observers of all the religious ceremonies of their nation, and therefore they attended the yearly festivals at Jerusalem, especially Joseph, as the law required. The Feast of the Passover was to commemorate the rescue of the Israelites in Egypt, when the angel of death slew the first-born of the Egyptians. Jesus had been left at home probably, during these annual visits to the capital, until he was twelve years of age, when he was permitted to accompany his parents to the Feast of the Passover, which continued eight days; one day for killing the paschal lamb, and seven days for the Feast of Unleavened Bread; this festival occurred about the middle of April.

During the national festivals, large numbers of the Jews from all parts of the country and other lands where they had settled went to Jerusalem to celebrate these feasts. At the close of the Passover, Joseph and Mary left for their home in Nazareth, but Jesus remained in Jerusalem without their knowledge, they supposing he was in the company of their friends and neighbors. It is a little surprising the parents did not watch over the lad more closely, as there was so great a multitude of visitors at the capital. In such journeys, friends and acquaintances often formed companies and travelled together, and the parents of Jesus probably thought their son was with some of their friends, but it is a little remarkable they should have made a day's journey before inquiring for him.

Not finding the missing child they returned to Jerusalem in great anxiety, feeling, perhaps, they had been too negligent in not seeking for him before. They continued their search in this state of mind until the third day, when they found him in the court of the Temple with the rabbis or religious teachers, listening to their instructions and asking them questions about the law and the prophets. These learned doctors and all others who heard him, were astonished at his questions and remarks, which indicated a remarkable understanding. One of the rabbis, according to tradition, was so fascinated with the boy, that he invited him to his house and cared for him until he was found by his parents. When they saw him in such company they were astonished, for they had not supposed his mind was sufficiently developed to comprehend subjects none but the learned men of the nation were expected to understand.

His mother said to him in a reproving tone, "Why hast thou dealt with us thus? Thy father and I have sought thee sorrowing." They had been three days separated from him. Though Joseph was not his father, Mary spoke of him as such, since Jesus was considered his legal heir. The parents were, perhaps, too hasty in their reproof, since God had revealed to them the future mission of the child. The reply of Jesus to his mother was as remarkable as his interview with the doctors:

"Do you not know that I must be about my Father's business?" meaning his Heavenly Father. At this early age he understood his relation to God and the work he came to accomplish, though he did not enter upon his public mission until many years later. His parents did not understand his meaning, but Mary thought about his words and "pondered them in her heart," as it is expressed, which proves she was a quiet, thoughtful and discreet woman, of deep piety and ardent maternal love. Jesus returned with his parents to Nazareth and was subject to them, and as the sacred historian expressed it, "he grew and waxed strong in spirit, filled with wisdom, and the grace of God was upon him."

Augustus, the Roman Emperor, died 14 A. D., and as Jesus was born four years before the beginning of the present era, he was at that time eighteen years of age. Tiberius, the successor of Augustus, reigned from 14 A. D. to 37 A. D., therefore he was emperor during the remaining years of the life of Christ. The Roman Empire at that period embraced a vast territory equal to 2,700,000 square miles, and a population of 100,000,000 as previously stated, hence an immense standing army was needed; the imperial system was, in fact, a military organization. The expense of maintaining such a government was very great, hence the necessity of levying heavy taxes to support it. This demand kept the people in comparative poverty, which was especially the case in Palestine.

Jesus was poor, and said of himself, "The foxes have holes, the birds of the air have nests, but the Son of Man hath not where to lay his head," and one of the

CHRIST AT THE AGE OF TWELVE YEARS.

sacred writers said of him, "Though he was rich, yet for our sakes he became poor, that we, through his poverty, might become rich." His poverty was shown when he commended his mother to the care of one of his disciples while on the cross. It is probable that Joseph died without wealth, otherwise Jesus, being the first-born of his mother, would have been given some of the estate of her husband. After finishing his school education, the Saviour labored at the business of a carpenter, which he learned from his reputed father, and probably earned sufficient for his support, until he was thirty years of age, when he entered upon the work of an evangelist, dependent upon the gifts of the people for whom he labored.

Whatever he did in any period of his life was, doubtless, complete in itself, for there was no want of thoroughness in his work, whatever he undertook. Every part was doubtless perfect, just what it claimed to be, therefore it is probable his labor was sought by builders who had confidence in his fidelity. The high estimation in which he was held by business men awakened a feeling of envy among the laborers of Nazareth, who never forgave him, but cherished this spirit until it led them and other Nazarenes to seek his death at a later period. Jesus, until the age of thirty, worked at the carpenter's trade, and during that time, he conscientiously attended to all the duties of the national religion, being present at the services in the synagogues, and at the yearly festivals in Jerusalem. Even in his private life as a mechanic, it is presumed he lost no opportunity of doing good, even to the most abandoned sinners whom he could influence and many profligates may have reformed by his benevolent efforts. His gentle, forgiving and loving spirit, his readiness to assist the poor, the friendless and the suffering, won him many friends. His heart was so tender and sympathetic that he often wept on account of the sins and sufferings of humanity, and there never was one so ready to forgive an injury or an insult. Jesus was respected by the Romans, especially the officers of the Roman Government, who frequently came to Nazareth and vicinity and he was sometimes doubtless employed by them to do the work of a carpenter.

The dwellings of the wealthy classes in the time of Christ were splendid, and generally constructed according to the Greek style of architecture. The palaces and elegant mansions were made with turrets and surrounded by walls and the roofs were flat, as was the case with other houses. Parts of the buildings were made of wood, such as the doors with their bars, the gates, lintels of the windows, and the roofs, but stone, which was abundant in Palestine, was used for the main part of the structure, and sometimes polished marble was the material employed. The most common woods used were the sycamore, remarkable for durability, acacia, palm, fir, olive and cedar, and sometimes the oak or terebinth, but the most valued was the almug tree. Our Lord during his labors as a carpenter became familiar with all these varieties used as timber, and doubtless skilfully employed them in different parts of the buildings.

The life of Jesus as an obscure mechanic, considering his exalted character and mission, inspires one with amazement; it is beyond human comprehension. But there was a divine purpose for this, and one lesson taught is, that honest labor is not degrading, but, on the contrary, any industrial art, if in accord with the rules of good morals, and faithfully and honestly pursued, is as noble as any of the learned professions, at least in the estimation of God. This truth is taught by the example of Jesus, the Son of the Highest, who did not appear as one of the learned doctors of his nation, but as an humble mechanic. How so many years of obscure labor were conducive to fit him for his wonderful future career is a mystery not explained.

The brothers of Jesus, called James, Joses, Simon and Judas, were, doubtless, in their childhood, as well as in their later years, very different from him. They had the faults common to other children, sometimes wayward and quarrelsome, and sometimes disobedient, and when they saw the gentle, submissive Jesus could not be enticed to do a wrong act, even in their childish sports, they regarded him with envy and jealousy, and after he entered on his public ministry and performed wonderful miracles, they did not believe in him. They would not admit his claim to being the Christ. How sad the thought that his kindred rejected him!

It is not probable that the Saviour, until the age of thirty, was free from mental suffering and anxiety on account of the future, since he understood for what purpose he came into the world; he was fully aware of what he must endure, and the ignominious death he would die. He was familiar with the prophecies concerning himself and doubtless often wept on account of the sin of his countrymen in rejecting him, but he had voluntarily offered himself a sacrifice for the redemption of the race, before he left his Father and resigned the glory he had with Him before the creation, as he said himself, yet these thoughts did not cause him to regret the work he had undertaken. A supreme love for sinners and a perfect acquiescence in the will of his Heavenly Father sustained him in considering his future labors and sufferings and when the period arrived, he began his work, the most important ever accomplished in the history of the human race, and one absolutely essential to their salvation.

CHAPTER VII.

THE PUBLIC MINISTRY OF CHRIST.

THE Jews expected their Messiah, as previously stated, would come as a conqueror and free them from the yoke of Rome, but he did not appear as a general or as a prince, and not even as a native of Jerusalem, surrounded by the splendors of courtly etiquette, but when he entered upon his public career he appeared as the compatriot of the rude Galileans, the fishermen and the laborers. The babe in the manger found no favor with those who were expecting a conqueror or a royal prince. "Where did Christianity originate?" it has been asked. "In a stable," is the answer, "with its rough floor, its unfinished walls, its cattle-stalls whence issued the sounds of their inmates at intervals, day and night, mingled with the coarse and loud voices of the herdsmen."

The time had come when the carpenter of Nazareth must assume the responsibilities and encounter the hardships and dangers of his public ministry. He was not ignorant of what the future would be, for before his advent, his work was planned in heaven, when he offered himself as the Redeemer of the world, though by this voluntary offering he must eventually surrender his mortal life. At the age of thirty, he left his home in Galilee, his friends and his business, and travelled on foot to Judea, where John was baptizing his converts in the Jordan. The Saviour in his preaching tours always journeyed on foot, and there is only one instance mentioned in his public labors of his riding, and that was when he entered Jerusalem as a Prince and a Conqueror, according to the declaration of the prophet.

The distance from Nazareth to Judea was considerable, and it was necessary to pass through Samaria or cross to the region east of the Jordan. The object of the Saviour was to be baptized by John, but when he asked to have the rite administered, the prophet said, "I have need to be baptized of thee, and comest thou to me?" By this he meant it was more becoming that he should be baptized with the baptism of the Holy Spirit, than that the Saviour should be baptized in water by him, since he — John — was a sinful man and unworthy of this honor. Jesus said "suffer it to be so, for it is proper to fulfil all righteousness" that is, all divine appointments. John complied with the request of Jesus, and when he was baptized the heavens were opened, and as he prayed, John saw the Spirit of God descending in the form of a dove and resting upon the Saviour, while a voice was heard saying, "This is my beloved Son, in whom I am well-pleased."

That the Jews were familiar with the rite of baptism before the Christian era is implied in the question addressed to John by those sent to him from Jerusalem asking, "Why do you baptize if you are not the Christ, nor Elias, nor that prophet?" meaning the Messiah. The Jewish rabbis, both in earlier and later times,

CHRIST REASONING WITH THE SCRIBE.

THE PUBLIC MINISTRY OF CHRIST. 77

bear witness to the custom of baptizing proselytes, and other writers as well as Jewish afford the same testimony. It has been considered that the baptism of John was introductory, and designed to prepare the way for the gospel dispensation. John himself said, "Christ should be manifest to Israel, therefore I am come baptizing with water."

An important part of John's ministry and baptism was to point out the Messiah to the Jewish people. This rite was not administered by John in the name of the Father, Son and Holy Spirit, for there were some who had been baptized by him who had never heard of the Holy Spirit, and who afterwards were rebaptized by the apostles, therefore it appears evident that his baptism was an introductory rite to prepare the way for the Messiah's kingdom. The personality of Christ is a subject of which nothing positive is mentioned in the gospels, but there must have been an irresistible attraction about him to draw such crowds in his preaching, and that so great multitudes followed him wherever he went, and who listened to him with the closest attention though not always approving of what he said. The ignorant and the learned, the rich and the poor, persons of rank and those in the lowest walks of life, the moralist and the profligate, men, women and children were his auditors and were more or less affected by his preaching, "Never man spake like this man" said one of his hearers, and his remark was literally true.

The Saviour has been represented in art by the most gifted painters and sculptors of the world, but it is not possible that human skill can perfectly represent the divine effulgence of the Son of God. His appearance was more striking, it is presumed, on account of his spirituality than for his physical aspect, though in the latter he may have been attractive. It is presumed he possessed the characteristics of his nation in features and complexion, while his figure was probably commanding, his voice clear and distinct with the power of being heard by multitudes. Sometimes he spoke in the most tender and gentle tones, and again in the most solemn and impressive manner, according to the nature of the subject and the character of his audience. There was never anything repulsive in his manners; his most attractive charms were his tender love, sympathy and pity for the suffering and the erring and grief for the impenitent. His national attachments were remarkably conspicuous, as shown on several occasions. What a tender, loving and sympathetic disposition he manifested at the grave of Lazarus, when he saw the grief of the sisters; he wept, though he knew what he would do for them. This spirit was frequently exhibited on other occasions, but with all his tenderness and willingness to forgive, he very forcibly expressed his condemnation of sin, and was especially severe in his bold censure of hypocrisy, as witnessed in his denunciation of the scribes and Pharisees.

The Temptation. — Although Jesus had submitted to the ordinary baptism, as preliminary to his public labors, yet he was not permitted to begin his duties until he had been subjected to a very painful ordeal, administered by Satan, the great adversary of God and man. This could not have been necessary so much for his own sake, as for the encouragement of his followers. The sacred writer says, "He," meaning Christ, "was tempted in all points as we are, yet without sin, that he might know how to succor those who are tempted." This ordeal had the divine permission, for it is said, "he was led by the Spirit into the wilderness" for this purpose. Jesus was still in the desert of Judea, that is a region of hills, mountains and forests, where the soil was comparatively barren and the land untilled. He went to one of the mountains where he remained without food, during forty days, and spent the time, doubtless, in solitary communion with his Heavenly Father, and meditation upon the important work he had undertaken. It was a subject requiring such sacrifices, and was so momentous in its consequences, that no created being, angelic or human, could possibly fully comprehend.

The thought is suggested, how did Satan know of Christ's fasting in the wilderness? No doubt he closely watched the Saviour from his birth in Bethlehem, in order to devise some plan to thwart the divine purpose, and prevent the mission of Christ from being successful. Before Satan's fall, it may have been known among the angels of heaven that a world would be created and inhabited by a race of beings who would rebel against their Creator, therefore subject to death both physical and moral, but that God would, in his mercy, plan a way for their redemption, by offering his beloved Son to die as a sacrifice for the guilty, and that in the course of time the Beloved of the Father would voluntarily assume a human condition, that he might give his life a ransom for the rebels. Satan, perhaps, was not sure that Jesus was that promised Redeemer, therefore he determined to ascertain the truth about it.

Jesus, after fasting forty days and nights, felt the demands of hunger, therefore it was a favorable time for the Tempter to assail him by his artful devices. The Saviour had been publicly declared by a voice from heaven to be the Son of God, hence Satan said to him, "If thou art the Son of God," or the Messiah, "here is a good opportunity to prove it. You have fasted a long time and are hungry, therefore command that these stones lying about be changed into bread." The advice seemed plausible, since no injury or loss would be sustained by any one, and there was no food to be had in the desert. Why should not the Saviour perform the miracle to avoid starvation? He, however, met the temptation by a passage of Scripture, showing that God could supply the wants of human life in other ways than by bread. Though the Saviour had been in the wilderness with the wild beasts that had not been allowed to do him any injury, and had been sustained forty days without food, and had resisted the temptation of Satan, yet he must pass through further trials and be again assailed by the Adversary. He was therefore conducted to Jerusalem, and placed upon a pinnacle of the Temple, that is a porch or piazza which, on the south side, was one hundred and fifty feet in height and overlooked a valley more than seven hundred feet below. Satan proposed that Jesus should cast himself down from this height, and if he was the Son of God, no harm would come to him, for, said the Tempter, it is written, "He shall give his angels charge of thee, and in their hands they shall bear thee up, lest at any time thou dash thy foot against a stone." This suggestion of Satan was not only audacious, but also absurd, for what possible advantage was to be gained by such an act. To this bold temptation the Saviour replied, " Thou shalt not tempt the Lord, thy God"; meaning the Lord does not promise to protect those who needlessly and rashly place themselves in danger for it would be in defiance of the laws of nature.

The next and third temptation was the most powerful, and, to human ambition, the most difficult to resist. Satan well knew that love of power was one of the strongest passions of the human race, and was the cause of his own fall and of those who rebelled under his leadership. Jesus was accompanied by his enemy to the top of a high mountain, probably near Jerusalem, and commanding a wide prospect, so that from its summit could be seen a large part of Palestine, and, perhaps, some adjacent regions. This position afforded a magnificent view with its numerous cities, rich cultivated fields, fertile valleys and high mountains, and embraced a great part of the dominions of Palestine, under the term of " all the world "; and these Satan claimed to own or to have a jurisdiction over them, which, from a moral point of view, was not far from the truth, and he asserted his right to bestow them upon whomsoever he pleased. If Jesus was the Messiah, his foe may have supposed he had come to take possession of the country, but he was without followers and without an army, therefore the Tempter proposed to place him at once in possession without delay, if the Saviour would acknowledge him as lord, or in other words, fall down and pay him the homage due only to God. This was the boldest and most audacious temptation the enemy offered, and which would have been the most effectual with a merely human being. It seems impossible that Satan could have understood the true character of the Son of God, when he tried to seduce him to perform an act of idolatry. Jesus met the temptation with so decided a rebuke, that his enemy left him. He said, " Get thee hence, Satan, for it is written, 'Thou shalt worship the Lord, thy God, and Him only shalt thou serve.'" It is said by one of the evangelists, that the devil left him for a time, implying that he renewed his temptations. The Saviour said to his disciples, just before his crucifixion, "The prince of this world cometh and hath nothing in me," and it may have been in the Garden of Gethsemane when Jesus was enduring his fearful agony. Satan had, doubtless, great influence in arousing the Jews against the Saviour, and in causing his arrest, condemnation and death. After his adversary left him in the wilderness, angels came and comforted him, and ministered to his physical wants. This scene in the wilderness is one of the mysteries in the life of Christ, and can never be fully comprehended. Why the immaculate Son of God, the dearly Beloved of the Father, should be subjected to such an ordeal is a question none can solve, but it affords some useful lessons, such as "no one is so pure as to be free from temptation; that when the tempter assails us, God will give us grace to resist if we look to him; that the tempter will adapt his plans to circumstances and make them appear plausible; that one of the best methods of meeting the danger, is by suitable passages of the Sacred Scriptures, and that when one is confronted by temptation, he should resist it, promptly, firmly and indignantly. And it is a source of comfort to the Christian to know that his Master, having been tempted, can sympathize with his followers in similar circumstances, and is able and willing to shield them from such perils."

CHAPTER VIII.

PREACHING IN GALILEE. THE APOSTLES.

THOUGH the baptism and temptation of our Lord, preliminary to the beginning of his public labors, that is, preaching the gospel and performing miracles, occurred in Judea, he did not remain in that region, perhaps on account of the strong opposition he would encounter if he began his ministry among the learned doctors and religious sects that centered at the capital. When he heard of the imprisonment of John the Baptist, he immediately left for Galilee, guided by the Holy Spirit. Here his preaching was attended by wonderful results; his fame spread throughout that region and his words were repeated from one to another, with admiration. At length Jesus came to Nazareth where he had been brought up and where Mary his mother still lived. She, of course, had heard of the success of her Son and his great popularity, and, as was natural, she was happy and felt honored. He had been faithfully trained in the religion of his nation, therefore was accustomed to attend worship in the synagogues, as well as observing the annual festivals at Jerusalem.

Though sacrifices could not be offered except in the

Tabernacle or the Temple, yet other religious ceremonies could be performed at any place. During the Babylonish captivity, the Jews were instructed by the leading men of their country, who read to them from the Sacred Book containing the history of their nation to that time. The origin of the synagogues is somewhat obscure; they are referred to as being in use sometime before the advent of Christ, and in his and the apostle's time they were found in every country where Jews lived. It is stated that before the Roman conquest, there were in Jerusalem alone, four hundred and eighty synagogues. They were constructed in imitation of the Temple, having in the centre a pulpit or place for reading the law, which was kept in an ark or chest. The audience sat facing the reader or speaker, and when the Scriptures were read, the one officiating rose, but when he expounded them, he was seated; the Saviour, when teaching in the synagogues, observed the same rules.

Jesus at length came to Nazareth, and on the Sabbath entered the synagogue for the purpose of instructing the people. When he rose, the minister or the keeper of the book or parchment containing the law of Moses and portions of the Scriptures from the prophets, gave it to him. Jesus unrolled it until he came to the passage in Isaiah, lxi, 1, 2, which is as follows: "The Spirit of the Lord is upon me; He hath annointed me to preach good tidings unto the meek; He hath sent me to bind up the broken-hearted and to proclaim liberty to the captive, to open the prisons to them that are bound, to proclaim the acceptable year of the Lord, to comfort all that mourn," etc. Having rolled up the parchment, he gave it to the keeper, and sat down, intimating that he was about to expound the passage, when every one listened attentively to hear what he had to say, and "every eye was fastened on him," so that nothing should divert the attention. The preacher opened his discourse by saying, "This day is the Scripture fulfilled in your ears," to which he added further remarks.

His hearers were at first astonished at his gracious words and said, "Is not this the son of Joseph, the carpenter? How then can he utter such words? he preaches like one of the prophets, or the learned doctors, and is very different from our teachers, the scribes and Pharisees." Resuming his discourse, the Saviour said, "Ye will repeat to me this proverb, 'Physician, heal thyself.' Whatsoever we have heard that thou hast done in Capernaum, do also in your city." It appears that Jesus had wrought miracles in Capernaum, a town on the north shore of the Sea of Tiberius or Galilee, not very far from Nazareth. Perhaps some persons who had witnessed his labors there were present at his discourse in the latter place.

At the risk of losing the admiration he had won, and of exposing himself to the dangers of an angry mob, the Saviour proceeded to tell them some plain and pungent truths that applied to his hearers. "No prophet," said he, "is accepted in his own country." He then mentioned, as examples, the widow of Sidon, in the days of Elijah, and Naaman, the Syrian, in the history of Elisha, to prove that foreigners were sometimes more worthy of divine favors than natives, and that the prophets were more highly esteemed by them

CHRIST DISPUTING WITH THE DOCTORS.

than they were by their own countrymen. His hearers applied the sermon to themselves and, in their anger, rose *en masse*, rushed to the speaker, seized him and hustled him to the edge of the hill upon which their city was built, with the intention of throwing him over the precipice, and thus putting an end to his life. It is possible there were other Nazarenes who were not in the synagogue, that became involved in a conflict with the intended murderers, so that Jesus quietly passed from their hands and was saved. This incident teaches the lesson that popular favor cannot be relied upon. It also shows that the wickedness of the human heart when not restrained will lead to fearful crimes. The common impression that the character of the Nazarenes was generally dangerously lawless is correct, and the better class of citizens must have found Nazareth an undesirable place to dwell in, yet Jesus spent the greater part of his life there.

After this event, the Saviour for a time confined his labors to Capernaum and the adjacent regions, and the people, who came in crowds to hear him, were filled with amazement. His thoughts, language and doctrines astonished them, especially those who had previously known him as the carpenter of Nazareth, and had, perhaps, employed him in that capacity. Capernaum, where Jesus spent considerable time after he began his public ministry, was in the region assigned to the tribes of Zebulon and Naphthali, on the northeastern shore of the Sea of Tiberias as before stated. The prophet Isaiah, referring to this region as it would appear in the time of Christ, said, " The people who sat in darkness saw great light, and to them who sat in the region and shadow of death, light is sprung up." Though the Saviour labored faithfully and wrought wonderful miracles in the vicinity, yet many of the people did not appreciate their great privileges, since he denounced these cities where he preached, in very severe language, especially Capernaum "which," said he, "though exalted to heaven, shall be brought down to hell," or Hades, meaning the shades of death. This prophecy was fulfilled in the utter destruction of the city.

The Sea of Tiberias, called also the Sea of Galilee, the Sea of Chinnereth, and the Lake Gennesareth, is about fifteen miles long and from six to nine miles wide. The River Jordan flows through this sea without mingling with its waters, and as the lake abounded with fish in the time of Christ, it gave employment to some of his followers. The environs of this body of water are said to surpass in beauty every other region of Palestine, therefore several populous cities were built on its shores, including Tiberias, Bethsaida, Chorazin and Capernaum. It was from this place that Jesus chose the apostles who were to proclaim the gospel, and here in the neighborhood of the laboring class of fishermen was laid the foundation of Christian missions. It was highly important that the Saviour should commit the work of propagating his doctrines to men selected by himself for this purpose, since he thoroughly understood the character of every one and knew who were best adapted for this purpose, and to give them a proper training, he made the selection at the beginning of his ministry.

The Saviour was in the habit of separating himself

from the crowd and spending the time in private devotion, meditation and communion with nature. The mountains, forests, meadows, river and lakes afforded scenes for contemplation to a thoughtful and poetical mind like that of our Lord's, and his appreciation of the works of creation is constantly appearing in his discourses. As he was walking on the shore of the Sea of Tiberias, doubtless engaged in deep study, his attention was attracted by two fishermen who were casting their nets. Such an event was a daily occurrence, and to an ordinary observer there was nothing remarkable about it. These fishermen were brothers named Peter or Simon, and Andrew, who were ready to obey promptly the call of their future Master. They had heard of the fame of Jesus, and, perhaps, had listened to his preaching, when they became so impressed with his teaching, that they believed he was a remarkable prophet, if not the Messiah himself. Jesus said to them, "Follow me," when they immediately left their nets, or their occupation, and without a question obeyed his command.

Walking farther on, the Saviour saw other fishermen who were in a boat with their father, mending their nets; their names were James and John, sons of Zebedee. When Jesus called them to follow him, they directly left the boat, their father and their business, and joined the company of the Saviour, Simon and Andrew. These four fishermen were the first apostles chosen, to whose number were added eight others soon afterwards.

Peter, James and John were admitted to a more intimate relation with their Master than the others, and were the only ones present on some important occasions. The apostles had confidence in the Saviour and his divine mission for, had it been otherwise, sincere, honest men like them, with one exception, would not have forsaken their business and have followed a pretender. They were convinced, after witnessing his miracles and listening to his preaching, that he was the Son of God, as he claimed to be.

The first and leading doctrine of Christ's teaching, and which he enjoined upon his apostles to proclaim, was repentance, "the foundation of the whole system of Christian ethics." The reason for this is the fact that all men are sinners, and must repent if they would avoid the consequence of sin, which is death morally and spiritually.

The names of the other apostles were Philip, Bartholomew, Matthew, Thomas, James, the son of Alpheus, Thaddeus, Simon the Canaanite, and Judas Iscariot. Jesus named James and John, the sons of Zebedee, Boanerges, meaning "sons of thunder." Some have supposed the name was given to them because they asked him to call fire from heaven and consume a certain village of Samaria, as an act of vengeance, but it is more probable the reason was on account of some personal trait, perhaps a fervid and glowing eloquence.

Zebedee, their father, was a fisherman of Galilee, and probably owned some property since he had servants or laborers in his employ. Their mother was Salome, who attended the Saviour in some of his journeys and was one of the women who ministered to his wants. John was the youngest of the apostles and seems to have been more generally known than the other disciples. He was the author of the Fourth Gospel, three Epistles and the Book of Revelation, and is supposed to have been the only apostle who died a peaceful death, and at an advanced age. When Jesus was on the cross he commended Mary his mother to the care of John who brought her to his own home, where she lived until her death about fifteen years after, it is supposed. John has been called the "beloved disciple" because he was admitted to peculiar favor and friendship by his Master. There is a tradition that he was a relative of Joseph, the husband of Mary, whose first wife left seven children, namely, James, Joses, Simon and Judas, and three daughters, called Martha, Esther and Salome, the mother of John, therefore she was considered the sister of Jesus, and John was his nephew; for this reason the sons of Joseph were called the brothers of our Lord.

The apostle John was a native of Bethsaida in Galilee, and is supposed to have been a disciple of John the Baptist before he was called by the Saviour. He was one of the four to whom Christ revealed the tidings about the destruction of Jerusalem, and was one of three present at the restoration of the daughter of Jairus to life and the scene in the Garden. He was the only apostle mentioned as present at the crucifixion, and was one of those to whom Jesus appeared at the Sea of Galilee after his resurrection, and who, with the other apostles, witnessed his ascension. After Jesus had declared that one of the disciples would betray him, Peter requested John to inquire of their Master who the traitor might be, knowing that he had the confidence of his Lord. John began to preach at Jerusalem and was imprisoned on this account, first with Peter and again with the other apostles. After his release, he was sent by his brethren to the Samaritans converted by the labors of Philip, to assist in the work of the Lord. In his Book of Revelation, John says he was banished to the Island of Patmos, in the Ægean Sea, by order of the Roman Emperor. During the last part of his life he lived in Asia Minor where he established churches at Smyrna, Pergamos, and other places, and in this evangelistic labor he incurred the hatred of the Roman Government. He is supposed to have lived until 100 A. D. and died at the age of ninety-six, during the reign of the Emperor Trajan. It is believed he wrote his gospel in Asia Minor, the leading doctrines of which are, that Jesus is the promised Messiah, that he is Divine, and that eternal life may be obtained by faith in his name. Besides his Gospel, as before mentioned, John wrote three Epistles and the Book of Revelation or the Apocalypse, addressed to the Seven Churches of Asia, which is a record of what he saw when in the Island of Patmos. These letters contained predictions of the most remarkable events in the Christian church from the time of the apostles to the final consummation of all things.

James, the brother of John, was called the Greater or Elder, to distinguish him from another disciple of Christ, designated James the Less or the Just, son of Cleophas. Herod Agrippa caused James the brother of John, or James the Greater, to be seized and executed at Jerusalem.

Matthew, called also Levi, a native of Galilee, was a publican or tax-collector under the Roman Govern-

JOHN THE BAPTIST IN THE WILDERNESS.

ment. Soon after his call to the apostleship he gave an entertainment at his house to Jesus and some of his disciples, at which the Jews were offended. After the ascension of our Lord, he continued with the other apostles and proclaimed the gospel for some time in Judea. No further authentic account is given of Matthew, but according to tradition he preached in Parthia or Persia, where he suffered martyrdom. He was the author of the First Gospel which, it is supposed, was written about 38 A. D. before he left Judea for his missionary work.

A distinctive feature of his gospel is the minuteness of detail with which he relates some of the events in the life of the Saviour; for example, his sermon on the Mount, his instructions to his disciples, the visit of the Magi, the escape to Egypt, the massacre of the Innocents, the parable of the ten virgins, and some of the scenes of the resurrection omitted by the other evangelists. He describes the second coming of Christ and the day of judgment in very impressive language and minuteness of detail.

Peter, the son of Jona, was a native of Bethsaida. His original name was Simon, which Jesus when he called him to the apostleship changed to Cephas, a Syriac word signifying a stone or rock, corresponding to the Latin word *petra*, meaning the same, whence the name Peter. He was the brother of Andrew and the only one of the apostles spoken of as a married man, though some of the others may have been and probably were. His family, including his mother-in-law, occupied a house in Capernaum. When the two brothers had passed a day with the Lord Jesus, they left him and returned to their occupation as fishermen. This was before he had called them to become apostles, but when he saw them again and said "Follow me, and I will make you fishers of men!" they immediately left all and followed him. The apostles manifested a remarkable spirit of self-denial and implicit obedience when they left their friends and business directly after being called to do so, and followed their Lord. They knew not what trials and losses they might have to bear, yet they never raised a question nor hesitated to obey. Peter left home, family and business without a doubt or a regret, so far as is known, and after his call he exhibited a strong faith in Jesus as the Messiah, and was prompt to avow his attachment to him, but, sad to say, he denied his Master three times when he was on trial, though he promptly repented of his sin with deep sorrow and bitter tears, and was forgiven. When Jesus, in a private interview with his disciples, asked their opinion of himself, Peter with characteristic ardor replied, "Thou art the Christ, the Son of the living God." With James and John, he was admitted to a close intimacy with the Saviour on several occasions. This apostle was hasty in temper sometimes, for instance, when in the fervor of his zeal, he drew his sword and cut off the ear of the High Priest's servant, at the time an armed band came to arrest his Master in the Garden. When Jesus arose from the grave, he commanded the joyful tidings to be made known to his disciples, and mentioned Peter especially, perhaps to assure him that he was forgiven for denying his Lord. From that time, this apostle exhibited the greatest zeal and fortitude in the service of his Divine Master. No mention is made of him in the "Acts of the Apostles," after the Council at Jerusalem, but he is referred to in the Epistle to the Galatians as present with Paul at Antioch. It is supposed he suffered martyrdom at Rome by being crucified with his head downward, according to his own request, not being worthy to die as his Master died. Peter is the reputed author of the two epistles bearing his name. The First Epistle was addressed to the strangers scattered throughout Pontus, Galatia, Cappadocia, Asia and Bithynia, and the Second Epistle was written to Christians in general.

Andrew, a son of Jona, and brother of Peter, was at first a disciple of John the Baptist, and was present when this prophet said of Jesus, "Behold the lamb of God that taketh away the sin of the world." Meeting his brother Simon, Andrew said, "We have found the Messiah," and conducted him to Jesus. Andrew, then leaving John the Baptist, followed the Saviour. Nothing is known of his future career from the Scriptures, but some of the early Christian writers believed he preached the gospel in Scythia, while others supposed he went to Greece and the neighboring regions to labor, and that he suffered martyrdom at Byzantium. The modern Greeks consider him as the founder of the church at the latter place.

But little is known of the other apostles. Philip was a native of Bethsaida in Galilee, the home of Andrew and Peter, therefore they may have been acquaintances from their youth. He was early chosen by Christ, when he immediately went to find Nathaniel and said, "We have found him of whom Moses and the prophets did write, Jesus of Nazareth, the son of Joseph." Nathaniel doubted, and replied, "Can any good thing come out of Nazareth?" Philip did not argue the question nor explain anything, but very wisely said, "Come and see"; that is when he had seen him, he could judge for himself. This was the more judicious method to overcome the prejudices of Nathaniel.

When Jesus saw him coming he said in his hearing, "Behold an Israelite indeed, in whom is no guile." "Whence knowest thou me?" inquired Nathaniel. "Before Philip called thee, when thou wast under the fig-tree, I saw thee," said Jesus. Nathaniel replied, "Rabbi, thou art the Son of God, and the King of Israel." Jesus said, "Do you believe because I said this? Thou shalt see greater things than these. Hereafter thou shalt see the heavens open, and the angels ascending and descending to the Son of Man."

Philip is mentioned several times in the gospels. He was present at the wedding in Cana of Galilee, in company with Peter, Andrew and Nathaniel, when Christ performed his first public miracle, though they had not then been called to the apostolic office. He appears again at the feeding of the multitude, when Jesus inquired where they could purchase bread for so great a crowd. On another occasion certain Greek proselytes who come to attend the feast at Jerusalem, having heard of the fame of Jesus, went to Philip and said to him that they wished to see him. Philip told Andrew about their request, when both of them went to inform the Saviour. At another time, Philip said to his Master, "Show us the Father and we shall be satisfied." By this question he manifested a want of faith, and the Saviour gently rebuked him by saying, "Have I been so long with you, Philip, and do you not know me? He that hath seen me hath seen the Father also."

Bartholomew is supposed to have been identical with Nathaniel. John, in his Gospel does not mention Bartholomew among the number of the apostles, while the other evangelists do not speak of Nathaniel as one of them, which is regarded as proof that they were idenitcal.

The sacred writers seem to have arranged the apostles in pairs, perhaps because the Seventy were sent out in this manner to preach the gospel. Philip and Nathaniel are mentioned together by John, and Philip and Bartholomew by the other three evangelists. There is a tradition that Bartholomew went as a missionary to India and some of the northern and western parts of Asia and that he finally suffered martyrdom.

Thomas, one of the Twelve, was also called Didymus, a Greek word for twin. No particular events of his life are known until A. D. 33, but according to tradition, when the apostles were sent to proclaim the gospel in different countries, Thomas was assigned to the Parthians and some other nations. He is supposed to have suffered martyrdom, as all the other apostles probably did except John and Judas Iscariot.

When Jesus told his disciples that Lazarus was sick, Thomas said, "Let us go to where he lives that we may die with him." He supposed that if they returned to Judea the Jews would stone them. On another occasion, when Jesus said, "I go to prepare a place for you, and whither I go ye know and the way ye know," Thomas replied, "We know not whither thou goest, and how can we know the way?"

Thomas has been called the "doubting apostle," for the following reason: When Jesus appeared to his disciples on one occasion after his resurrection Thomas was absent and when told by the others that they had seen the Lord he would not believe it, and required some definite proof of their story, but a few days after he was convinced of the fact when the risen Lord again appeared and gently rebuked him for unbelief. This apostle is mentioned in connection with Peter, Nathaniel, James and John, the sons of Zebedee, and two others who had returned to their former occupation at the Sea of Tiberias, after the resurrection of Christ, therefore the inference is that he was a fisherman.

James the Greater or Elder, the brother of John and son of Zebedee and Salome, is generally called the Greater to distinguish him from James the son of Alpheus, called James the Less. He was a native of Bethsaida, and a fisherman by occupation, and when called to follow the Saviour he immediately obeyed and was a faithful witness of his Lord's public life until his ascension. He was one of the apostles who was present at the Transfiguration on the Mount, and with Peter and John was admitted to a close intimacy with his Master. On one occasion he manifested a rash zeal, for which he was rebuked by the Saviour.

As he was going to Jerusalem Jesus sent a messenger to prepare a place for lodging and entertainment in Samaria, but the inhabitants of the village refused to accommodate them because they were Jews. James and John, indignant at the treatment of their Master, asked him to command fire from heaven to consume them and their village, when he reproved them for their spirit of revenge, saying, " You know not what wrong feelings you manifest. You should have understood that the Son of Man came not to destroy men's lives, but to save them."

A few days after the resurrection, James with his brother John returned to the Sea of Tiberias, to resume their former occupation, when they saw their risen Lord and afterwards witnessed his ascension. It is believed this apostle preached to the dispersed tribes of Israel. About 47 A. D., during the reign of the Emperor Claudius, Herod Agrippa began a persecution against the Christians during which he killed James, the brother of John.

James the Less, called the brother of our Lord, was the son of Cleophas or Alpheus, and the sister of Mary, the mother of Jesus, therefore a relative of his. He was surnamed the Just on account of his upright life, and is said to have been a Nazarite. According to the First Epistle to the Corinthians, Jesus, eight days after his resurrection, appeared to him, and when Paul came to Jerusalem after his conversion James was there and voted in the council held to settle a question of dispute.

About 63 A. D. it is said that James was commanded by the Jews to proclaim from a gallery of the Temple that Jesus of Nazareth was not the Messiah, but, instead of complying with the order, he declared him to be the Son of God and Judge of the world, and for this confession he was thrown from the battlement, and while praying for his enemies was stoned to death. In the Epistle ascribed to James, the object of the writer was to encourage the Jewish Christians to bear with patience and fortitude the sufferings they might be called upon to endure on account of their faith and to enforce the true doctrines and practices of the gospel. He urges them to observe conscientiously all the Christian duties.

Judas, or Jude, called also Thaddeus and Lebbeus, one of the twelve apostles, was the son of Alpheus and brother of James the Less, therefore was called a near kinsman of the Saviour and is supposed to have been a husbandman with a family. A Judas surnamed Barsabas was sent to the church at Antioch to report the decision of the apostles at Jerusalem about the non-observance of the Mosaic law by the Gentile Christians, 54 A. D., and another individual by the same name is mentioned in connection with some events of the early church. It is probable that after the descent of the Holy Spirit at the Pentecost Judas called Lebbeus or Thaddeus preached the gospel and wrought miracles, as did the other apostles, in the name of Christ — first in Judea, and then to both Jews and Gentiles in other countries. According to tradition, he labored in Arabia, Syria, Mesopotamia and Persia, and suffered martyrdom in the last-named country, but there is no record of his travels or any account of his death. He is the reputed author of the Epistle of Jude, written probably between 64 and 66 A. D.

Simon the Canaanite was another of the apostles, but it is not known why he was called the Canaanite. It may have been from Cana, a town in Galilee, or perhaps, with more probability, from the Hebrew word *cana*, meaning zealous, since he was named Zelotes. One of the brothers of our Lord, so called, was named Simon, who may have been the son of Joseph, the husband of Mary. Some historians have considered Simon identical with Simeon, son of Cleophas and bishop of Jerusalem, but no authentic record is given of his labors or his death.

The history of Judas Iscariot, the traitor, is given in connection with the last scenes in the life of Christ. Matthias, who was chosen to take his place after the fearful death of the traitor, was one of the followers of Jesus, and it has been thought by the Greeks that he preached at Colchis, where he died. He was one of the two candidates to fill the place of Judas Iscariot, the other being Joseph called Barsabas surnamed Justus. After praying over the subject, the apostles cast lots that they might know which candidate to install in office, when the lot fell to Matthias, therefore he was numbered with the eleven.

CHAPTER IX.

THE MIRACLES OF CHRIST.

It was important that Jesus should give some infallible proof that he was the Messiah sent from heaven to accomplish the great work of redemption, as predicted by the prophets. The most convincing evidence that could be given was a power to work miracles, and this gift the Saviour exercised on so many occasions, often in the presence of multitudes, that there could be no reasonable grounds to doubt their genuine nature. They were of a different character in most instances, and performed in different places. It is probable that some of the miracles of our Lord were not recorded by the sacred writers, for it is said "He went through all Galilee preaching the gospel and healing every kind of disease," so that there were brought to him persons afflicted with different maladies, and he healed them all.

The miracles specially described are the following, with the places at which they occurred designated:

1. Water changed to wine. Cana of Galilee. John ii.
2. Cure of the nobleman's son. Cana of Galilee. John iv.
3. Draught of fishes. Sea of Galilee. Luke v.
4. Cure of a demoniac. Capernaum. Mark i.
5. Cure of Peter's mother-in-law. Capernaum. Mark i.
6. A leper healed. Capernaum. Mark i.

CHRIST.
(Represented by Carlo Dolce.)

THE MIRACLES OF CHRIST. 103

7. Centurion's servant healed. Capernaum. Matt. viii.
8. Widow's son brought to life. Nain. Luke vii.
9. Tempest on the Sea of Galilee calmed. Matt. viii.
10. Demoniacs restored to reason. Gadara. Matt. viii.
11. Man cured of the palsy. Capernaum. Matt. ix.
12. Daughter of Jairus restored to life. Capernaum. Matt. ix.
13. A woman cured. Capernaum. Luke viii.
14. Two blind men restored. Capernaum. Matt. ix.
15. A dumb man cured. Capernaum. Matt. ix.
16. A man cured at Bethsaida. John v.
17. A man cured of dropsy on the Sabbath. Galilee. Luke xiv.
18. Man having a withered hand cured. Judea. Matt. xii.
19. A demoniac cured. Capernaum. Matt. xii.
20. Five thousand fed. Decapolis. Matt. xiv.
21. Daughter of a Canaanite restored. Near Tyre. Matt. xv.
22. Deaf and dumb man cured. Decapolis. Mark vii.
23. Four thousand fed. Decapolis. Matt. xv.
24. Blind man restored to sight. Bethsaida. Mark xiii.
25. A boy possessed with a devil cured. Tabor. Matt. xvii.
26. Man born blind cured. Jerusalem. John ix.
27. A woman diseased eighteen years cured. Galilee. Luke xiii.
28. Ten lepers healed. Samaria. Luke xvii.
29. Lazarus brought to life. Bethany. John xi.
30. Two blind men restored. Jericho. Matt. xx.
31. The fig-tree withered. Mt. Olivet. Matt. xxi.
32. Ear of Malchus healed. Gethsemane. Luke xxii.

AFTER THE RESURRECTION:
Jesus walking on the Sea. Galilee.
Draught of fishes. Sea of Galilee.

Matthew records the largest number of miracles, 16.
Mark " 5.
Luke " 7.
John " 6.

The first recorded miracle of the Saviour was at a wedding feast in Cana. This was a small town of Galilee about six miles northeast of Nazareth, and to distinguish it from another town of the same name in the tribe of Ephraim it was called Cana of Galilee. A marriage feast was given at this place to which Jesus and his mother were invited. The ceremonies attending a wedding among the Jews were somewhat as follows:

When the day arrived the bride was adorned in rich apparel and costly ornaments, and her head was encircled with a crown. The bridegroom prepared a feast, which, if he was wealthy, was prolonged through the week. Clothed in rich robes and attended by a company of young men and with songs and musical instruments, he went to conduct the bride from her father's house to that of his father. The bride, closely veiled, was also accompanied by virgins near her own age. In case it was evening, the way before them was lighted by flambeaux or torches carried by some of the attendants. Having arrived at the place where the nuptials were to be celebrated, the guests of both sexes indulged in gay pleasures; the women in apartments by themselves.

Marriage ceremonies in the East were celebrated with great pomp and splendor and generally prolonged through several days, including the festivals attending them. Both the bride and bridegroom were carried in palanquins and attended by friends, and after the ceremony a feast lasting seven days was given at the house of the bride's father and at the close the groom conducted his wife to his own home. Beside the company that attended the bride, another band went from the home of the bridegroom to welcome them.

The Saviour illustrated the marriage customs of his time by the parable of the ten virgins, who went to meet the wedding party with lamps, that is, torches made of rags wound about some incombustible substance, which was hollow to contain oil. The virgins waited until midnight, when the marriage procession appeared. As they kept their torches burning all this time, their oil would become exhausted, therefore the five thoughtful virgins supplied themselves with an extra quantity for such an emergency, but the foolish ones, having neglected to do so, were as a consequence excluded from the feast.

The bride of Cana was probably a relative of Mary, the mother of Jesus, therefore she, with him and the disciples Peter, Andrew, Philip and Nathaniel, was invited, but as Joseph is not mentioned, he was, it is presumed, not living. The Saviour had not to this time wrought any public miracles to confirm his divine mission, but it would be important that he should, to prove to his followers that he was really the Son of God. As the festival continued several days, the wine used on the occasion became exhausted, when there arose the question about supplying the large number of guests present. This perplexity was made known to Mary, who appears to have been a confidential friend of the bride or the groom. She told Jesus of their dilemma and perhaps exhibited too great anxiety about it, but it appears from what followed that she had confidence that her Son was able to relieve the parties of all embarrassment. He attempted to quiet her fears and said the moment had not come for him to interfere and there was no need of haste. When he addressed his mother by the word *woman* he did not intend any disrespect, and it is evident she did not understand it as such. She believed he could meet the difficulty, therefore she told the servants to follow his directions.

It was customary for the Jews to keep vessels or water-pots made of stone to hold the water used for the purpose of bathing and other necessary appliances. There were six of these stone jars containing two or three firkins apiece, or perhaps a little more than seven gallons. The Saviour told the servants employed at the feast to fill these vessels with water, which they did, even to the brim, so that no more could be poured in. As the water-jars were filled by the servants, it could not be said the disciples of Jesus had filled them with wine so as to make it *appear* a miracle had been wrought. After this was done Jesus told the servants to draw from the jars and carry the contents to the governor or the one who presided on the occasion, and who sat at the head of the table. No one at the feast, however, knew whence the wine was brought except the servants, therefore, when the governor tasted the wine and found it excellent, he addressed the bridegroom, saying that it was customary to use the best wine first, and afterwards that of a poorer quality, but on this occasion the best had been reserved for the last. The wine used in Palestine was the pure juice of the grape, not fermented as at the present day. It is probable that only the water which was drawn from the jars became changed to wine. Later, Jesus performed another miracle at Cana, the healing of the nobleman's son who was ill at Capernaum.

It has been supposed that after Jesus left Nazareth, he removed with his mother, first to Cana and then to Capernaum. As this region of Galilee is connected with the life and labors of our Lord, a brief description of it may be interesting. Mt. Tabor, lying between Nazareth and Cana, rises from the Valley of Jezreel or the Great Plain, about nine miles west of the Jordan. The mountain is oblong in shape from north to south, and is of considerable height, with a plain on the summit where there was once a city. The Plain of Esdraelon or Jezreel extends from twenty-three to twenty-eight miles from west to east, and is from nine to thirteen miles in width. The road from Nazareth lies between low hills, and after some distance it descends into the Plain. Mt. Tabor, about six miles from the early home of Jesus, stands almost isolated, and is somewhat rugged. The ascent is difficult and several circuits must be made to reach the summit. This mount is among the highest in Palestine and affords a magnificent prospect from the top. On the northwest the Mediterranean can be seen, while at the base are spread out the beautiful plains of Esdraelon and Galilee. Towards the south are the mountains of Gilboa, and on the east the Sea of Tiberias. A little to the north appears what has been called the Mount of Beatitudes, and beyond are the snow-crowned mountains of Antilibanus, while on the southwest are Mt. Carmel and Samaria. The summit of Mt. Tabor was covered with small oaks, plants and flowers. This whole region, with its variegated scenery, was familiar to the Saviour, who travelled through it during his missionary tours, and doubtless he employed these scenes as figures of speech in his sermons.

Jesus was accustomed to attend the festivals at Jerusalem, as every Jewish male was required to do, and on one occasion, when returning to Galilee, he went to Cana where he had performed his first miracle. A certain nobleman or officer at the court of Herod Antipas, who resided at Capernaum, had a son ill with a fever and lying at the point of death. The anxious father, having heard of the fame of Jesus, — for those who had attended the festivals at Jerusalem had spread the news throughout Galilee, — believed that this remarkable teacher could restore his dying child to health; therefore, he left his business and went to Cana, about a day's journey or from twenty to thirty miles from Capernaum, to persuade the Saviour to come to his home and cure his son. To test his faith, Jesus replied " Except you see signs and wonders, you will not believe." The distressed father said in beseeching tones: "Sir, come down, ere my child dies." He evidently supposed the presence of Jesus was necessary for the performance of a miracle, but he was taught that the *word* of Jesus could heal him. The Saviour said, " Go, return to thy son, for he shall live." The nobleman believed His word, and on his journey home he was met by his servants, who were eager to communicate the glad tidings of the recovery of the invalid. The father inquired when he began to amend and they replied, "yesterday, about the seventh hour (that is, about one o'clock P. M.) the fever left him." That was the time that Jesus assured him that his son would not die. As the result of this miracle, the nobleman, who may have been a Roman, and all his household believed in Jesus.

Miracles at Capernaum. — The Saviour, having called Andrew, Peter and John to follow him, went with them to Capernaum and, on the following Sabbath, he

CHRIST AND HIS MOTHER.

entered the synagogue where he addressed the people, who were astonished at his preaching, so different from the teachings of the scribes. In the midst of his sermon, a great excitement occurred on account of the ravings of a madman who was possessed of an evil spirit that caused the maniac to exclaim, " Let us alone, Jesus of Nazareth, Thou art the Holy One of God, art Thou come to destroy us?" Jesus rebuked the evil spirit and commanded him to come out of the man, which he did after inflicting all the injury he could upon the wretched victim, leaving him in a state that seemed like death. Wicked spirits, it appears, believed that Jesus was the Son of God and had power over them. Those who witnessed the miracle were amazed, for the power of casting out devils they had not known before, especially of one's performing such a miracle in his own name. The fame of Jesus consequently spread throughout all the region.

After the services of the synagogue were closed, Jesus, with Andrew, Peter, James and John, entered the house of Peter, whose wife's mother was ill of a fever. When Jesus was informed of her illness he approached the bed of the invalid and took hold of her hand, when the fever immediately left her and she arose and prepared a meal for the company. In the evening, there were many brought to him that were possessed with evil spirits or otherwise afflicted, and he cured them. It was not lawful for the Jews to bring even the sick to be healed on the Sabbath until after sunset, but when that time arrived, they brought the invalids to be restored, thus fulfilling a prophecy of Isaiah, " He took our infirmities and bore our sicknesses." It is said "all the city gathered at the door," that is, of Peter's house.

The miracle of healing a leper occurred in Galilee, but it is not specified at what place, probably one not far from Capernaum. The leprosy was considered one of the most dreaded diseases mentioned in the Scriptures. It first appeared in spots of different colors on the skin, sometimes white, and sometimes black or red. These spots gradually spread over the whole body, and affected the bones and joints. The disease continuing, eventually caused death, though the sufferer might live twenty or even fifty years in dreadful misery. The hands, feet and joints lost their power until, finally, the body collapsed to a hideous form, or the members dropped off one by one. The disease is contagious and hereditary. The law of Moses was very strict in regard to the spread of this fearful malady. The leprous person was separated from the congregation, and the priest alone watched the development of the disease and pronounced the cure of the patient, if that was ever attained.

There came a leper to Jesus, while in Galilee, and kneeling before him besought his help, saying, "If thou wilt, thou canst make me clean." The tender heart of Jesus was moved with pity, and he immediately extended his hand and touched him, which, according to the law, was forbidden, saying, "I will; be thou clean." Immediately the leper was cleansed, when the Lord told him to go directly to the priest without stopping to tell any one by the way, and then make the customary offering, which consisted of two birds, cedar wood, scarlet wood and hyssop, and after eight days, two male lambs, one ewe lamb, fine flour and oil. These were offered to prove to the people that he had been cured. The man restored to health was joyful at his recovery, though he did not go directly to the priest, but delayed, that he might proclaim the miracle to the public, which drew such crowds to the town in which it was wrought that Jesus considered it best to withdraw to the desert, where large multitudes could listen to him without the danger of a mob. After laboring several days, the Saviour returned to Capernaum, when the news of his arrival spread rapidly, and soon a crowd gathered, so that no place was large enough to hold the people, and it was difficult to get standing room about the door. Whether it was in a dwelling-house or a synagogue is not intimated, but from what followed it was probably a dwelling-house.

While Jesus was addressing the multitude four men appeared, bearing on a couch one afflicted with the palsy to be cured by him. When they saw it was impossible to approach the Saviour on account of the great number of people, they were troubled and in doubt what to do, whether to abandon the attempt and return with the paralytic without being cured, or resort to some other method to secure their object. At length one of the men solved the difficulty.

The houses of Palestine were constructed with flat roofs, which could be used for various purposes, especially in the cities where the buildings joined one another. They afforded a retreat for private conversation, for devotion, for witnessing any public scene, and, in warm weather, for sleeping. The roofs were surrounded by a breastwork or wall to prevent any one from falling; it was this wall that was removed to lower the invalid into the open court which was in the centre, usually covered with a curtain or awning that could be removed at pleasure; the roof was reached by stairs on the outside. The man afflicted with paralysis was taken to the roof and lowered on his bed to where Jesus was addressing the people in the court.

When he saw what confidence they placed in him, he said to the invalid, "Son, thy sins be forgiven thee." The language of the Saviour suggests the idea that the man's disease may have been the result of some vice. A number of scribes were present who said to themselves, "This man has uttered blasphemy. Who can forgive sins but God only?" Jesus, who could read their thoughts, saith, "Why do you reason thus in your hearts? Is it not as easy to forgive sins as to give a paralytic the power to walk?" He then said to the man, "Arise, take up thy bed and go to thy house," a command he immediately obeyed to the astonishment of all, when they said, "We never saw anything like this before.

Another miracle wrought at Capernaum was at the request of a Roman centurion stationed at that place. He was probably a pagan, yet he had confidence in the power of Jesus to perform miraculous cures. This Roman exhibited some noble traits of character; for example, his care for his servant who was sick with the palsy, his faith in the Saviour's power and willingness to cure even a Roman's servant, and his humility in confessing that he was not worthy to entertain him under his roof, though Jesus was a Jew belonging to the nation subject to the Romans, the centurion's countrymen. When the Saviour said, "I will come and heal him," the Roman replied, "Speak the word only and my servant will be healed, for as my soldiers obey me, so at thy word will diseases obey thee."

When Jesus heard the declaration of the centurion, he said to the Jews near him, "I have not found so great faith in Israel." He then intimates that this Roman would not be a solitary example, but that many pagans from the East and the West would accept the gospel and be saved, while many of the Jews would be lost. Jesus at length told the centurion his request would be granted. When he arrived at his home, he learned that his servant was restored to health precisely at the time the Saviour declared the fact.

This incident in the life of our Lord is given by another evangelist mainly as follows: After the Sermon on the Mount, Jesus returned to Capernaum, where he made his home for two years and a half of his public life. A centurion of the Roman army stationed in that region had a bond-servant or slave, dear to his master, sick with the palsy. The Roman law gave a master absolute control over his servant or slave, even the power of life and death. This officer was, however, a kind and humane master, therefore he sent to Jesus some of the elders of the Jews to beseech him to come and heal his servant. The messengers earnestly entreated him, saying, that this centurion is worthy of favors from our nation, for he is very kind to us and has built us a synagogue. It is possible he may have become a Jewish proselyte.

It is said that at the modern Tell Hum, on the site of ancient Capernaum, there are the remains of a large synagogue, which was seventy-five feet in length, and fifty-seven in width, with walls ten feet thick; the interior was divided into five aisles by four rows of pillars. This may have been the one built by this Roman. Jesus told the messengers he would go with them and heal the servant, but when he had nearly reached the centurion's house, the latter sent other messengers, saying, " Lord, do not trouble thyself to come any farther, but speak the word and my servant will be healed, for I am not worthy to receive you at my house"; and to illustrate his idea, he said, "though I am under superior officers, yet there are those whom I command by a word, and who obey my orders, though I am not present." As previously stated, the servant was healed.

CHAPTER X.

THE MIRACLES OF CHRIST — CONTINUED.

The town of Nain was about twenty-five miles southwest of Capernaum, and seven miles north of Nazareth. Jesus left Capernaum the next day after healing the centurion's servant, and went to Nain, where he arrived the following day. As usual, he was accompanied by a large company, and when they came near the gate of the city they met a funeral procession attended by the customary exhibitions of mourning. A widow of the city had lost an only son who was being carried to his grave, followed by a large procession of the citizens. The occasion was a very sad one. A young man in the prime of life, upon whom the mother was dependent, had been taken, and she was left alone and unprotected. To pay due honors to the dead was regarded as a religious duty, and on such occasions the mourners who followed the bier expresssed their grief, real or ostensible, in loud lamentations, while eulogists and musicians rehearsed the virtues of the departed, accompanied by solemn music. Coffins were not in use among the Jews, though they were employed by the Egyptians and Babylonians. The corpse, instead of being placed in a coffin, was wrapped in folds of linen and laid on a bier, carried by four or six persons. While the mourners, on this occasion, were bewailing the deceased in the usual manner, Jesus approached and touched the bier, when the bearers stopped. He then said, "Young man, arise!" and immediately he was restored to life and spoke, and, being unbound, was conducted to his mother.

It was the custom in Oriental countries to express grief for the death of a person by noisy demonstrations, such as wailing and crying bitterly, tearing the hair, and sometimes by lacerating the flesh, but the Jews were forbidden by the law of Moses to tear their hair or cut their flesh, though they could express their grief by lamentations, by rending their outer garment, by casting dust into the air, and by abstaining from washing or anointing themselves, or conversing with any one. There were persons of both sexes engaged to mourn for the dead, who accompanied these demonstrations with instrumental music, while the women of the family joined in such exhibitions in a prolonged and mournful cry ending in sobs. These displays of grief usually continued eight days, and upon the death of a king or any other eminent person, they were generally prolonged for a month. This ostentatious mourning was exhibited during the procession to the grave, while the lamentations of the friends or the hired mourners rent the air.

Jesus had crossed the Sea of Galilee to the west side, on a certain occasion, and the people in great crowds gathered to hear him. Here he was invited to a feast given by Matthew, called also Levi, and among the guests were publicans, as the master of the feast had himself been a publican, or tax-gatherer, under the

Romans, an office held in abhorrence by the Jews. When Jesus was conversing with the guests, a ruler of a synagogue, that is, one who had charge of it, whose name was Jairus, came, and kneeling before him as a subject paying homage to his sovereign, besought him to restore his daughter, who was very ill and "who, perhaps, is now dead," said he, " but come and lay thy hands upon her and she shall live." While Jairus was talking with Jesus, there came one of his servants, who said to him, " Thy daughter is dead, why should you trouble the Master any further?" The Saviour said to the father, " Be not anxious, only believe." When the ruler of the synagogue presented his petition, Jesus, with Peter, James and John, immediately left the feast and went with him, but while on the way an incident occurred of special interest.

Before the servant of Jairus had arrived to inform him of his daughter's death, a certain woman who had been afflicted with a troublesome disease during twelve years, and had spent all her fortune to pay her physicians, but to no purpose, for she was daily growing worse, appeared on the scene. She had heard of the miracles Jesus had performed, and resolved to approach him, notwithstanding the crowd, with the hope that he would heal her malady. She believed that if she could only touch the hem of his garment she would be cured. The Jews were required by law to have their outside garment fringed to distinguish them from other nations. It was this fringe, or "hem" as it is called, that this woman wished to touch, therefore making her way through the crowd she came behind him, so as not to be observed, and touching the hem of his garment, she was immediately restored to health. Jesus, knowing what had been done, turned about and said, "Who touched my garments?" His disciples said, "The multitude press around you, is it then strange they should touch you?" When the woman perceived her act was known, she was afraid, and, trembling, cast herself at the feet of Jesus, and confessed the truth. He knew, of course, who touched his garment, and for what purpose, but he wished to lead her to make confession for the benefit of others. When she had done this, he said, "Daughter," using a term of gentle tenderness, "go in peace: thou art cured," — that is permanently.

During this delay Jairus had been impatiently waiting for Jesus to proceed on his way, fearing it might be too late to save his child, when, to his dismay, a messenger arrived with the fearful tidings that his daughter, who was twelve years of age, was actually dead. When Jesus arrived at the house of the bereaved father he entered the room where the corpse lay, and said, "Talitha cumi," which means "Damsel, arise!" This was in the Syro-Chaldean or Aramean dialect, the common language used by the Jews at the time. The maiden directly arose and walked, when Jesus told the parents to give her something to eat, probably to confirm the fact that she had been really restored to life. There were five witnesses to this miracle, namely, the parents of the damsel, and Peter, James and John.

When Jesus arrived at the house of Jairus and witnessed the tumult usual on such occasions, he told the people to be quiet, for the damsel was not dead, but was asleep. He could not have meant she was not physically dead, but that her soul or spirit was still

JESUS, MARTHA AND MARY

alive. When he made this declaration a scornful laugh arose from the crowd, for they were sure she was dead. There may have been Sadducees present, who believed death ended all, and that there was no soul or spirit, consequently she could not be raised. When Christ spoke of death as a sleep he implied there is a resurrection.

Those who saw the miracle were much astonished, as they had never seen anything like it before, but the Saviour strictly charged them to tell no one about it. His reason for this is not given, but it may have been to avoid the appearance of ostentation and giving the multitude cause for saying that he performed miracles to gain popularity. Jairus, who was well known to the public, received the congratulations of his friends, and not even the Sadducees dared to deny the miracle.

After Jesus left the house of Jairus he was followed by two blind men who heard the crowd say that he was passing by. They were, probably, accompanied by some one who had compassion on them in their sad misfortune. These blind men had heard of his wonderful miracles and believed he was the Son of God, and could restore their sight. Raising their voices above the noise of the multitude, they said, " Thou Son of David " — a term applied to the Messiah — " have mercy on us." Jesus having entered the house, probably to avoid the tumult in the street, was followed by the blind men; when he inquired whether they believed he was able to restore their sight, they said " Yea, Lord." He then touched their eyes, saying, " According to your faith, be it unto you," when their sight was immediately restored. Though the Saviour said to them "Tell no man," yet as soon as they left the house they, being so overjoyed at the miracle, spread abroad his fame all through that region, and another unfortunate was brought to him to be cured. This was a man possessed with a devil and was dumb. Jesus commanded the evil spirit to leave his victim, when the dumb man recovered his speech. This miracle increased the astonishment of the people, who said, "Nothing like it was ever seen before in Israel."

Decapolis was a region of ten cities, as the name implies, lying mostly on the east side of the Jordan in the province of Gaulonitis, which belonged to Herod Antipas. Though located in Palestine, it was largely inhabited by foreigners, and this may account for the herds of swine in that region, since the Jews were forbidden by the law of Moses to raise these animals. Jesus visited this region, where he performed some of his miracles.

When he heard of the execution of John the Baptist, he considered it prudent to leave the place where he was laboring, therefore he crossed the Sea of Galilee in a ship or boat, to the east side, and withdrew to a desert place, that is, a region with a scattered population and extensive fields of meadow land. It was, however, impossible to remain separated from the multitude, for as soon as the people learned about his movements, they followed him on foot. To accomplish their purpose, they went around the head of the lake or sea, consequently were obliged to travel some distance, but in their haste to depart, they neglected to supply themselves with food to satisfy their immediate wants.

This throng comprised five thousand men, besides

women and children, who probably increased the number to ten thousand or more. There were, in this vast company, different classes of people with different views and motives; some believing that Jesus was the Son of God, others scornfully spurned that idea; a part were led by curiosity, others were expecting to gain some worldly advantage, for, if Jesus was really the Messiah, he would establish his royal power and then, perhaps, they might be honored by an appointment to an office under his government. Another class comprised Romans who still adhered to the customs and religion of their nation, yet were surprised at the remarkable events that had stirred all Galilee and the adjacent regions. The children were crying for food and the mothers were exhausted by carrying their infants in their arms during the long and tedious journey, while their cheeks were bathed in tears.

A crowd of ten thousand persons afforded an exciting scene; for there were the aged and the young, the feeble and the vigorous, children carried in the arms of their parents or led by the hand and invalids assisted by their friends with the hope of reaching the Great Physician. The intense interest of the masses in the person and work of Christ was exhibited on this occasion, as on so many others. When they brought to him the sick, he healed them; those afflicted with the heavy burdens of life he comforted and never treated with contempt the poor, despised outcast, while his tender heart was so moved with pity, he said, "They were like sheep without a shepherd," meaning they had no one to care for or instruct them in the truth, since their teachers only led them astray.

The Saviour instructed the people until near the close of day, when his disciples requested him to send them to the neighboring village to buy food for themselves. He said to them, "We must feed them. How many loaves have we on hand?" They replied "only five, and two small fishes, but what are these for so great a multitude?" Jesus then inquired of Philip where they could purchase the needed supply for the company, when he told his Master that it would require two hundred pence, a sum equal to about twenty-eight dollars, and this amount was more than the common purse contained. Some barley loaves, a cheap kind of bread used by the poor, were in the possession of a lad accustomed to attend to their supply of food when they were travelling about the country, and the fishes were, perhaps, those caught in the lake by the disciples, and had been cooked ready for use, but neither they nor the loaves could, naturally, satisfy the hunger of the multitude on this occasion.

There was a large space of ground in the vicinity, covered with grass, and the Saviour gave directions to have the people seated. It required some time to do this, but they were quiet and did not crowd one another. The disciples acted as ushers and designated the places each group comprising, some fifty, and others one hundred persons, should occupy. The position at meals was that of reclining on the left side, and that may have been the attitude taken on this occasion, since the season was warm and vegetation fresh. There was some surprise at the movements going on, as it was not understood what the Saviour intended to do.

After the company was quietly seated, Jesus took the

bread, and raising his eyes to heaven asked a blessing. By this act he acknowledged the goodness of God in providing the food. He then broke the bread into separate pieces and passed them to the disciples for distribution. It was the custom of the Jews to invoke the blessing of God at their meals in the following words: "Blessed be thou, O Lord our God, the King of the earth and the vine," etc.

The expression "breaking bread" as used in the Scriptures may need an explanation. Bread was of two kinds, leavened and unleavened. The loaves or cakes were round and nine or ten inches in diameter, the leavened were about one inch thick, while the unleavened were much thinner, and could be broken instead of being cut.

After the distribution of the bread, the fishes were given out, and when the people had eaten all they needed, there were left twelve baskets full, enough to supply the disciples for some time. These baskets, so called, were such receptacles as travellers used to carry their provisions, for as there were few public houses or hotels, it was necessary for one on a journey to carry his own supplies. The command of Jesus that the fragments be gathered that nothing be wasted teaches a practical lesson easily understood.

The effect of the miracle was important, since many of those who witnessed it believed that Jesus was the Messiah, or the Prince they had been expecting, and they were ready to compel him to be proclaimed and crowned, therefore he resolved to leave the place as soon and as privately as possible. After dismissing the multitude he directed his disciples to embark and cross the

Sea of Galilee or Tiberias to the other side and wait for his coming, but he withdrew to a solitary mountain for private devotion. The Saviour loved to hold communion with his Heavenly Father, and in the midst of his urgent duties, his labors for others, and his remarkable popularity, he never omitted frequent and prolonged seasons of prayer and meditation.

When Jesus was alone on the mountain during the night there arose a storm, such as was common on the Sea of Galilee, and the disciples were tossed in their little boat and in danger of being wrecked, for the wind blew so furiously in the opposite direction they could make no headway. While in this perilous condition their alarm was increased by seeing through the darkness the form of a man walking on the turbulent billows, and in their fear they exclaimed "It is a spirit." Jesus, who was the form they imagined a spirit, said to them, "Be of good courage, it is I." They at once recognized his voice, when Peter, the impulsive disciple, said, "If it be thou, bid me come to thee." To show him his rash presumption and his want of faith, the Master said, "Come" Peter immediately left the boat and attempted to walk on the water, but as the rolling waves tossed him about and he began to sink, he cried in a beseeching tone, "Lord, save me." Jesus immediately extended his hand and caught him, and at the same time administered a gentle rebuke, saying, "O thou of little faith, why didst thou doubt?" They were both taken into the boat or ship as it is called, and directly it came to land, although it was in the middle of the sea that the incident occurred.

It is said that Jesus appeared in the fourth watch of

CHRIST WITH LITTLE CHILDREN.

the night. The Jews in earlier times divided the night into three divisions of four hours each, but in the days of our Saviour it was divided into four watches of three hours each, the change having been made by the Romans. The first watch was from 6 until 9; the second, from 9 to 12; the third, from 12 to 3; the fourth, from 3 to 6. The first was called evening; the second, midnight; the third, cock-crowing; the fourth, morning. As Jesus appeared to the disciples in the fourth watch, it is evident he had spent most of the night in prayer on the mountain.

The following is a picture of the scene as one has drawn it. "A dark night, roaring wind, tossing waves, a little boat some miles from the shore, the crew in momentary expectation of sinking to the bottom of the sea, a person walking upon the waves, a sudden calm, and instant approach to land." It is not surprising the ship's crew came to Jesus to pay him homage and said, "Of a truth thou art the Son of God." When they came to the region of Gennesareth west of the sea, and the people who had heard of his miracle in Decapolis and of his return to Galilee were aware of it, all the invalids were brought to Jesus that they might touch the border of his mantle and be restored to health.

After the miracle of feeding the multitude and of walking on the sea, the scribes and Pharisees came to Jesus with complaints about his disciples, because they did not wash their hands before eating. He reproved them for such scrupulous exactions, at which they were offended and were determined to be avenged, therefore he went to the region of Tyre and Sidon on the coast of the Mediterranean, probably for concealment, and entered the house of a friend; he did not wish the people of that region to know it, but he could not remain concealed, since his fame had preceded him.

The Jews regarded all nations except their own as Greeks or Gentiles. The Phœnicians were the descendants of the Canaanites, and their country was called Syro-Phœnicia. It was conquered by Alexander the Great, and in the time of Christ the cities of this region were considered Greek and the inhabitants were pagans. While the Saviour was there, a Syro-Phœnician woman, who had heard of the wonderful miracles he had performed, came to him for a favor. She had a daughter possessed with a devil, and in her maternal anguish, she said, "O Lord, thou Son of David," thus acknowledging his Messiahship, "my daughter is grieviously vexed with a devil." She intended to say more, but the Saviour apparently gave no attention to her and made no reply. It was not because he felt no pity for her, but he wished to test her faith.

The disciples besought their Lord to send her away, for they considered it a public scandal to have anything to do with a heathen. Jesus at length said to her that he was sent to preach the gospel to the Jews only, but this reply did not silence her, and coming nearer she fell at his feet, saying, "Lord, help me." He replied, "It is not proper to take the children's bread and cast it to dogs." The Jews, to express their contempt for the Gentiles, called them dogs. The woman was not repelled by this remark, but said, "It is true, Lord, yet the dogs eat the crumbs which fall from their master's table." Jesus did not intend a sneer in his reply to the woman, but he meant, "Are you willing to receive a favor from a nation that designates your people dogs?" "Yes, let me be considered a heathen dog, yet I entreat thee to grant this favor to one not worthy of it." "O woman, great is thy faith; thy request is granted," said Jesus, and the daughter was immediately restored to her right mind. When the mother returned to her home, she found her lying upon her bed perfectly sane.

It was not because the Saviour had little sympathy for the calamities of other nations that he was apparently unmoved at first, but he wished to prove to others the faith this pagan had in him and, perhaps, teach the doctrine that the gospel was to be proclaimed to the Gentiles as well as the Jews.

CHAPTER XI.

THE MIRACLES OF CHRIST — CONTINUED.

Jesus returned to the Sea of Tiberias, after his miracle in Phœnicia, then ascended one of the mountains or hills in the vicinity and, wearied by his travels, sat down, when he was directly surrounded by a great multitude of people who had been waiting for him. If the Saviour needed rest he was not allowed to take it, for there were brought the lame, blind, maimed and others afflicted with diseases, and laid at his feet to be healed. These unfortunates had been gathered from different places, and some from great distances, and comprised all classes, but the larger number belonged to the poorer and lower ranks, including men, women and children. Jesus healed them all, one by one, and when the spectators saw these miracles, they praised the God of Israel, who had given such power to the Healer.

The crowds were not inclined to disperse, though they had been three days without their regular meals. The tenderness of Jesus was again manifested for the physical comfort of the people, when he said to his disciples, "I will not send them away fasting, lest they faint before reaching their homes." The disciples, forgetting that five thousand men had been fed on a previous occasion, said, "Where can we purchase, in the wilderness, food for so large a company?" Jesus inquired how many loaves they had, and they replied, "Seven, and a few little fishes." He said "Seat them on the ground," which they did as on a similar occasion when they were to be fed. The number this time was four thousand men, besides women and children, or perhaps six thousand persons or more in all. The food was distributed, and after the people had finished their meal, seven baskets of the fragments left were gathered. This miracle was performed on the east side of the Sea of Tiberias or Galilee, in or near the vicinity of the first one of feeding the multitude. After the people had been sent to their homes, the Saviour embarked with his disciples and came to Magdala on the western side. Both these miracles had been performed in Decapolis, east of the sea.

When travelling from Galilee to Jerusalem to attend the annual festivals, Jesus passed through Samaria, and in his journey, on one occasion, as he entered a certain village, ten lepers standing afar off were waiting for his coming, with the hope of being cured of their fearful malady. They were not allowed to enter the village on account of the nature of their disease, therefore they exclaimed in a loud voice, " Jesus, Master, have mercy on us." He answered their appeal by saying, "Go show yourselves to the priest." They directly obeyed, and as they proceeded on their way they were suddenly cured. Among these lepers was a Samaritan, the others being Jews, who, when he learned that he was cured, returned to the Saviour and in a loud voice, so that all could hear, glorified God, and, falling upon his face, gave thanks for his recovery. Jesus said, "Were there not ten who were cleansed, but where are the nine?" Only this stranger or foreigner returned to give God the glory for being cured, while the Jews who ought to have expressed their gratitude were all silent.

When Jesus was at Jerusalem on a certain occasion an incident occurred which excited the wonder of the multitude and the hatred of his enemies; this was the restoration of sight to a man born blind, a cure that had not ever been known before, but since the Saviour's day it has been done by a surgical operation; the first instance of the kind, it is said, was performed in the early part of the eighteenth century. The Saviour had just finished an address to his countrymen, in which he said they were not the true sons of Abraham, as they with their pride claimed to be, since it conferred upon them great honor and superior advantages. This declaration so aroused their anger that they attempted to kill him. The repairs on the Temple made by Herod were not then completed, and loose stones were lying about, which in their excitement the Jews seized with the intention of stoning him to death, but Jesus managed to pass through the turbulent crowd and escape the danger. As he was leaving the Temple he saw a blind man asking charity, an intimation that his parents were poor.

The Jews believed that all personal calamities were the consequence of sins committed either by the sufferer or his ancestors. As this man was born blind, they were in doubt whether his blindness was caused by his own sin before his birth, since they believed such a thing possible, or whether it was through the sin of his parents. Jesus told his disciples when they asked the question, that the man's blindness was not caused by either, but was so ordered by Divine Providence to manifest the power of God in his restoration by a miracle. When he said that neither the man nor his parents had sinned, he meant that their transgressions had not caused his blindness.

It was the Sabbath, yet the Saviour did not consider it a violation of the Fourth Commandment to cure this man on that day. He had placed his life in danger, but he did not hesitate to pause and restore this blind beggar even on the Sabbath. He said that he was doing the work his Father had assigned him and that he must labor while the day lasted, that is, his earthly life which was drawing to its close. He was in the moral world, what the sun is in the natural world; that is, he was the Sun of Righteousness that came to illumine the spiritual life. Jesus then applied to the eyes of the blind man a clay made by mixing the soil with spittle. Like the prophets, Jesus sometimes used symbols in performing miracles, and it may have been in this instance he intended to signify that the power of healing came from himself.

After annointing the blind man's eyes, he told him to go and wash in the Pool or Fountain of Siloam, situated at the foot of Mt. Zion near the King's Garden, which was surrounded by a wall, and supplied a large part of the water for the city. The blind man, led by some of his friends, immediately complied with his directions and his eyes were opened. This man was well known, as he had been accustomed to resort to public places for the purpose of soliciting charity, therefore his neighbors were surprised and inquired, "Is not this the blind man who sat by the wayside begging?" Some thought it was he, while others said, "He resembles him." As they were discussing the question he said, "I am he." "If you are the man, how did you recover your sight?" He then related the circumstances, when they inquired "Where is he?" that is, the one who cured him; "I know not," he replied.

The man restored to sight was conducted to some of the members of the Sanhedrim, perhaps with the intention of accusing Jesus of violating the Sabbath, when they inquired how he was restored to sight, and he repeated the circumstances as related. There was a division among the members of the Great Council, some asserting that Jesus could not be a good man, because he did not observe the Sabbath, while others said, "How could a sinner perform such miracles?" They said to the man, "What is your opinion of him?" The reply was "He is a prophet." The Pharisees did not, or pretended they did not, believe he was born blind; therefore they sent for his parents and inquired whether he was their son and whether he was born blind, and if he was their son, how he was restored to sight. They confessed he was their son and was born blind, but they could give no positive information in regard to the miracle, since they did not witness it; they must ask him about it, as he was old enough to bear legal testimony. A person thirteen years old and upwards, among the Jews, could be a witness in courts of law. It is probable the parents did believe that Jesus performed the miracle as represented, but they did not dare to acknowledge it, since the Pharisees had decided that if any one confessed he was the Christ, he should be put out of the synagogue that is, be excommunicated. There were three different kinds of excommunication: *First*, For lighter offences, when the accused was suspended for thirty days and not allowed to enter a synagogue, or have any intercourse with others, not even the members of his own family. *Second*, The excommunication denominated the *curse*, uttered with imprecations in the presence of ten witnesses. It excluded the criminal from all intercourse with his countrymen, who were not allowed to sell him anything, not even the necessaries of life. *Third*, This degree was still more severe, when the offender was secluded absolutely from all other persons and left entirely to the justice of God. It is probable the second degree was the one administered to those who acknowledged Jesus the Son of God.

The Pharisees again called the one restored to sight and said to him, "Give God the praise; we know this man (meaning the Saviour) is a sinner." He replied that he would not attempt to decide the question, but "One thing I know," said he, "that I was once blind but now I see." With the intention of making him contradict himself, they inquired again how his eyes were opened. "I have told you already, why do you ask me? Will you become his disciples?" Their pride and indignation were aroused, and they reviled him and with a contemptuous sneer said, "Thou art his disciple but we are the disciples of Moses, and know that God spake by him, but as for this pretender, we know nothing of his origin and family. We do not know whether he is mad or under the influence of the Evil One." "It is marvellous that you do not know whence he is, and yet he has opened my eyes. It is admitted that God does not answer sinners, and only those who worship him and do his will have the gift of working miracles. Now if Jesus had not been sent of God, he could not have performed such a deed."

The exasperated Pharisees made answer, " Thou wast born in sin," that is, in a state of blindness, "and hast thou the presumption to teach us?" Then they cast him out of the synagogue, that is, excommunicated him.

When Jesus heard of it, he sought for the man and asked him whether he believed on the Son of God. "Who is he, Lord, that I may believe on him?" "Thou hast seen him and he is now talking with thee." Previously the man but imperfectly understood the true character of Jesus, though he believed he was able to restore his sight. As the Saviour explained the subject more fully, the man said, "Lord, I believe," and prostrating himself at the feet of Jesus he worshipped him as the Messiah. Jesus closed the interview by saying that he came to declare the gospel of salvation, and his preaching would give sight to the spiritually blind who accepted it, while it would increase the blindness of those who excluded the light.

There were three great annual festivals held at Jerusalem, as previously stated, namely, the Passover, Pentecost and the Feast of Tabernacles, each to commemorate some important event in the history of the Jewish nation, and as all male Jews were required by law to attend these feasts, Jesus, of course, conformed to this practice. It was during one of these festivals that he

LITTLE CHILDREN BROUGHT TO CHRIST.

performed the miracle of curing the man who had suffered from some disease which rendered him unable to walk for thirty-eight years. At the time of Christ there was a pool or fountain called Bethesda, meaning "house of mercy," which was supposed to possess medicinal properties. It was near the Sheep-gate, the one through which the animals were driven intended for sacrifice. This pool had five porches or covered apartments for invalids who came to the waters to be cured. There were usually great numbers waiting for an opportunity to descend first into the fountain, which descent was by steps. There were paralytics and others afflicted with various diseases, waiting for the "moving of the waters," or its agitation, which occurred at intervals. It was then the fountain contained an unusual amount of water impregnated with strong medicinal properties. A tradition existed that an angel agitated the water at certain seasons, and after this whoever first descended into the pool was cured. The Jews believed in the ministry of angels in human affairs, and it is written in the Scriptures, "Are they not ministering spirits sent forth to minister to those who shall be heirs of salvation?"

The invalids at the fountain were not, probably, healed instantly but gradually. The first one stepping in after the agitation of the water received the benefit, while the others were compelled to wait until a similar event occurred again. There was nothing miraculous about the healing properties of this pool, for there are medicinal springs at the present day which cure diseases supposed incurable by the usual methods. When at Jerusalem the Saviour passing near this pool saw a man lying in one of the porches, or apartments, waiting for an opportunity to descend into the water; he understood his case and said, "Wilt thou be made whole?" The invalid did not know who addressed him, but he replied, "Sir, there is no one to assist me, and when I am trying to descend, another less helpless steps down before me." Jesus said, "Rise, take up thy bed and walk," thus proving that he was cured. What was called his bed was a light mattress and could be easily carried. This was on the Sabbath, and the Jews were forbidden by their law to carry burdens on that day, therefore they told the man he was violating the law. He replied, "The one who healed me said, 'take up thy bed.'" He had not inquired the name of his Physician who, afterwards finding his patient in the Temple, said to him, "Behold, thou art made whole; sin no more, lest a worse thing come upon thee." This injunction seems to imply that the invalid's disease was the result of some evil course, perhaps in his youth. The man cured told the scribes and Pharisees that it was Jesus who had cured him, when they laid plans to kill the Saviour because he had performed the miracle on the Sabbath. Jesus vindicated his conduct by saying, "My Father works on this day, therefore I also work," that is, in doing good to others. This made his enemies still more angry because he had not only violated the Sabbath in their estimation, but had also called God his Father, thus making himself equal with God. Jesus continued his remarks, confirming the truth of his claim.

At one time when Jesus was at Capernaum, there were brought to him so many persons to be cured that he became weary, and proposed to his disciples that they should cross the sea, for the purpose, undoubtedly, of being more retired, but previous to their going on board the boat, a certain scribe came and said he would follow him. The Saviour told him of his poverty, and illustrated it by saying, " The foxes have holes, and the birds of the air have nests, but the Son of Man hath not where to lay his head." It is possible this scribe was influenced by worldly motives and expected some temporal advantages by following him. Another of his hearers said he would follow him after he had performed the funeral rites for his deceased father, but the Saviour may have known that if he returned to his home he would not come back, hence he said, " Let others perform these duties, and do you leave your home and follow me now." These incidents teach the lesson that the first and most important duty is to follow Christ, that is, become one of his disciples, even if in so doing great sacrifices must be made, for as the Saviour declared, whoever was not willing to forsake all his friends, his home, his possessions, if necessary, could not be his disciple, and further, he must resign his own life if the sacrifice was demanded.

CHAPTER XII.

THE MIRACLES OF CHRIST — CONCLUDED.

It was night, and Jesus, wearied after the labors of the day, said, "Let us pass over to the other side of the lake," perhaps with the desire of obtaining rest. He had been instructing from the boat the crowd who stood on the shore, and the multitude had been sent to their homes, when he and his disciples sailed away; but some of the people, determined to follow them, embarked in other boats for this purpose. The Saviour retired to the stern of the ship or boat and reclining on a pillow fell asleep. The Sea of Tiberias was subject to storms, and at this time there arose a great tempest with violent wind, so that the billows dashed against the little bark and the crew and passengers were in danger of being wrecked or drowned. The disciples, as well as others on board, were greatly alarmed, and going to their Master awoke him, saying, "Lord, save us or we shall all perish." He mildly rebuked them and asked, "Why are you afraid, O you of little faith? You should have felt safe for the Son of God is on board." Then he arose and commanded the winds and the waves to be quiet, when immediately there was a perfect calm. The scene just before was

THE MIRACLES OF CHRIST.   139

fearful: the darkness, the dashing waves, the roaring winds, the tossing ship, the terror of the sailors and passengers, all combined to render the situation appalling. No wonder the people were greatly surprised and said, "What manner of man is he whom even the wind and sea obey?" The disciples, of course, who had witnessed so many of his miracles and believed he was the Son of God, were not astonished, but the event must have impressed them with reverence and admiration for their Divine Master.

After crossing the sea, they came into the country of the Gergesenes or Gadarenes. Gadara was a city east of the Sea of Tiberias or Galilee, about eight miles from the shore. Gergasa was not far from Gadara, and both places were in a region containing tombs, hewn in the rocks, though in the time of Christ they were not used for that purpose, but had become the resort of people afflicted with various maladies and were considered the outcasts of society. The tombs or sepulchres of the Jews were generally in groves or mountainous, uninhabited regions, sometimes far below the surface and reached by a flight of steps. They often became the resort of the insane and bands of robbers.

After Jesus came into this region, inhabited by a mixed population of Jews and Gentiles, there came from one of these tombs or caverns two men so fierce and dangerous that no one ever ventured to pass that way unless properly guarded; they were naked and under the influence of evil spirits. One of these lunatics had been a citizen of Gadara and a person of some distinction and wealth, therefore those who had known him felt sympathy for him and his friends, though they did not dare to approach him. He was so dangerous, it was necessary for the safety of himself and others to bind him with chains, but in his ravings he always succeeded in breaking them. Finally, he escaped to the wilderness or sparsely inhabited region, where he kept up his cries and wounded himself with stones. When these maniacs saw Jesus, they fell to the ground and cried in a loud voice, "What hast thou to do with us, Jesus, thou Son of the Most High? Art thou come to punish us before the time? We beseech thee to torment us not."

The Saviour commanded the evil spirits to leave the men, but they asked him not to send them to the place of final punishment, but to allow them to enter a distant herd of swine feeding. Jesus asked one of the maniacs his name, and he replied "Legion," implying there were a large number of demons tormenting him. Jesus gave the evil spirits permission to enter the swine, when the whole herd, numbering two thousand, ran violently down the steep bank of the sea and were drowned. When the men attending the swine saw what was done, they were alarmed and fled to the city with the astonishing news. The citizens, offended on account of the losses they had sustained, came to Jesus, perhaps with the intention of arresting him for causing the destruction of their property, but when they saw him they were so awed by his presence, they did not lay violent hands upon him, but they entreated him to leave their country. Keeping swine was illegal for the Jews, and the Gentiles were aware of the fact, therefore the owners had no just cause for complaint. The evil spirits cast out

CHRIST PREACHING FROM THE BOAT.

had their revenge in causing the loss of property, besides attempting to counteract the influence of Christ's miracle.

When the people of the city saw the most dangerous of the maniacs sitting at the feet of Jesus, clothed and in his right mind, they were astonished and impressed with awe. The man restored besought Jesus to allow him to remain in his company, but the Saviour told him to return to his own home and show what had been done for him. He went as requested and proclaimed to the whole city the miracle which had been performed. Jesus directly left Gadara, recrossed the lake and came to Capernaum, his resident city. The people meanwhile had been anxiously waiting his return, and when he appeared they welcomed him with joyful demonstrations.

While Jesus was teaching in a synagogue of Galilee on a certain occasion, he noticed a woman in the audience who had been afflicted with a disease for eighteen years, which rendered her unable to stand or walk upright. She was an object of pity and perhaps aversion to some, yet she was a constant attendant upon the public services of religion. The Saviour came to her and tenderly laid his hands upon her, saying, "Woman, thou art free from thine infirmity," when, to her amazement, she was directly restored, and standing erect, she praised God for her recovery. This was witnessed by all in the synagogue, but the ruler was offended because Jesus had performed the miracle on the Sabbath. He said to the people, there are six days when it is lawful to work, that is, to come for healing, but it ought not to be on the Sabbath. Jesus accused him justly of hypocrisy, for, said he, "every one leads his animals to water on the Sabbath; ought not then this woman, a daughter of Abraham, therefore a Jewess, be set free on the Sabbath?" This reply silenced the ruler and his associates, being condemned by their consciences, but the rest of the audience were greatly amused at their discomfiture.

Jesus had been on the Mount of Transfiguration, where a scene of ineffable glory was witnessed by Peter, James and John. The Saviour chose these disciples to accompany him to a high mountain, supposed to have been Mt. Tabor in Galilee, to witness his Transfiguration. It was a place Jesus had often visited for the purpose of secret prayer and communion with his Father. The scene, as described by the evangelists, was wonderful, when the countenance of our Lord "shone as the sun, and his garments became white as the light, or as snow." Two persons long since dead, appeared talking with him, that is, Moses, the great Law-giver and Leader of the Israelites, and Elijah the prophet, who had been translated to heaven without suffering death.

It is probable the Transfiguration occurred during the night, for the witnesses of this remarkable scene fell asleep, and when they awoke, they were so entranced by the heavenly vision that Peter desired to remain, and proposed to erect three tents, one for his Master, one for Moses, and one for Elias or Elijah. While he was speaking a cloud enveloped them, and a voice was heard saying, "This is my beloved Son, in whom I am well pleased; hear Him." The disciples were so astonished at the wonderful scene that they fell to the ground on their faces, being greatly alarmed, but Jesus came and touched them, saying, "Arise, and do not fear," and when they arose the vision had disappeared and they saw no one except their Lord who charged them to repeat the event to no one, until the Son of Man had risen from the grave. The effect of this miraculous incident was to confirm the faith of Peter, James and John, in Jesus as the Messiah.

The multitude had been waiting for the appearance of the Saviour, not knowing where he was nor the cause of his absence. In the crowd were some of his disciples, and the scribes were making inquiries about their Master, his birth, family, manner of life, and doctrines, not in a spirit of candor, but with the artful design of proving that he was not the Son of God, that is, the expected Messiah. When the people saw Jesus coming, they left the scribes and hastened to meet and welcome him, and one came and kneeling before him as an act of homage, said, "Lord have mercy on my son, for he is a lunatic, and I brought him to thy disciples but they could not cure him." This son was an only child and very dear to his father, whose tender affection led him to weep on account of his affliction. When under the influence of evil spirits, he was dumb and thrown into convulsions, foamed at the mouth, gnashed his teeth, sometimes falling into the fire, and but for constant care and watchfulness would have been killed. This fearful condition came upon him in his childhood. The father said, "If thou canst do anything for him, have compassion on us and help us." There seemed to be some doubt in his mind about the Saviour's power to cure his son, perhaps because his disciples had failed to restore him. Jesus said, "If thou canst believe; all things are possible to those who believe." The distressed father said with tears, "Lord, I believe; help my unbelief."

The people came running to see what was going on, when Jesus rebuked the evil spirit and commanded him to leave his victim, saying, "Thou dumb and deaf spirit, I charge thee to leave him and return no more." Before obeying the command, the fiend inflicted further injuries upon his victim so that he appeared to be dead, and some of the witnesses said he was dead, but Jesus took him by the hand and he arose from the ground to which he had been thrown. After the Saviour entered a house, his disciples came to him privately, and inquired why they were not able to cast out the evil spirit. His reply was in substance, because they had not faith.

About two miles northeast of Jerusalem, on the declivity of the Mount of Olives, was a village called Bethany, the home of a pious family comprising a brother named Lazarus and two sisters, Martha and Mary. When in Judea, the Saviour made his home with this family, whose members were among his most intimate friends, and whom he regarded with peculiar affection. They were devotedly attached to Jesus, and considered it a great honor to entertain him as their guest.

When he was at Betharbara beyond the Jordan, a day's journey, or thirty miles from Bethany, Lazarus was taken ill, and his disease assumed alarming symptoms, therefore the sisters sent a message to the Saviour expressed in these words, "Lord, he whom thou lovest is sick." They probably thought their Master would immediately come to aid and comfort them by restoring the invalid. When Jesus received the news he said to his disciples, " This sickness is not unto death," by which he evidently meant a permanent death, but it was to prove the power of the Son of God. Though the Saviour had a strong attachment for the family at Bethany, yet he remained two days at Betharbara, after the messenger arrived, instead of going at once to the anxious sisters. It is probable that Lazarus died soon after the courier left. It required one day to go to Betharbara, and one day to return, and Jesus waited two days before he left for Bethany, therefore when he arrived Lazarus had been dead four days.

When he was ready to go the Saviour said to his disciples, " Let us go into Judea again." They replied, " Master, the Jews lately " — about four months before — " attempted to stone thee, and will you venture to go there again?" The Lord taught them by his reply, that his Father would defend him until the appointed time of his death, therefore he would safely go among his foes trusting in Him. At length he said to his disciples that " Our friend Lazarus sleepeth, but I will go and awake him." Not understanding his meaning, they replied, " If he sleeps, he will recover." Sleep was regarded a favorable symptom in sickness. Then Jesus told them plainly, without metaphor, " Lazarus is dead, and I am glad for your sakes, I was not there; nevertheless we will go to him." Thomas said, " We will go and die with him," meaning the Lord, probably, since his life was threatened.

Many of the friends of Martha and Mary came to comfort them in their deep affliction. Their parents, it is evident, had been taken from them, perhaps when they were children, therefore they regarded their brother as a father to them, and depended upon him for protection and support. When Martha heard that Jesus was coming, without telling her sister, she went to meet him and said to him, "Lord, if thou hadst been here, my brother would not have died, but even now, whatever thou wilt ask of God, he will grant it." Jesus replied, "Thy brother shall rise again." She understood him as referring to the general resurrection. After further conversation, Martha returned and privately said to Mary, "The Master is come and calleth for thee," when she hastily left her friends and went to meet him; they supposed she had gone to the grave of her brother to weep. As Mary approached the Saviour, she prostrated herself at his feet and repeated the words of her sister, that is, "If thou hadst been here my brother had not died." When Jesus saw the sisters and their friends weeping, he was greatly agitated and said, "Where have ye laid him?" They said, "Lord, come and see." When he arrived at the tomb, he was so much affected that he could no longer restrain his tears. The evangelist expresses the emotions of our Lord in the concise language, "Jesus wept." Those present said, "Behold, how he loved him! Could not he who opened the eyes of the blind have saved him from death?"

When Jesus came to the grave, which was a cave with a stone placed at the entrance, he commanded it to be removed. This was the fourth day after the death of Lazarus, therefore Martha said, "By this time putrefaction must have begun." It is probable she did not expect he would be raised from the grave, but that Jesus paid this visit to his tomb from sympathy and to see where his friend was laid. He then reminded Martha of what he had said about his resurrection. After the stone had been removed, Jesus offered a prayer and then in a loud voice exclaimed, "Lazarus, come forth!" and immediately he arose and came out of the tomb enveloped in his grave clothes. The Saviour said, "release him so that he can walk."

Many of the Jews who witnessed this wonderful miracle believed in Jesus, but there were others who went to the Pharisees and related the event they had observed, for the purpose of arousing opposition to him. The chief priests and Pharisees called a council to consider what course to pursue, "for," said they, "if this man is allowed to go on as he has done, the consequence will be a war, and the Romans will come and overthrow our nation." They plotted among themselves how they might put him to death, and even later they considered the question of murdering Lazarus, because he was a living witness of the miracle; Jesus, therefore, considered it prudent not to appear publicly in Judea, on account of the enmity of the Jews, and retired to a city or town called Ephraim, about five miles north of Jericho, which was a city nineteen or twenty miles northeast of Jerusalem, and six miles west of the Jordan. It was called the "city of palm-trees," on account of the large number of this species of trees growing there. A small stream flowed through the valley of Jericho, whose salt and bitter waters were sweetened by the prophet Elisha.

This was the first city of Canaan taken by Joshua

after crossing the Jordan, when he pronounced a curse upon the one who should rebuild it, but a little more than five centuries after Hiel undertook to restore it, and when laying the foundation, Abiram, his eldest son, died, and after he had nearly completed it, his youngest son, Segub, died. These calamities were considered judgments as a punishment for Hiel's audacity. There was, however, a city of Jericho built on or near the site of the ancient town, mentioned in the time of the Judges, and during the reign of David it was a place of some importance. In the time of Christ Jericho was the second city in Judea and contained a school of the prophets. It was here that Herod the Great died.

The mountains in the vicinity were some of the highest in Judea, while the road from this city to Jerusalem was infested by highway men, thus making it dangerous to travellers. Sometimes the road led by steep precipices where the first misstep might prove fatal, while in other places it wound through passes overshadowed by projecting rocks. Such a road was favorable for robbers to attack an unarmed man travelling alone, as was the case mentioned in the account of the Good Samaritan.

Jesus had been teaching in Galilee and on his way to Judea he came to Jericho attended by his disciples and a great multitude, as was usual in his journeys. After leaving the city he passed two blind men sitting by the wayside to solicit arms. They were poor and helpless and had no other means of obtaining the necessaries of life. One of these men was called Bartimeus, that is, the son of Timeus, as the name signified, and was well known to the public. When the blind beggars heard the tumult caused by the crowd, they inquired the cause, and were told that Jesus of Nazareth was passing by. They had heard of him and the wonderful miracles he had performed, and believed he was the Son of God, who could restore their sight. They raised their voices above the noise of the crowd, saying, "Jesus, thou Son of David," that is, the Christ, "have mercy on us." The people standing near reproved them and told them to be quiet, but giving no heed to the rebuke, they became more importunate and would not keep silence.

Jesus stopped and commanded them to be conducted to him, when some compassionate friend said to Bartimeus, "Be comforted, for he called for thee," when they both arose and casting aside their loose outer garments, so as not to be impeded in their haste, they were led by some one in the crowd to Jesus, who inquired what they desired him to do for them. "Lord, that our eyes may be opened." He then touched their eyes and immediately their sight was restored, and they followed the Saviour.

Another incident, though not miraculous, occurred during the Lord's visit to Jericho. One of the citizens named Zaccheus, a publican, having heard of his wonderful deeds, which were known throughout the country, had an earnest desire to see him, but the crowd was so great that he, being low in stature, could not get a sight of Jesus; but he did not, however, abandon the attempt, and thought of a plan that proved successful. Though a wealthy man and an officer under the Roman Government, he ran ahead of the multitude and climbed into a sycamore-tree growing by the wayside, that he might get a sight of the One who was so popular.

When the Saviour came to the tree, he looked up and said, "Zaccheus, make haste and come down from the tree, for to-day I must abide at thy house." This was an honor the publican was not expecting, for he had only sought to see him, and now he was to entertain him as a guest. This, of course, was displeasing to some, because Jesus was to dine with a publican, a class considered by the Jews as sinners. When they had reached his home, Zaccheus said, "Lord, I will give half of my goods to the poor, and if I have taken anything unjustly from others, I will restore to such fourfold." The Saviour declared that salvation had been bestowed upon the publican and his family, and that he was a worthy descendant of Abraham.

Bethsaida was a city on the Sea of Tiberias or Galilee, and on account of its proximity to the lake or sea it became the home of fishermen, as of Philip, Andrew and Peter. After the miracle of feeding the four thousand Jesus embarked on board a ship or boat, and crossing the sea to the west side, he went to Dalmanutha and Magdala, places near each other, thence to Bethsaida, a short distance north of the latter. As soon as he arrived there a blind man was conducted to him by his friends, who besought the Saviour to restore his sight. Jesus took his hand and led him out of the town, perhaps to avoid the crowd — for the Pharisees were plotting to take his life on the charge of sedition — and prevent a dangerous mob. Our Lord never attempted to arouse public excitement to gain popularity, but, on the contrary, many times he tried to avoid noto-

STILLING THE TEMPEST.

riety. For some unexplained reason, Jesus in this instance did not perform the miracle by a word or a touch, but chose a more gradual process. He moistened the eyes of the blind man and then placing his hands upon them inquired whether he saw anything. The man replied, "I see men walking, but so indistinctly they might be taken for trees." The Saviour placed his hands again upon his eyes and told him to look up, when his sight was fully restored and he saw objects clearly. Jesus told him to return to his home without going into town to relate the miracle to any one, lest it should arouse the enmity of the Pharisees, and thus increase the danger to himself, as they were planning to take his life.

When Jesus was arrested in the Garden of Gethsemane, Peter very hastily drew his sword and cut off the ear of Malchus, servant of the High Priest, who was with the crowd. The Saviour told the apostle to put his weapon into its sheath, for he did not wish his disciples to use any violence in his defence. He then performed the miracle of healing or restoring the ear of Malchus. The disciples of Jesus were not usually armed, but on this occasion they had two swords among them, for when travelling they were sometimes obliged to defend themselves against robbers, who were encountered in some regions. When attending the festivals at Jerusalem, people were accustomed to carry weapons concealed under their robes. Peter had done a rash act, since he alone attacked a whole band of officers, and Jesus told him his imprudence might cause his own destruction, besides, his deed implied a distrust of Divine protection. If necessary, God could afford more efficient aid than he could, for, said Jesus, "My Father could give me more than twelve legions of angels for my defence," that is, more than seventy-two thousand. But it was necessary that the Saviour should die, since it was the Divine plan for the redemption of the world.

The miracles above mentioned are those recorded by the evangelists as wrought by the Saviour during his life, though it is implied that he performed many others of which no account is given; but after his resurrection the miraculous draught of fishes occurred at the Sea of Galilee, of which a particular account is given in another chapter.

CHAPTER XIII.

THE PARABLES OF CHRIST.

The word parable, derived from the Greek language, signifies "to compare together." It is a similitude taken from a natural object or event to illustrate a moral or spiritual subject. It is not essential that the figure should be literally true and that was understood, so there was no dishonesty or deception. The design of speaking in parables was to convey truth in a more interesting and impressive manner, in order to arrest the attention of the common people, or present an offensive subject or a pointed rebuke; for instance, the parable of Nathan to David, and some of the Lord's parables to the Jews. Both the prophets and heathen writers in the early ages employed this mode of illustration, and in the time of Christ it was in common use.

The parables of Jesus, it has been said, " are distinguished for clearness, purity, simplicity and power, calculated to awaken the attention of his hearers and impress the truth upon their minds and hearts." They were impressive object-lessons and largely based upon the common affairs of life, therefore understood by all classes. They were related in a simple and clear style, so that every one could understand them.

The largest number of Christ's parables were uttered in Galilee, where he performed more miracles and delivered more discourses than in Judea. The evangelists vary in the number of parables recorded, Matthew and Luke giving the most. The following is a list with the names of the places where they were uttered:

1. The Sower. Capernaum. Recorded by Matthew.
2. The Mustard-seed. Capernaum. " " Mark.
3. About Leaven. Capernaum. " " Matthew.
4. The Found Treasure. Capernaum. " " Matthew.
5. The Costly Pearl. Capernaum. " " Matthew.
6. The Net. Capernaum. " " Matthew.
7. The Two Debtors. Capernaum. " " Luke.
8. The Unmerciful Servant. Capernaum. " " Matthew.
9. The Good Samaritan. Near Jericho. " " Luke.
10. The Rich Fool. Galilee. " " Luke.
11. Servants Waiting. Galilee. " " Luke.
12. The Barren Fig-tree. Galilee. " " Luke.
13. The Lost Sheep. Galilee. " " Luke.
14. Lost Piece of Money. Galilee. " " Luke.
15. The Prodigal Son. Galilee. " " Luke.
16. The Dishonest Steward. Galilee. " " Luke.
17. Rich Man and Lazarus. Galilee. " " Luke.
18. The Unjust Judge. Perea. " " Luke.
19. The Pharisee and Publican. Perea. " " Luke.
20. Laborers in a Vineyard. Perea. " " Matthew.
21. The Pounds. Near Jericho. " " Luke.
22. The Two Sons. Jerusalem. " " Matthew.
23. The Vineyard. Jerusalem. " " Matthew.
24. The Marriage Feast. Jerusalem. " " Matthew.
25. The Ten Virgins. Jerusalem. " " Matthew.
26. The Talents. Jerusalem. " " Matthew.
27. The Sheep and Goats. Jerusalem. " " Matthew.

Jesus had been performing miracles and preaching to the people in the vicinity of the Sea of Tiberias, when, weary and sad, on account of the obduracy and enmity of the Pharisees who were plotting against his life, he left the house and rested on the bank of the lake. He could not, however, long remain alone, and soon there gathered so great a company of people, that many of them could not get near enough to hear him, therefore he entered a boat and sat down, intimating he was about to address them. The boat was rowed a short distance from the shore, so he could be heard by all his large audience, standing or sitting on the bank; it was on this occasion that the Saviour gave his parable of the sower, a lesson all could understand, for the Jews were an agricultural nation and familiar with the process of tillage; Jesus himself was a close observer of Nature in all her varied aspects, hence many of his metaphors were taken from the visible works of creation. It was possible there were laborers in the vicinity at the time, sowing seed for the wheat harvest. There were, doubtless, rocks and weeds in some parts of the field, and as the farmer scattered the seed right and left, some fell upon the beaten paths and became food for the fowls, especially ducks, abundant in that region. Some of the seed was cast upon rocky soil, and though it sprang up, the roots could not strike deep enough to reach the moisture necessary for their growth, consequently they withered under the hot rays of the sun. Other seeds were scattered among thorns and weeds, which absorbed all the nourishment from the soil, leaving nothing for the wheat, but the larger part of the field contained rich and fertile ground, which yielded from thirty to one hundred fold. Jesus explained the parable in the following manner:

The seed represents the word of God, revealed in the Scriptures and in Providence, by the Holy Spirit and by preaching. The fowls that gathered the seed by the wayside represented the Wicked One who does not suffer it to produce any results. Those who hear the truth and for a time rejoice in it, but are deceived, have no root in themselves, and when trials and temptations occur, they fall, while those whose minds and time are so occupied with worldly cares that they neglect to secure the true riches, are represented by the seed among thorns. That in the fertile soil is intended to apply to those whose hearts are prepared to receive the seed or the word of truth, therefore they yield an abundant harvest.

The parable recorded by Mark about a husbandman planting seed, etc., is also founded on agricultural methods, and intended to illustrate the truth that the gospel Jesus came to announce would take root, spring up, and bear fruit, though no one but God could understand its secret operations in the heart of the believer. The word translated *corn* means wheat or barley. Here is a farmer, who, having planted seed, must trust Providence for the harvest. He does not understand the secret laws of Nature, but leaves all speculation about them and attends to other duties. In the mean time the seeds germinate, the wheat springs up, first the tender shoot or blade appears, then the ear or stock of the grain, and after a time, the ripe wheat when it is ready for the harvest. The lesson taught is that the growth of religion in the regenerate soul is gradual, and understood by none but the Omniscient One.

THE CRY OF PETER.

No human mind, either scientist or philosopher, however cultivated, has ever been able to explain the mysterious growth of plants. They know what is essential for this, such as fertile soil, rain and sunshine, but they can go no further. Jesus was a close observer of the operations of men in their various occupations, and made use of these employments to illustrate his teachings. At the same time, he perfectly understood the laws of Nature, for it is said that "all things were created by him, and without him nothing was made that exists or ever existed."

The darnel or tares was a vegetable growing abundantly in Palestine, which closely resembled genuine wheat, but it yielded a harmful grain. Its leaves were so much like those of wheat, they could not be separated when growing together. If the seeds of the darnel are mixed with the genuine grain, they will produce intoxication when made into bread and eaten. The cultivator does not attempt to separate the tares or darnel from the wheat until the harvest, when it is collected in bundles and burned, and if any seeds accidentally become mixed with the genuine grain, they are separated by winnowing.

The Saviour may have known an actual case of the kind when he uttered the parable of the tares, which was nearly as follows: There was a certain husbandman who had a neighbor that was his enemy. Perhaps he was jealous on account of the success of this husbandman, whose crops yielded an abundant harvest, therefore, after he had sowed his field with wheat and retired to rest at night, his envious neighbor went over the ground and scattered the darnel seeds among the wheat.

No one suspected him of such baseness until the wheat and tares sprung up together, when the owner of the field was convinced his enemy had done the mischief. His servants inquired whether they should not attempt to pull up the tares, but the master, knowing their qualities, said, "Let both grow together until the harvest, for if you attempt to uproot the tares, you may destroy the wheat also. We will then burn the tares with other useless weeds."

After Jesus had sent the multitude away he entered the house, when his disciples requested an explanation of the parable, which was as follows: "The field is the world, the Son of Man is the sower of the genuine seed, the good seed are the children of the kingdom, that is, Christians, the tares are the children of the wicked one, that is, Satan, who sowed the darnel seed, the reapers are the angels. As the tares are gathered and burned in the fire, so shall it be at the end of this world." The Saviour closed his explanation with the most solemn declaration ever uttered, which is briefly as follows: "The Son of Man shall send forth his angels to gather the wicked from every part of the world, to be cast into a furnace of fire, where there will be inexpressible suffering, but the righteous shall shine as the sun in the kingdom of their Father."

The parable of the leaven is similar in significance to that of the mustard seed. Leaven or yeast, as is well known, is a substance intended to produce fermentation. The process of making leavened bread among the Jews was similar to that of the present day, which is by placing the yeast in the meal moistened by some liquid and then left to ferment. The parable was intended to illustrate the silent and secret influence of religion in the soul.

The seed of the mustard plant is one of the smallest in the vegetable kingdom, yet the plant itself, in Oriental countries, requires several years to reach maturity, when it attains a size sufficient to be climbed like other trees. In the parable a man is represented as sowing a mustard seed from which, though exceedingly small, will spring a plant of such size that the birds alight in its branches. So the beginning of piety in the heart is small, but it gradually increases by culture. The same is true of the Christian Church, which was feeble at first, but at length spread and is destined to pervade every part of the world.

The occasion of the parable of the hidden treasure may have been an actual event; it may have referred to a tradition, or been simply imagined, but whatever the facts may have been the incidents are such as might naturally occur. A certain speculator whose chief desire was to acquire wealth heard that an owner of real estate had a piece of ground which, it was rumored, contained a hidden treasure, perhaps a gold or diamond mine, though he was not aware of it. The speculator, by some means, learned that the land actually contained a valuable treasure, therefore he was anxious to purchase it, but unfortunately he had not the means to pay for it. After thinking upon the subject, he decided to sell all his property and invest it in a land speculation, but he kept his reasons for doing so a profound secret. The land was bought at the usual price of real estate and the purchaser became a wealthy man.

His method had not been perfectly honorable, and the

Saviour did not commend his conduct in this respect, but he meant to illustrate one feature of the transaction, namely, that of sacrificing everything to obtain the hidden treasure. Its application is, that the gospel is a valuable treasure and to obtain its blessings one should relinquish all earthly riches, if necessary, to secure them. They are of more value than silver or gold, while sometimes they are hid and need to be sought for earnestly.

The parable of the pearl is similar in its teaching to that of the hidden treasure, and illustrates the truth that seeking the kingdom of heaven may be compared to the methods of a dealer in pearls.

These beautiful gems obtained from the pearl oyster have always been highly prized for jewelry and other decorative purposes, and consequently are of great value. Sometimes a single pearl is considered equal to a fortune.

A merchant or dealer in precious stones is represented as coming across one of these gems which attracted his attention. Being an expert in the business and understanding the value of this specimen, he sold all his possessions to gain the means to purchase it. The merchant may not have been judicious in a worldly sense, but he wished to be the owner of so priceless a treasure.

The parable of the net differs from the preceding in method and design. Its meaning is similar to that of the tares, and the scene depicted was very familiar to Galilean fishermen. The gospel is compared to a fishing net which had been dragged along through the waters of the lake, and filled with different kinds of fishes. The men engaged in the business drew the net to the shore, and sat down to select the valuable fish from those unfit for use; the good ones they placed in their boat to be taken home, but the bad they threw away. Jesus explained the parable thus: At the end of the world the angels shall separate the wicked from the just, and shall cast them into the fiery furnace; the condition of the righteous he had mentioned in a former parable, which was that "they shall shine as the sun in the kingdom of their Father."

Jesus then inquired whether his hearers had understood the lessons he had taught them. They replied, "Yea, Lord," but to enforce his instructions he said, "Every scribe instructed in the kingdom of heaven is like a householder who, having placed his valuable possessions in his treasury or place of deposit, obtains from his safe whatever is needed in any emergency." The truth taught was what one has acquired of valuable knowledge should not be concealed, but made known for the benefit of others.

After teaching by parables in different places, Jesus came to Nazareth and taught in the synagogue, but the citizens sneered at his instructions, saying, "Is not this man the carpenter's son, and is not his mother called Mary, and are not James, Joses, Simon and Judas his brethren? And are not his sisters with us? How can he preach and perform such mighty works?" The people of the city were disgusted on account of his humble birth, and so prejudiced that they could not or would not judge him or his works fairly, therefore it would be useless for him to attempt to instruct them.

When the parable of the two debtors was related,

Jesus was in Galilee, probably at or near Capernaum or the Sea of Tiberias where he had been preaching and performing miracles. A Pharisee named Simon, who had heard him and was impressed with his teaching, made a feast to which he invited Jesus and his disciples as guests. After they were placed at the table, which was by reclining on the left side, an incident occurred which led the Saviour to relate the parable of the two debtors. When walking the Jews protected the soles of their feet by sandals, or shoes as they were sometimes called.

While partaking of their banquet, a certain woman of the city regarded as an outcast and excluded from respectable society came to the table where the Saviour was reclining and performed an act that showed her repentance and faith in him. She, perhaps, noticed that the servant of the host had omitted the usual courtesy bestowed upon the guests at an entertainment, that is, washing their feet, therefore she would perform the ceremony, and while doing this her head was bowed low and her tears were falling. She had probably unbraided her hair and it fell over her shoulders, so that it might be said she wiped his feet, over which she was weeping, with her loose hair. Having finished the bathing, she kissed her Lord's feet and annointed them with a precious substance she had brought for the purpose in an alabaster box. This was a perfume of spikenard or liquid nard, which afforded an agreeable odor. The nard from which this perfume is obtained is an East Indian plant, with a slender stalk and a large root both of which yield the odor. The woman, having broken the seal of the box or vessel containing the perfume, poured the contents on the Saviour's feet. A similar scene occurred in Bethany, at the house of Simon the leper, but they were not identical and the actors were not the same.

When the Pharisee who gave the entertainment saw what the woman had done, he thought if Jesus was a prophet, he would have known the character of this woman, and not have allowed her to touch him. Jesus, knowing what his host thought, said, "Simon, I have something to say to thee." "Master, let us hear it," was the reply.

"There was a certain creditor who had two debtors; one of them owed him five hundred pence, and the other fifty, but as neither of these debtors was able to pay his debts, the creditor generously and promptly cancelled them. Which of these men owed him the most gratitude?" Simon replied, "I suppose the one whose debt was the greater," Jesus told him he had answered correctly, but he probably did not understand how the parable applied to himself, therefore the Saviour said, "Simon, do you see this woman? I came to your house, but you made no arrangements for washing my feet, according to the general custom, while she bathed them with her tears and wiped them with her hair. You gave me no kiss, the common mode of salutation, but she kissed my *feet;* you did not anoint my head, while she performed this ceremony upon my feet, thus affording proof of her ardent attachment to me." Then speaking to the woman he said, "Thy sins are forgiven; thy faith hath saved thee; go in peace." When the guests at the table heard this they said to themselves, "Who is this man? Who is able to forgive sins except God alone?"

CHAPTER XIV.

THE PARABLES OF CHRIST — CONTINUED.

WHEN Jesus was in Galilee on a certain occasion, he related the parable of the unmerciful servant, with the object of teaching the duty of forgiving those who injure us. Peter came to him with an important question, namely, "How often must I forgive my brother, or fellow-creature, who has injured me? Shall I forgive him the seventh time?" The Jews taught that one should forgive an injury repeated for the third time, but not for the fourth. Peter had extended the number to seven. The Saviour's reply was not only seven times, but seventy times seven, or four hundred and ninety times, by which he meant that forgiveness should not be limited to any definite number of times, that is, if a person injures us and *asks* to be forgiven, tell him that he is, and if he does not ask to be forgiven, we are not at liberty to take vengeance, or cherish malice towards him. When the apostles heard the Saviour's views on the subject, they said, "Lord, increase our faith." They understood how difficult it is to forgive injuries and insults. With a majority of persons, probably, it is the most perplexing question of what is duty, and Jesus illustrates it by the following parable. The circumstances may have been taken from real life, or they may have been imagined, but the lesson taught was the principal thing.

A certain king wished to settle his accounts with his servants, by whom may have been intended small tributary princes or collectors of revenue. It was common among ancient rulers to "farm out" or sell for a specified sum, the taxes of a particular province, a custom which sometimes gave occasion for oppression and injustice by the collector of the taxes. There was brought to this king one of the subordinates who owed him 10,000 talents, equal to about $15,180,000. This vast sum proves the debtor was a tributary prince. As he had no means of paying this enormous debt, the king commanded the man, his wife and children and all his property to be sold to settle the account. The Hebrews were allowed by their laws to sell debtors with their families, to labor as servants for a time, to pay a debt.

This was a grievous calamity, since it would require a very long period of servitude to pay this enormous sum, therefore the distressed debtor came to the king and falling down before him, said, "Lord, have patience with me and I will pay thee all." He may have expected to gain the means by some profitable business transaction, or perhaps he intended to extort the money from his own dependents. The king was moved with compassion and cancelled the debt. Such noble generosity should have awakened in the heart of the debtor a tender sympathy for others in similar circumstances, but this was far from the truth, for this same man when he found that one of his fellow-servants owed him one hundred pence, or about fourteen dollars, seized him by the throat in a barbarous manner, and in an imperative tone said, "Pay me what thou owest." The servant in terror fell down at the feet of his creditor, and earnestly plead with him to have patience and he would pay him, but he would not grant his petition, and sent him to prison to remain there until the debt was paid.

When his associates learned what had been done, their sympathy for the prisoner and indignation against his oppressor were great, therefore they went to the king and informed him, when the offender was summoned to his lord's presence, who said to him, "Thou wicked servant, I forgave thee all thy vast debt when asked, ought you not to have had compassion on your fellow-servant for a small debt?" The king then delivered him to the jailer to be kept in prison until he should pay his own debt. The moral lessons taught by this parable are that "our sins are many; that God freely forgives them when, in penitence, we ask him; that the injuries received from our fellow-creatures are comparatively small, and we should freely forgive them, and if we do not, God will justly withhold his forgiveness from us."

The parable about the "Good Samaritan" was delivered on the following occasion: Jesus was preaching in Galilee, and in the audience was a certain lawyer, or one skilled in the Mosaic laws, and who expounded them to the people. During the sermon, the lawyer rose in the assembly to ask a question, as if for instruction, but really, without doubt, intending to lead the Saviour to give an opinion contrary to the

FEEDING THE MULTITUDE.

teachings of the law, that he might have an opportunity of accusing him before the Sanhedrim, or Great Council.

The question was, "What shall I do to inherit eternal life?" The Jews believed that one must keep the commandments, in order to be saved. Jesus said to the lawyer, "What is written in the law? How do you understand it?" The reply was, "Thou shalt love the Lord thy God with all thy heart, soul and strength, and thy neighbor as thyself."

Jesus replied, "That is the truth, and if you do this you shall have eternal life." The lawyer evidently had been trusting in his good works and upright conduct, and wishing to justify himself, inquired, "Who is my neighbor?"

His countrymen believed that Jews only were their neighbors, and that the Gentiles had no claims upon their charity or sympathy. To show that all the human race were kindred, and that kindness should be impartially extended to all, of whatever nation, Jesus related the parable of the Samaritan, one who belonged to a people whom the Jews hated, yet who showed more kindness to one of the latter than a priest and a Levite, who were consecrated to religious services, showed to a suffering countryman.

A certain man was on his way from Jerusalem to Jericho, about fifteen miles distant from the capital. He was travelling on foot and alone, therefore was exposed to danger, for the solitary, mountainous region was the favorite resort of highwaymen, who were constantly watching their opportunity to assault and rob travellers, and in case of resistance, kill them.

As Jericho was pre-eminently a city of priests, and as their duties called them frequently to Jerusalem, they were daily passing over the road between the two cities.

This solitary traveller was attacked by a band of robbers who stripped him of all his garments, the only plunder they could get, and in his struggles with the highwaymen he was beaten and wounded so severely that he lay upon the ground bleeding and unconscious. While in this condition, a priest who had been attending services at the Temple was returning to his home in Jericho, when he saw this man lying by the side of the road, but instead of ascertaining whether he was dead, or in case he was alive, giving him any assistance, he crossed to the other side and went on, apparently entirely unmoved by the sad spectacle. Soon after he had gone, a Levite, who had been officiating also at the Temple, passed this way, and seeing the man lying on the ground, had the curiosity to stop and look at him, but instead of affording any relief, he crossed to the other side of the road and passed on perfectly indifferent about the fate of the sufferer.

The wounded man must have died soon, had not a Samaritan, who was riding over the same road, saved him. The sight of the injured man, whom he recognized as a Jew, awakened his sympathy, and all his national prejudices were forgotten. He raised the stranger, dressed his wounds very carefully, and when consciousness was restored, placed him upon his own beast and walking by his side conducted him to an inn, and nursed him through the night. Before his departure the next morning, the Samaritan paid the innkeeper a certain sum for the man's immediate wants, and said, "Take care of him, and if you spend more for the invalid, I will pay you when I come this way again."

Having told this interesting story, which may have been founded on facts, Jesus asked the lawyer the appropriate question, "Which of the three," that is, the priest, Levite or Samaritan, "was neighbor to the one who fell among the thieves?" He replied, "The one who showed mercy." He did not say the Samaritan, for his Jewish prejudices would not allow him to designate the philanthropist by his Gentile name. The Saviour then told the lawyer to go and imitate his example. He taught by this parable that a Samaritan might be a neighbor to a Jew, and that mutual kindness should be practised by both nations.

The vine and the vineyard and whatever is connected with them are often employed by the sacred writers as figures of speech, to represent some important and spiritual truth. The cultivation of the grape was one of the leading industries of Palestine, for which the soil was well adapted. The vines were so productive that sometimes a single cluster of grapes weighed several pounds, requiring two men to carry it, as was the case with the spies sent by Joshua to explore the land. The grapes were generally red, whence the phrase "blood of grapes." Some vines ran on the ground, others grew upright, often to a considerable height so that one could sit under them, thus explaining the text, "Sitting under one's vine and fig-tree." Vineyards were usually planted on the declivity of hills and mountains, and were defended by a wall or hedge, and sometimes by thorn-bushes. A tower, perhaps eighty feet high and thirty feet square, was erected in the vineyard for the keepers stationed there to protect the vines against thieves and animals, especially dogs and foxes. The grapes were not to be gathered the first three years, and in the fourth they were devoted to sacred purposes, but the fifth year they were allowed to be gathered for use. Sometimes the grapes were dried in the sun, and when soaked in wine and pressed they yielded sweet wine, or new wine as it was called.

The manner of preparing a vineyard was nearly as follows: The soil was loosened and the stones removed, then the young vines were planted and wound about trees or a stake. Narrow trenches were dug around the running vines to prevent the shoots from intertwining with one another. The vintage in Palestine sometimes began as early as June or July, while there were three different periods of gathering the grapes, lasting until November or December. The time of vintage was a joyful occasion, when with mirthful demonstrations the fruit was gathered and taken to the wine-press, which consisted of two receptacles built of stone or hewn out of a rock. The grapes were put into the upper receptacle, and the juice was trodden out by five men, when it flowed into the lower one. Treading the wine-press was very laborious, and the garments of those employed were stained with the red juice, yet it was a time of merriment attended by singing and music, when those performing the labor jumped up and down, exclaiming, "Ho, up." Gathering grapes and treading the wine-press were sometimes used as metaphors to signify battles, great slaughter and suffering. The Saviour is represented as treading the wine-press *alone*. The kingdom of heaven, or the church, is compared to a vineyard, and by the parable of the laborers in this vineyard, Jesus taught the lesson that rewards would be given to his followers according to the value of their labors.

This parable was spoken in Perea, a town east of the Jordan, when Jesus was on his way to Jerusalem, and was substantially as follows: There was a certain householder, or the master of a family, who owned a vineyard, besides other possessions, for he seemed to have been a person of considerable wealth. He needed laborers to cultivate his vineyard, therefore early in the morning he went to seek help. There were many persons standing on the streets, even at that time of the day, waiting for an opportunity to be employed, consequently the householder met with no difficulty in securing laborers, whom he engaged for one penny a day. This was a Roman coin known as the denarius, equal to about fourteen cents, and was the common wages per day of a Roman soldier, and the price paid to other laborers. This coin was stamped with the representation of the heads of the Roman emperors, as alluded to in another place.

The workmen hired in the early part of the day were sent into the vineyard, but the owner, needing more help, went out about the third hour of the day, or 9 o'clock, A. M., and found others waiting in the marketplace for some one to employ them. He told them to go and labor in his vineyard and he would pay them what was right, but did not specify the sum. Again, at 12 o'clock A. M., 3 o'clock and 5 o'clock P. M., the master saw other men standing idle and inquired why they were not at work. They replied, "No man has hired us." He then said, "Go work in my vineyard and whatever is right ye shall receive."

When the day ended at the twelfth hour, the lord of the vineyard told his steward, who was entrusted with the care of paying the laborers, to call them together and give them their wages, beginning with the last ones hired. There was a reason for this, since, had he paid the earlier laborers first, they would have gone away satisfied and the object of the parable would not have been gained. Though the householder had not stated the price he would pay the later workers, yet he gave to each class the same. When those hired first saw that all received the same compensation, they found fault, supposing their wages would have been advanced. They said, "We have worked from morning through the heat of the day, yet these who came late have received the same wages as ourselves." "Friends," said the owner, "I have not wronged you. Did you not agree to work for a penny? Have I not the right to do as I please with what belongs to me? If I chose to give anything to others, have you a right to complain?" We learn from this parable that some who are called late into the kingdom of Christ may be first in usefulness, hence their reward may be equal to that of those called before them.

Jesus had been instructing the people in Jerusalem, though his home when at the capital was in Bethany with the family of Lazarus. When he was in the Temple, the chief priests, scribes and elders came to him and inquired, "By what authority hast thou cast out of the Temple the buyers and sellers and overthrown the tables

THE TRANSFIGURATION.

of the money-changers and the seats of those who sold doves? Who gave thee authority to do these things?" Though the Saviour was not of the priestly order and had neither civil nor ecclesiastical authority, yet he came as a prophet, while his miracles were sufficient proof of his Divine power. He said to them, "I will ask you a question, Whence was the baptism of John, from Heaven or from men?" After discussing the subject among themselves, they answered, "We cannot tell." "Neither will I tell you by what authority I have done these things," said Jesus, and then related the parable of the two sons.

A certain man who had two sons, said to the eldest, "Go and work in my vineyard to-day." For a moment the son forgot his filial obligations and very discourteously said, "I will not." After thinking about his conduct and his obligations to his father, he regretted his uncivil reply and went to labor in the vineyard. The father came to the younger son and made the same request and the answer was, "I will go, sir," but he did not do as he promised. Whether he intended to deceive his father or whether he changed his mind, preferring ease and pleasure to duty and labor, is not intimated. Jesus then inquired which son obeyed the will of the father. They replied "the first." The elder son was intended to represent the publicans and sinners who repented and believed, while the younger son represented the scribes and Pharisees who, though observing the external rites of religion, were disobedient to the calls of the gospel. None are so difficult to reach with the truth as the self-righteous and prejudiced. Both John the Baptist and the Saviour gained more converts from the masses, or the common people, than from the higher classes, especially the educated and the priestly orders, a condition that has always existed in Christian communities.

Jesus was at Jerusalem when he delivered the parable of "the vineyard," which was nearly as follows:

A certain householder planted a vineyard, enclosed it by a wall, built a tower, made a place for a wine vat, etc., that is, he made every preparation for the cultivation of the grape and the manufacture of wine, and then rented it to husbandmen or cultivators, with the understanding that he would receive a certain per cent. of the profits. At the time of the vintage the owner, who lived at a distance from the vineyard, sent one of his servants to collect his dues, but the husbandmen, instead of granting his just demands, seized the servant and after beating him sent him away without any of the fruits of the harvest. The householder then sent another servant on the same errand, whom they treated with greater severity, stoning him and inflicting a severe wound on his head, and after treating him in this barbarous manner sent him back to his master, who, with remarkable forbearance sent a third messenger, whom they killed. He still sent others, some of whom were severely beaten and others were murdered.

It was surprising the owner did not punish these wicked men with the utmost severity, but being exceedingly humane and forgiving, he granted them another trial. He had an only son, very dear to his father, and the object of his devoted love. The father said, "They will certainly respect my son, therefore I will send him on the same errand," but when these wicked husbandmen saw him at a distance they recognized him and laid a plan to take his life, for, said they, "He is the heir to his father's estate, and if he is put out of the way we can seize his possessions." When the young man arrived they caught hold of him, drew him outside of the vineyard and put him to death.

Jesus then inquired of his listeners what the lord of the vineyard ought, in justice, to do with these murderers? They replied, "He should kill them and let his vineyard to others who would deal honestly." The object of the parable was to lead the scribes and Pharisees to condemn themselves and admit the justice of the punishment that was coming to their nation by the conquest and destruction of their city.

The Saviour said, "Have you not read in the Scriptures that the stone which the builders rejected has become the chief corner-stone?" This figure refers to the methods of architects, who select a stone of superior size and excellence for the corner of the building. Jesus is the corner-stone of the Church, yet the Jews rejected him. "Therefore," said he, "the kingdom of God shall be taken from you and given to a nation that will yield fruit. Whoever falls against this stone will be injured, but he upon whom it may fall, will be ground to powder." Death by stoning was a mode of execution well understood by the Jews and was attended by the following circumstances: A scaffold was erected twice the height of the condemned person, and when standing on the edge of the scaffold he was violently thrown off by one of the witnesses. If he was killed by this act, that ended the affair, but if he was not, a heavy stone was thrown on him which at once ended his life. In the above parable the householder represents God the Father; by the servants were meant the prophets, and the son was Jesus Christ; the vineyard referred to the Church, the husbandmen were the Jews who rejected and put to death the Son of God.

When the chief priests and Pharisees perceived the parable was spoken against themselves they were very indignant and laid their plans to arrest the Saviour, but they did not think it prudent to attempt it then, for fear a mob would collect to prevent it, as the people, generally, believed he was a prophet. There never had appeared one who was so popular, or who was followed by such a crowd of attentive listeners as Jesus. In all his long journeys he was attended by multitudes of both sexes and of all ages and conditions in life, and this was one of the principal causes of the jealousy and hatred of the Jewish rulers. As they were determined not to accept him as the Messiah, they persistently closed their eyes against the overpowering evidence he gave of his Divine mission by his miracles, his parables and his preaching, confirmed by his devout and holy life.

The parable of the barren fig-tree applied to the Jews illustrated the dealings of God with them.

A certain man whose business was agriculture planted a fig-tree in his vineyard, though the common practice was to cultivate the fig with the grape. The owner, who perhaps resided in a city, came to his vineyard at the time of gathering fruits, but found none on the fig-tree, and this had occurred for three years in succession, therefore, presuming the tree would never yield any figs, he told the dresser of the vineyard to cut it down, because it absorbed the moisture needed for the growth of the vine. The one who had the care of the vines replied, "Lord, let the tree remain this year, and I will take special pains to fertilize the soil about it, then, if it yields no fruit, let it be cut down."

CHAPTER XV.

THE PARABLES OF CHRIST — CONTINUED.

THE parable of the lost sheep was given in Galilee. "Publicans and sinners" had gathered in large numbers about the Saviour to listen to his teaching, and some of them had entertained him at their homes. The scribes and Pharisees found fault with him on this account, and considered it a dishonor for him to treat these classes with courtesy, especially to eat with them. They felt it would be a disgrace for *them* to do so, and if Jesus associated with publicans and sinners he must be in sympathy with them, and no better than they. Jesus, knowing their thoughts, related to them the parable of the lost sheep.

The business of a shepherd was so well understood by the people, since raising sheep and goats was one of their leading industries, that many of the Saviour's metaphors were derived from the occupation. He supposes a case in this instance, yet it was what may have happened very frequently. One of the sheep in a flock, probably a lamb, had strayed away, and was wandering alone in the desert, exposed to the danger of starvation or wild beasts.

When the flock which had comprised one hundred

sheep was gathered into the fold, and the sheep counted, as was the practice, one was missing. What must be done to rescue the wanderer? The shepherd was not long in deciding. He left the ninety-nine safe in the fold, and went himself to find the lost one. Perhaps he was obliged to go some distance and search long, but after diligently seeking for the wanderer, he heard a mournful cry, and following the direction of the sound, he finally saw the lost one coming towards his tender shepherd who had been calling him, when he raised the weary lamb and placed it upon his shoulder.

When the shepherd reached his home with his precious burden, he related his adventure to his friends and neighbors who knew of his loss, saying, " Rejoice with me, for I have found my lost sheep." The recovery of a lost object of small value often affords, for a time, greater joy than the quiet possession of things more valuable. Jesus expounded the parable by saying, " Greater joy will be expressed by the angels of heaven over one sinner who repents, than over ninety-nine persons who are already saved."

The interesting parable of the prodigal son was also uttered when Jesus was in Galilee. He had been severely criticised for associating with "publicans and sinners" when he taught the lesson that it was just and proper to rejoice over a penitent sinner, which was illustrated by the joy of a father over the return of a wandering and dissolute son.

A certain wealthy and respected citizen had two sons, both of whom had arrived at the age when they were considered competent to manage their own affairs. The law of the Jews allowed the eldest son to inherit twice as much of his father's estate as his younger brothers. The junior of these two brothers came one day to his parent, saying, "Father, give me my portion of the property, that I may use it as I please." He expressed a wish to travel in foreign lands, and perhaps he hoped to make a fortune and become as wealthy as his older brother would be when he came into possession of his inheritance. The father granted his request, and gave him his share of the property in money, or something he could exchange for it.

Having arranged his affairs the young man started on his journey and came to a distant country inhabited by a people who had a low standard of morals. The stranger soon joined a dissolute company, and yielding to their influence he spent his money in dissipation. After a time a great famine spread throughout the whole country and there was much suffering. This calamity may have been the result of the idle and dissolute habits of the natives, who neglected to cultivate the land. The young stranger was in trouble: he had spent all his means of living in dissipation and vice, and now want stared him in the face. What could he do? He had never been accustomed to labor, while begging was repugnant to his pride, but to die from starvation was fearful. Finally, he resolved to seek employment, therefore he engaged to labor for a citizen of that region, who sent him to tend or look after a herd of swine in a distant field. This was a very repulsive service for a Jew, since he was never allowed to keep swine.

His employer was under obligations to supply him with proper and sufficient food, but this he failed to do, therefore his hired laborer was suffering from hunger and would gladly have eaten some of the food given to the swine, that is, the husks, which may have been the fruit of the carob-tree, used for these animals and by the poor, but no one gave him any of it. Though dissolute in his habits, the young man was scrupulous about appropriating for his own urgent wants what did not belong to him, nor would he solicit charity. A certain quantity of food was measured out to the swine daily, therefore he was not at liberty to use any of it for himself.

His condition was deplorable, and while attending to his duty in the field he had time for reflection. He thought of his childhood, and the happy days spent in his father's comfortable home; of the servants ready to wait upon him, while now he was one of the most despised and wretched of slaves. These thoughts continued to occupy his troubled mind until, after reflecting upon the subject a long time, he came to a decision. He said to himself, "My father's numerous servants have food enough and more than they need, while I am dying from hunger." Finally, he resolved to return to his father, whom he had left without his approval, and had disgraced by his sinful career, and say to him, "Father, I have sinned against heaven and against thee. I am not worthy to be treated as a son, make me one of thy hired servants." By this resolution the prodigal exhibited deep humility, attachment to his early home and confidence in his father, whom he found to be more tender and ready to forgive than he expected.

He left the swine he was tending in a foreign country, a poor, ragged, hungry wayfarer, and came to his native land. As he journeyed on foot, weary and dejected, his thoughts troubled him. "Would his father receive his wayward son, even as a servant?" But he had greatly misjudged the character of his parent, who, as he was directing the labors of his servants in the field, chanced to see a lonely wanderer a great distance off, and immediately recognized the stranger as his son. The anxious father had never heard from him during the long years of his absence, and knew not whether he was still alive, yet, strange to say, he knew the forlorn and weary traveller was his son and he pitied him. He did not wait until he came near, but *ran* to meet him and throwing his arms about his neck, he kissed him as a sign of affection and reconciliation. The prodigal son said to his father what he had planned to tell him, but met with a most cordial welcome.

The wanderer was dirty, ragged and barefoot, therefore he must be clothed in proper garments. The father gave orders to his servants to bring the best robe used for festal occasions, and clothe him, to cover his bare feet with sandals, and place a ring on his hand as a mark of wealth and dignity. The father had him arrayed not as a servant, but as a son whom he delighted to honor.

Nor was this all; there must be a feast given to celebrate the event, therefore the "fatted calf" was killed and an entertainment was made, accompanied with music and dancing. The latter exercise, among the Jews, was an exhibition of joy, and sometimes practised as a religious ceremony. The feast was intended as a joyful occasion, for, as the father expressed it, "My son

CHRIST LAMENTING OVER JERUSALEM.

was dead, and is alive again; he was lost and is found"; that is, he feared he might have been physically dead, or perhaps morally dead, since he had wandered from home and he knew not where he was.

Near the close of the day, the eldest son, who was superintending the labors of the farm, returned to his home, and as he drew near the house he heard music and great rejoicing, which surprised him, and he inquired of one of the servants what it meant. He replied, "Thy brother has returned, and thy father has prepared a feast to express his joy at the unexpected event." The elder brother was angry and would not enter the house, when the father left the company, went out and entreated him to go in and join in the festivity, but he refused, saying, " I have served you faithfully many years, and have never disobeyed your commands, and yet you never gave me even a kid, which is of much less value than a calf, that I might entertain my companions at a feast, but as soon as this thy son" (he does not call him brother), "who has spent thy property in vice and dissipation, returned, thou hast killed for him the fatted calf."

This charge was true, yet the prodigal had repented, and wished to live a correct life, and the elder brother should have rejoiced at his return and reformation. The father's vindication of his own course was, "Son, thou art always with me, and all that remains of my property belongs to thee, therefore you have no cause to complain, but it was proper that we should rejoice at the return of one whom we supposed lost." By the elder brother, Jesus intended to represent the scribes and Pharisees, and by the younger, the publicans and sinners.

This parable may be called a beautiful, delightful and instructive poem. It teaches the lesson that it was proper for the Saviour to receive and forgive repentant sinners, while the complaint of the Pharisees was unreasonable.

The Unjust Steward. — The parable of the prodigal son was more especially intended for the scribes and Pharisees, but that of the rich man and his steward which immediately followed was addressed to the publicans who were the tax-collectors, an employment that encouraged a love of wealth, and tested one's honesty.

A steward held a responsible position in a household, as it was his duty to provide for the wants of the family, consequently he had control of the funds necessary for this object. The position of steward was commonly given to a slave as a reward for his fidelity during a long period of service. The office was one that afforded an opportunity for dishonesty and prodigality, as the master could not always be engaged in watching his servants.

A certain rich man had a steward who was suspected of having wasted or appropriated to his own use his lord's property. At length complaints reached the master, that his steward had been dishonest, when his lord sent for him and said, "Give an account of your stewardship," that is, his expenses and management, "and if the reports I have heard are confirmed, you cannot hold the office any longer." The steward did not attempt to vindicate his conduct, which was a proof of his guilt. He thought about his situation and said to himself, "What shall I do for a living if I am removed from the position of steward? I have not been accustomed to manual labor, and I am ashamed to beg." He was too proud for that, therefore, after reflecting upon the subject, he came to a decision. His plan was to bestow favors upon his lord's debtors, or tenants, before he was deprived of his position, that they might feel indebted to him. His scheme exhibited much shrewdness and worldly wisdom, but it was dishonest and selfish.

As it was his duty to collect the debts due his master, he sent for his lord's debtors and inquired how much they owed him. The first one said, "One hundred measures of oil," or nearly ten gallons, which may have been the sum due for the rent on the land. It was the oil of olives used for various purposes. The steward told him to take his bill or contract and quickly write fifty measures, or one-half the quantity due. The second debtor was asked the same question and he replied, "One hundred measures of wheat." A measure was about fourteen bushels, hence the whole amounted to some fourteen hundred bushels. "Take thy bill and write eighty measures," was the order. The object of the dishonest steward was to place the debtors of his lord under obligations to himself that they might offer him a home when he was deprived of his office.

The master commended the shrewdness and wordly wisdom of his steward, though he was dishonest in all his transactions, having defrauded his lord both on his own account, and also on that of the debtors.

The Rich Man and Lazarus. — The Saviour had taught the people by parables the danger arising from the loss of money, the deceitfulness of riches, and that what men highly esteemed was offensive to God, that those who did not use their property aright could not enter heaven, and that kindness should be shown to the poor. The design of the parable of the rich man and Lazarus was to impress these truths more forcibly on the mind, and to teach the Pharisees that, with all their wealth and position, and observance of religious ceremonies, they might be lost.

The rich man is not represented in the parable as immoral or as neglecting the observance of the law, but his great wealth was the chief danger to his spiritual welfare. He was clothed in purple, the color usually worn by princes, nobles and the rich, and fine linen, also an article of luxury worn by the same classes. He lived sumptuously, that is, his table was furnished, not occasionally, but every day, with all the luxuries that wealth could purchase.

Jesus did not charge him with any crimes, or intimate that his wealth had been acquired by dishonesty or oppression, neither did he insinuate that he was unkind, penurious or uncharitable. He was simply a rich man, but he neglected to make provision for the wants of his soul.

There were no charitable institutions in those days for the care of the poor and for invalids, consequently, they were often found at the gates of cities and doors of the rich and places of public resort, to receive charity. There was a certain poor man, called Lazarus, meaning "one needy," lying at the gate or door of the rich man's house, to be fed with the "crumbs" from his table, as it is expressed. He was not only destitute, but was covered with loathsome ulcers which the dogs came and licked. A more pitiable object could hardly be imagined; and what a contrast he afforded to the rich man, clothed in purple and faring sumptuously, yet he did not drive away the poor, diseased beggar, and the probability is that he had been fed by the rich man from his own table.

In the course of time Lazarus died and his spirit was conducted by angels to heaven, where he is represented as reclining on the bosom of Abraham, as it was customary for guests at table to lean on the breast of the one sitting near. The Jews believed that the spirits of the righteous dead were conducted to heaven by angels. Nothing is said about the funeral of Lazarus: he was too poor and ignoble to have any ceremony at his burial. Soon after, the rich man died, when there was a grand funeral attended by many distinguished persons.

At this stage of the parable, Jesus directs the attention of his hearers to the future world, and represents the rich man as in a place where the departed spirits of the wicked go, far from the abode of the righteous, and separated from them by an impassable gulf. It was a place of torment, and the suffering of the occupants was very great, represented by fire, from which there was no escape.

The rich man suffering inexpressible agony, seeing Abraham afar off in heaven, and Lazarus resting on his bosom, raised his voice, saying, "Father Abraham, have mercy on me, and send Lazarus that he may dip his finger in water and cool my tongue, for I am tormented in this flame." Abraham replied, "Son, remember that in thy lifetime thou hadst prosperity, luxury and honor, while Lazarus had only poverty, contempt and suffering. Now he is comforted and thou art tormented. Besides, there is a fathomless gulf or chasm between us, over which there is no passing." "Send Lazarus to my father's house," said the sufferer, "that he may warn my five brethren, that they may not come to this place of torment." Abraham replied, "They have Moses and the prophets, let them listen to them." "They will not hear them," said Dives, "but if one went to them from the dead, they will repent." "If they will not give heed to the teachings of Moses and the prophets, neither will they be persuaded though one rose from the dead," was the answer.

This parable delivered in Galilee is, perhaps, the most solemn and impressive of all those spoken by the Saviour. It teaches that the punishment of the wicked is fearful and eternal; that God has given them sufficient warning to prepare for death, as by the Scriptures, in the teachings of Christ, the influences of the Holy Spirit and by human messengers, therefore they are without excuse if they reject or neglect these aids.

The Wedding Feast. — On a previous occasion, Jesus had given the parable of the householder and his vineyard which the priests and Pharisees understood was against themselves, and which awakened in their hearts a desire to murder him. Though this design was understood by the Saviour, yet he gave another parable illustrating the rejection of the Jews, and the calling of the Gentiles, by a marriage feast. At Jewish weddings, the bridegroom had a bridesman called "the friend of the bridegroom," by the Saviour, whose office it was to attend to the ceremonials of the wedding, and have the care of providing for the guests. The bridegroom was attended by a number of young men during the days of

THE WOMAN OF SAMARIA.

the marriage ceremonies, while the bride was accompanied by young women who sang a bridal song at her door the evening previous to the marriage. The young people of each sex during the time occupied different apartments and sat at different tables. The ceremonies continued seven days if the bride was a virgin, and three days if she was a widow. The seven days were usually spent at the house of the bride's father, when at their close, she was conducted to the home of the bridegroom, sometimes with great pomp. Weddings were commonly performed in the evening, and after the procession from the bride's home, the guests, before being admitted to the hall where the entertainment was given, were examined, so that no stranger or person not clothed in raiment for the occasion should enter. If such was found, he was excluded. The wedding garment of the invited guest must be suitable to the occasion.

The son, perhaps the heir apparent, of a certain king had just taken a bride, and the father of the prince made a feast in honor of the event and sent invitations by his servants to those he wished to honor as guests. It was customary to send two invitations: the first to give notice without specifying the time; the second to notify the invited guest of the precise time of the wedding. When everything was ready, the king said, "Tell those invited that the preparations are completed; the oxen and lambs have been killed, come to the feast"; but instead of appreciating the royal munificence, the invited guests treated it with contempt, and each went to his usual business; some to their farms and others to their mercantile pursuits, while there were those whose hatred of the king led them to commit acts of violence, by treating his messengers spitefully, and even killed some of them.

When the king heard of it, he sent an army, destroyed the murderers and burned their city. Having made preparations for a sumptuous feast, he would not abandon his plan, therefore he sent other messengers to invite the poor, the neglected, the despised outcasts, such as are found in the highways, both "bad and good," so that the feast might be furnished with guests. When the king entered, he noticed that one of the company did not wear a wedding garment. Being questioned about it, the man was silent, for he could offer no apology. He was without excuse, for kings and princes in ancient times were accustomed to present changes of raiment to their guests, when they were expected to wear them in the presence of their benefactor. This man had come to the feast in his ordinary dress, such as he wore when taken from the highway, instead of asking for one provided by the king for the occasion. Calling his servants, he ordered them to bind the insolent intruder, and thrust him into the midnight darkness without. This parable, doubtless, referred to the rejection of the Jews and the calling of the Gentiles. The general truth taught is, that the gospel with its blessings, being rejected by the Jewish nation would be accepted by the Gentiles.

CHAPTER XVI.

THE PARABLES OF CHRIST — CONCLUDED.

The Ten Virgins. — Jesus was at Jerusalem, and the time was drawing near when the great tragedy was to be performed which would end the earthly career of our Lord. As he came to the celebrated capital for the last time he wept over it, knowing what a fearful calamity would, in that generation, befall the city and nation. Under these circumstances, he uttered the parable of the ten virgins.

On several occasions Jesus made use of marriage ceremonies to illustrate his teaching, by enforcing some moral or religious truth, or describing some important event, and under this similitude he represents his coming in the Day of Judgment. Ten virgins at a certain wedding, according to the custom of the Jews, took their lamps, that is, torches or flambeaux, and went to meet the bridal party. If these young damsels were thoughtful they would take an extra supply of oil, not knowing how long they might be obliged to wait in the night for the coming of the bridegroom. The lamps, so called, were made by winding rags about some incombustible substance, usually hollowed to contain oil, and fastened to a handle of wood.

After the marriage the bridegroom conducted the bride to his home in the evening, attended with great parade, and it was during this part of the ceremony that he was met by female friends who went forth to welcome the bride and bridegroom. Not knowing precisely when the bridal procession would appear, they started early, but were obliged to wait until late in the night, hence their wisdom or foolishness would plainly be exhibited in taking or neglecting to take an extra supply of oil. Five of these virgins were thoughtful and supplied themselves with what was needed, but the other five neglected to make any such provision.

As the bridal party was delayed, these maidens became weary and fell asleep, when at midnight they were aroused by acclamations of joy, and a shout, "Behold the bridegroom cometh, go ye out to meet him." The wise virgins awoke and "trimmed" their lamps by a fresh supply of oil, but the foolish ones found they had none, for their store was exhausted, therefore they requested their more judicious associates to supply them with oil, but the latter declined, fearing there was not enough for all, but advised them to purchase it from those who sold the article.

While they were gone to buy it the bridegroom and those who were ready entered the house, and the door was closed and fastened, so that no one who came afterwards could enter. It was not long, however, before the other virgins came and applied for admittance, saying, "Lord, Lord, open the door for us," but the bridegroom replied, "I do not know you," therefore they were not admitted. The impressive lesson taught is, that every one should be ready and watchful, since no one can tell the hour the Son of Man will come, either to judgment or at death. The Saviour closed this solemn lesson with the words, "Be ye ready, for in such an hour as ye think not the Son of Man cometh."

The parable of the talents was spoken to illustrate the manner Christ will deal with human beings when he comes to judgment, and is as follows:

A certain man, intending to travel in a distant country, and might be absent a long time, left the management of his worldly affairs to his servants, whom he called together and arranged his business in the following manner: He gave to each different sums of money to be invested on the best terms they could secure, so when he returned he might receive a profitable income. To the first servant called he gave five talents, or between $7,000 and $8,000; to a second, two talents, or more than $3,000; and to a third servant he gave one talent, or between $1,000 and $2,000. Having entrusted to the care of these servants different sums, according, perhaps, to their different capacities for business, the master started on his journey.

The first two employed their lord's money in trade or by judicious investment, thus increasing its value twofold. The servant who had received one talent, either from indolence, dissatisfaction, contempt or jealousy, made no attempt to invest his master's property, though he did not squander it or appropriate it to his own use. He was not dishonest in this respect, but he was unfaithful to the trust committed to him. Wishing to preserve the talent in safety to be returned to his lord, he secretly buried it in the ground, secure from robbers.

After a long time the master returned from his journey and summoned his servants for a settlement. The one who had received five talents brought his lord ten, as the result of his management, and received the commendation, "Thou hast been faithful over a little, as a reward, I will promote thee to more important trusts. Enter into the joy of thy lord," that is participate in the pleasures of the feast to celebrate his master's return. The one who received two talents brought his master four, and received the same commendation and promise of reward. The servant who had been given one talent came at length, and addressed his lord thus, calling him a hard master and accusing him of extortion, "therefore," said he, "I was afraid I might lose the talent in trade, and to keep it safe I hid it in the ground, and now return it to thee."

The master severely and justly rebuked him, saying, "Thou wicked and slothful servant, if thou knewest I was such a man, why didst thou not give my money to the exchangers (or those who borrow), that I might have received it with interest?" Then addressing his faithful servants he said, "Take from him the one talent and give it to him who hath ten, and cast the unprofitable servant into outer darkness, where shall be great sorrow and anguish." The expression "outer darkness," used as a metaphor to denote future punishment, may have been suggested by Roman prisons, usually constructed under ground, and were dark, damp and unhealthy, where the unhappy prisoners spent their time in weeping and "gnashing their teeth," with indignation. This parable was delivered by the Saviour when at Jerusalem.

The Sheep and Goats. — When Jesus, on a particular occasion, was on the Mount of Olives, whence a magnificent view of the city was obtained, he, with tears, delivered this prophetic lamentation, "O Jerusalem, Jerusalem, how often would I have gathered thy children together, as a hen gathers her brood under her wings, but ye would not. Behold your house" — the Temple — "is left unto you desolate, for the time will come when thine enemies" — the Romans — "shall besiege thee, throw down thy wall and capture the city." This prophecy was fulfilled in little less than forty years later, or in the year 70 A. D. This startling announcement was made in the presence of all the apostles, but Peter, Andrew, James and John came to the Saviour, and said, "tell us privately when these things shall be, and what shall be the sign of thy coming, and of the end of the world." There were three distinct questions asked: First, When would the predictions about the Temple and city take place? Second, What would be the sign of his coming? Third, What signs would indicate the end of the world was near? Jesus answered these inquiries, not as separate questions, but by combining the descriptions which could be expressed in the same language, in the parable of the sheep and goats, delivered on this occasion.

When the Son of Man comes to judge the world, he will appear as a king, in royal splendor, attended by a host of angels, when all nations will be gathered before him, not only those then existing, but all that have passed away, and that may exist to the end of time. The grave and sea will surrender their dead, for the momentous trial; not one human being can be absent from the vast assembly. No created mind can form an adequate idea of the importance of the occasion, or compute the vast number to be judged. They will be separated into two great classes — the righteous represented by sheep, and the wicked by goats, the former on the right hand of the Judge, and the latter on the left.

The Judge, who will be Christ himself, is represented as seated upon a throne, which will be raised above the multitudes to be judged so that he can be seen by all. No imagination can fully picture the scene in all its solemnity. The separation of the two classes will be so distinct, there will be no possibility of a mistake: both will comprise persons of all nationalities, ages and conditions in life. There will be emperors, kings, princes, conquerors, statesmen, presidents, men of business, the highly cultivated scholars, philosophers, poets, artists, the poor, the wealthy, the honored of earth, and the depised, the hypocrite and the self-deceived, but the only distinction observed by the Judge will be that between the righteous and the wicked.

He will open the court by calling for the Books in which have been recorded the deeds of those to be judged. To those on his right hand he will say, "Come, ye blessed of my Father, inherit the kingdom prepared for you from the foundation of the world," or from eternity. Then he will give the reason for his decision, which will be, not for their professions, but for their works, as evidences of their love to him, as, "I was hungry and thirsty and ye gave me food and drink. Ye clothed me when I was naked, and visited me when I was sick and in prison." Conscious of their unworthiness, the righteous will answer, "Lord, when have we performed such deeds of kindness to thee?" The Judge will reply, "inasmuch as ye have performed them to one of the poorest and most despised of these my brethren, ye have done them for me." What wonderful condescension, what amazing love, to call sinful mortals brethren!

Having decided the case of the righteous, represented by sheep, the Judge will then pass sentence upon those on his left hand, represented by goats, and expressed in the fearful words, "Depart, ye cursed," or those who deserve punishment, "into everlasting fire, prepared for the devil and his angels," and then will give as a reason for this sentence, their neglect to perform deeds of kindness and charity to him. In vindication of their conduct, they will say, "When have we seen thee hungry, thirsty, naked, sick or in prison and did not minister to thee?" "Inasmuch as ye did it not to these," on my right hand, "ye did it not to me." At the conclusion of the decisive trial, those found guilty will be sentenced to everlasting punishment, but the righteous will be rewarded by life eternal. This parable of the sheep and goats is one of the most impressive and solemn ever uttered, for it settles the most important question pertaining to the final destiny of the human race.

The Rich Fool. — When in Galilee, Jesus had been talking with the scribes and Pharisees, and a great crowd had gathered about him, so that some could not even get standing room sufficiently near to hear him. One man from the immense throng came near the Saviour and said, "Master, command my brother to divide the inheritance with me." He had probably disputed with his brother about the property, and now appealed to

Jesus as arbitrator in the quarrel. If he had any just claim, why not settle it by law? The answer of Jesus was a rebuke to him; he said, "Man, who made me a judge to settle disputes about your claims?" meaning it was not his business to settle controversies of this kind; he came to preach the gospel and left civil affairs to the magistrates.

This incident led the Saviour to relate a parable nearly as follows, as a warning against covetousness, of which one or both of these brothers were guilty: A certain rich man owned a farm that was very fertile, and yielded abundant crops, so that his granary, called a "barn," was not large enough to hold them. Granaries in the East were generally under the ground, where the grain could be kept safe for a long time. The farmer was troubled about a place in which to store his produce, but finally decided to enlarge his granary for storage. He reasoned thus: "I will pull down my barns and build greater ones, and there will I store my grain, and then I will say, 'Soul, thou hast an abundance laid up, enough to last many years; take thine ease, eat, drink, and be merry.'" But the Lord said to him, "Thou fool, this night thy soul will be required of thee, then to whom will belong the things thou hast provided?" "So is every one," said Jesus, "that layeth up treasures for himself and is not rich towards God."

The Seed Springing Up. — This parable was spoken in Capernaum, a city of Galilee, a region in which Jesus was brought into frequent communication with those engaged in agriculture. Many of his parables and the figures of speech used in his discourses referred to scenes in rural life, which proves he was a close observer of the

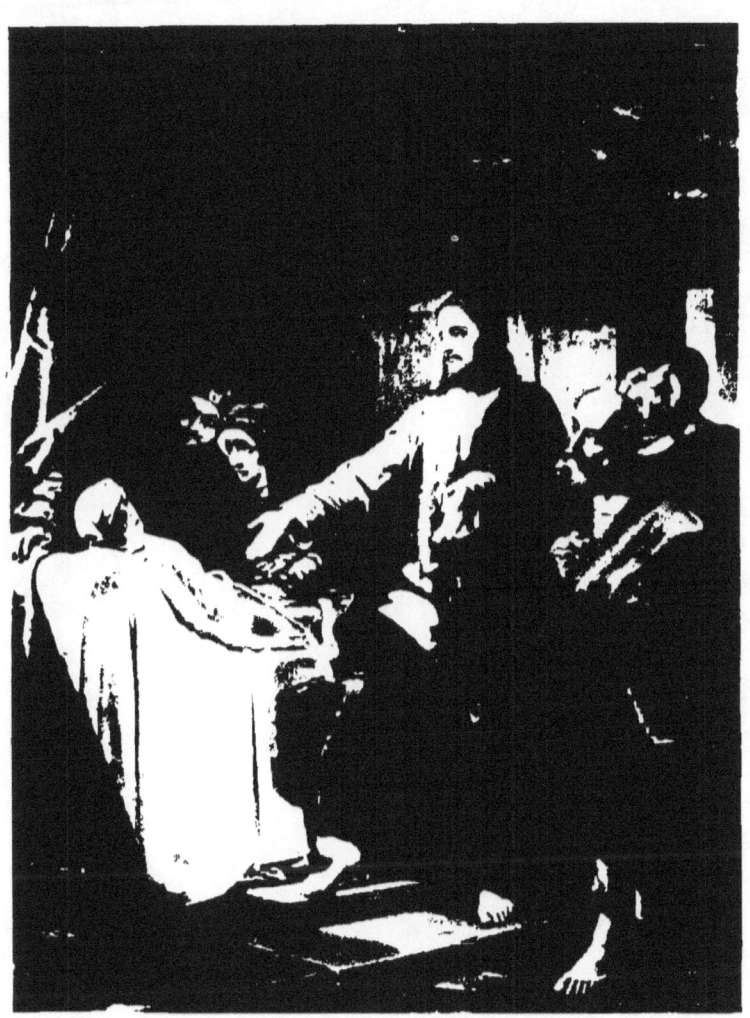

THE DAUGHTER OF JAIRUS.

works of nature. The gospel, in its influence upon the hearts of men, may very appropriately be compared to the labors of the husbandman, who plants his seed in the ground, and then leaves it to attend to other duties, or, as it is expressed, he sleeps at night, and rising in the morning goes about his usual occupations, without any thought of the buried seed; but in the mean time it germinates, springs up and bears fruit in the following order: first, the blade or tender shoot, which gradually becomes a stalk; after this, appears the ear or bud, and finally, the ripe wheat, expressed by the word corn.

These processes were not understood by the husbandman, for no one can fully comprehend the operations of nature, but when the wheat is ripe, he understands it is time to harvest it, therefore he sends his laborers to cut it with their sickles and store it in his granaries.

The lesson taught by this parable is, that religion in the heart of the believer is at first feeble and sometimes almost imperceptible, but it gradually advances until it comes to maturity, when he is removed from the earth to a more exalted state. A more general truth is, that the gospel had a small beginning in Judea, but finally it would spread to other regions and yield an abundant harvest. In the end Christ will send forth his angels and gather his disciples into his fold, which will occur at his second coming, when he will appear to judge the world.

Servants Waiting for their Lord. — This parable, delivered in Galilee, was under the similitude of a marriage feast, to which the master of a household was invited as a guest. He left his servants at home to watch for his return, so when he knocked at the gate, or door, for entrance, they might open it immediately and not keep him waiting. As their lord delayed his coming, the watchers became weary and sleepy, therefore some of them yielded to the demands of nature, and were taken by surprise when their master returned, but others by great effort succeeded in keeping awake. The faithful servants were honored in the following manner: Their master assumed the position of a servant, and girding himself, that is, by confining his long flowing robe with a girdle around his waist, he waited upon them at table. Here Peter interrupted his Master by the question, "Whether the parable applied only to them," that is, the apostles, "or to every one?" Jesus without answering his question definitely, replied by saying, "Who is the steward whom his lord chooses to rule his household?" It certainly is not the unfaithful servant who, finding that his master delayed his return, indulged his cruel disposition by beating the other servants, both male and female, and squandering his lord's property in feasting and drunkenness.

    The lord of such a servant will return unexpectedly, deprive him of his office as steward, and deliver him for punishment, for "The servant who knew his lord's will, but was disobedient, shall be corrected by many stripes, while those who through ignorance committed offences, will be chastised with few stripes." The Jews did not administer more than forty stripes or blows for one offence, and for smaller ones they inflicted only four, five, six, etc., according to the nature of the crime. The lesson of the parable is expressed in the following language, "Unto whom much is given, of him much will be required," that is, much will be expected of those who possess great talents and opportunities, while less will be required of those who have fewer advantages, and possess smaller talents.

The Lost Piece of Silver. — The recovery of an object lost, as previously stated, though of no great intrinsic value, frequently affords more pleasure to the owner than more valuable ones safe in his possession. This principle is illustrated by the parable of the piece of silver, spoken in Galilee. The Saviour represents a woman as having lost a piece of silver, or one drachm, worth about fourteen cents, a trifling sum, but probably she was poor and could not afford to lose it, as all her store mentioned was only ten pieces or drachms, equal to about one dollar and forty cents. She was very anxious about this misfortune, and made diligent search for the missing coin, which she may have dropped upon the floor or laid in some obscure place that she had forgotten. After searching in vain for some time, she lighted a candle and examined every dark corner, but without success, and then swept the house, thinking she might find it by this method. Finally, after searching a long time, she discovered the lost treasure in a very unexpected place, and in her joy she called her friends and neighbors who, perhaps, were aware of her anxiety, saying, "Rejoice with me, for I have found the lost piece of silver." The lesson taught is similar to that afforded by the parable of the lost sheep, namely, there is more joy in the presence of the angels over one straying sinner recovered, than for those who had not wandered.

The Unjust Judge. — Jesus had crossed the Jordan to the east side, and came to Perea, where he delivered the following parable: There was in a certain city a judge, or one appointed to decide cases brought before him for settlement. This judge was not influenced by moral principles, for he feared not God, nor regarded the feelings, opinions or rights of his fellow-creatures. These civil officers were under obligations, by the Jewish laws, to show special attention to the rights of widows, since they had no one to protect them, and were commonly poor and liable to be oppressed.

A certain widow, in the same city, came to this judge and said, "Avenge me of my adversary," that is, protect me in my rights against my oppressor, who is unwilling to do me justice. The judge for a time turned a deaf ear to her petition, yet she continued to repeat her request, until he became weary of her importunities, and said to himself, "Though I fear not God, nor regard men, yet I will avenge this widow who, by her frequent coming and persistent appeals, wearies me." Jesus then directs the attention of his hearers to what the unjust judge said, and adds, "Will not God avenge his own elect," or his chosen people who cry to him day and night, though he may delay to answer their petition in order to test their faith? One lesson taught is the power of importunity in prayer.

The Pharisee and the Publican. — This parable given in Perea was intended as a rebuke to those who trusted in their own righteousness.

Two men went to the Temple to pray, that is, in the court of the Temple, where prayer was usually offered. The Pharisee drew near the sacred building and stood, while he offered the following prayer: "I thank thee Lord, that I am not as other men, such as extortioners, unjust persons, adulterers, nor even as this publican. I fast twice in the week, and I give tithes of all I possess." According to his own declaration he had carefully observed the outward forms of religion, and had not been guilty of any unjust or immoral act.

The publican stood afar off, or in the most distant place of the court, from the Temple, and conscious of guilt, he would not raise his eyes to heaven, but smote upon his heart, as an expression of deep sorrow, grief and repentance, saying, "God be merciful to me a sinner."

The Pharisees would have said, the first man was the one approved by his Maker, but Jesus told them the publican was the most acceptable to God, "For whoever exalteth himself shall be abased, and he that humbleth himself shall be exalted."

CHAPTER XVII.

DISCOURSES OF CHRIST.

Interview with Nicodemus. — Jesus had gone to the capital to attend the Feast of the Passover, where large numbers of the Jews were present from all parts of the country. Many were persuaded that he was the Messiah on account of the miracles he had wrought, and some of these were, doubtless, sincere believers, while others yielded an intellectual assent, but their hearts were not affected, for they did not understand the spiritual nature of Christ's teaching. The principal object of John's Gospel was to prove that Jesus was the Messiah, and it would strengthen his argument if he could offer the testimony of one of the leading Pharisees, who were nearly unanimous in their opposition to the claims of the Saviour.

Nicodemus, a ruler of the Jews, that is, a member of the Sanhedrim or Great Council of the nation, came to Jesus in the evening, after the multitude had dispersed leaving him quietly alone. Both Jesus and the ruler were more at leisure at such a time, besides, he would be more likely to avoid strong opposition which might endanger both the Saviour and himself. The future conduct of Nicodemus bears evidence of his sincerity.

CHRIST ENTERS JERUSALEM AS A CONQUEROR.

He is mentioned twice afterwards; once as protesting against the unjust suspicions of the Jews by saying when Christ was accused, "Doth our law judge a man before it hears him?" and again when he came with Joseph of Aramathea, to remove the body of Christ from the cross, embalm it and place it in the sepulchre. When Nicodemus came to Jesus, he said, "Rabbi," a title of respect conferred on Jewish teachers, "we know that thou art a teacher come from God, for no one can do the miracles thou doest except God be with him." He came to be instructed, and this was his introduction.

Jesus begun by stating the fundamental and essential doctrine of his religion, namely, the new birth, or a change of heart. He said "Except a man be born again, he cannot see the kingdom of God," that is, he is not fitted to partake of its blessings. The ruler understood the Saviour's declaration literally, and inquired how could he be born a second time? Jesus explains his meaning by saying, it was necessary to be born of the spirit, signifying that the regeneration of the soul is through the influence of the Holy Spirit. He then begins a discourse on the subject, when Nicodemus said, How can these things be?" "Art thou a Master in Israel, and knowest not these things?" replied the Saviour. The doctrine of regeneration is taught in the Old Testament and being a teacher of religion Nicodemus ought to have understood it. Jesus then resumed his discourse in which he taught that his mission to the world was to save sinners.

The Woman of Samaria. — The life of Jesus was in danger in consequence of the malice of the scribes and Pharisees, therefore he left Judea for Galilee where he would be more safe, and in going thither, he must pass through Samaria as the most direct route. In his journey he came to the vicinity of the city of Sychar, about fifteen miles south of the city of Samaria, between Mount Ebal and Mount Gerazim, both celebrated in the history of the Israelites. It was one of the oldest towns of Palestine, formerly known as Shechem or Sychem, belonging to the tribe of Ephraim and was the place where Joshua assembled the people to renew their covenant with the Lord. After the death of Gideon, it became a place of idol worship, and was destroyed by Abimelech, who overthrew the city and sowed the ground with salt, but it was afterwards rebuilt and became the home of Jereboam, King of Israel. Jacob bought a piece of ground near the city, and here was Jacob's well.

It was the middle of the day, and Jesus, becoming weary with his journey, sat down by the well to rest while his disciples went to Sychar to buy some food. While waiting for their return, a Samaritan woman came to the well to draw water, and Jesus, being thirsty, said to her, "Give me some of the water to drink." The woman, recognizing him as a Jew, was surprised at his request, for the two nations had no dealings with each other, and said, "How is it that a Jew should ask a favor from a Samaritan?" He replied, that if she knew who he was, she would ask of him living water. She did not understand his meaning, but their interview was continued, in which the Saviour told her many truths, some of them relating to her personal history, when she replied, "I perceive thou art a prophet." She referred to a coming Messiah, when Jesus affirmed that *he* was the Messiah. He then instructed her in the true religion, and she became so impressed with his teaching, that she left her water-jar and returned to the city to inform the citizens about him, when many of them came to the well and found him still there.

In the mean time his disciples returned with food, and were surprised that he should hold any conversation with a Samaritan. They urged him to eat, but he said, " My meat is to do the will of Him who sent me." Many of the Samaritans believed on him, and urged him to remain with them. He tarried two days, and during that time many more believed, so that the gospel was preached to a foreign nation, during the ministry of Christ. After the two days spent in Samaria, Jesus resumed his journey to Galilee. The account of his discourse at Nazareth is given in another chapter.

The Sermon on the Mount. — Jesus had been preaching and performing miracles in Galilee, so that his fame spread throughout Syria, Phœnicia and some other countries, and as a result great multitudes followed him from different regions, as Galilee, Decapolis, or the ten cities east of the Jordan, Tyre, Sidon, Judea, and from Jerusalem. As only a few, comparatively, of so large a multitude could come near so as to hear his words if he stood on a level with his hearers, he ascended a hill or mountain in the vicinity, and occupied a position on the declivity, probably, where he could be heard by a large number. This eminence has been called the "Mount of Beatitudes," but its exact location is not now positively known. Tradition assigns a hill a short distance north of Capernaum as the Mount of Beatitudes.

After ascending the mount, the Saviour sat down, the common position among the Jews for preaching, as an intimation to the crowd at the foot of the hill, that he was about to address them, therefore those attending upon his ministry regularly came nearer, that they might hear all his words. What are called "beatitudes," comprised nine: First, a blessing for the poor in spirit, or the humble; Second, for those who mourn; Third, for the meek; Fourth, for those who earnestly seek for righteousness, represented by the hungry and thirsty; Fifth, for the merciful; Sixth, for the pure in heart; Seventh, for peacemakers; Eighth, for those persecuted for righteousness; Ninth, for those slandered on account of being Christians.

The Sermon on the Mount is the longest and most comprehensive delivered by the Saviour as recorded by the sacred writers, and contains some of the most vital principles of religion. It has been said there is no Christian duty it does not enforce, and may be considered an epitome of the whole duty of man, and a "perfect standard of Christian living."

Instructions to the Apostles. — When in Galilee, Jesus called together his disciples known as the apostles, in order to give them special instructions and power to work miracles. They were to preach the gospel to their own countrymen only, as the time had not come for labor among the Gentiles. These missionaries were sent out in companies of two each, that they might encourage and assist each other in cases of emergency. They were not to make any provision for their support, as they would be entertained by those who accepted their teachings. They were not to provide themselves with money, knapsacks, extra shoes or sandals, nor extra clothing, such as coats or tunics. They were, however, allowed to wear sandals to protect their feet during their travels, and to carry a staff, a necessary protection against danger. The reason given for these directions was that "the workman is worthy of his meat." Those who had walking sticks were to take them, but those who had none need not provide themselves with them.

"When you arrive at a city or town," said their Master, "inquire about the people to ascertain who will be likely to show you hospitality, and abide there during your visit, but do not go from house to house" like idle vagrants. "When you enter a house, salute the family to show the customary tokens of respect, and if the members are willing to receive you, let your peace come to it, but if they will not receive you, this blessing shall not be theirs. Whoever will not receive you nor listen to your words, when you depart shake off the dust from your feet as a witness against them, and it will be more tolerable for Sodom and Gomorrah in the Day of Judgment, than for that city." This was a fearful doom, but as the cities of Palestine in the time of Christ had greater light, their punishment for neglecting that light would be more severe. He warned them against dangers they would be likely to encounter, saying, "I send you as sheep in the midst of wolves; your innocence or philanthropy will not protect you, therefore be wise as serpents and harmless as doves." By this he meant they should exercise caution and wisdom, the serpent being the emblem of these qualities, and the dove of innocence. They should not, unnecessarily, expose themselves to danger, but they would, however, encounter greater perils than from wolves, since they would be from men, "For they will deliver you," said Jesus, "to the Council, or judicial tribunal, they will scourge you in the synagogues and bring you before governors and rulers on account of your attachment to your Lord."

Scourging or whipping was a common mode of punishment in ancient times, when the victim was laid on the ground with his face to the earth, and the blows were inflicted on his naked back, and sometimes he was tied to a post. A rod was used with thongs or lashes not unfrequently containing points of iron, called scorpions. The law of Moses forbade more than forty stripes to be inflicted at one time, therefore the Jews used a scourge with three lashes, and administered thirty-nine stripes only. Paul was scourged five times in this manner. The Romans did not observe this rule, but inflicted the number of blows that suited them, therefore the Saviour was scourged before his crucifixion until he became too weak to bear his cross. Christ's prediction that his disciples would be arraigned before kings and rulers was literally fulfilled. It is said that Peter was brought before the Emperor Nero, and John before Domitian, and other apostles appeared as criminals before different rulers.

The disciples whom Jesus sent to preach the gospel were obscure fishermen of whom the world knew nothing, yet when brought before emperors, kings and rulers they were not to be anxious about what they should say, for they would, on such occasions, be inspired from heaven. He then tells them what to expect. Families would be divided among themselves; for example, brother against brother, father against his child, and children against their parents; they would persecute one another even unto death, and his disciples would be hated by all men for his sake, but he that endured unto the end should be saved. Some of the methods of putting Christians to death have been the following: By crucifixion, casting them into boiling oil, burning at the stake, roasting alive, compelling them to drink melted lead, torn in pieces by wild beasts, covered with pitch and burned, as they were by the Emperor Nero, to light his gardens by night, and by many other fearful tortures.

When they were persecuted in one city, they were to escape to another, and this was to be continued, for they could not visit every city in their native land before the coming of the Son of Man, that is, before the destruction of Jerusalem and the end of the Jewish economy, which occurred 70 A. D. "The disciple is not above his master," said Jesus, that is, he must expect the same treatment, and if the world had called him Beelzebub, or the prince of devils, they must expect to be called the same. Beelzebub was considered the lowest and most offensive of all the heathen gods, therefore by applying the name to Christ, or attributing his miracles to the influence of this demon, his enemies expressed their greatest contempt for him. He told them not to fear their malicious foes, for their innocence would eventually be vindicated, and, as an illustration, he refers to the sparrows but little valued among the feathered tribe, yet their Heavenly Father cares for them, and not one falls to the ground without his notice; if then he has such care for them, his human children are dearer to him, since they are of more value than many sparrows.

Another illustration given was, that the Father knows the number of the hairs on our heads, and if he cares for such insignificant affairs, he will certainly provide for the personal comfort and safety of his children. Having received their orders from their Lord, the disciples started on their mission tour and preached the gospel, confirming their teaching by casting out devils, healing the sick and performing other miracles, and when they returned, related to the Master what they had done and the success of their labors.

Jesus was at or near Capernaum when he chose his apostles, and in their journeys they might become separated, therefore, when he wished to address them collectively, he called them to his presence to give them their instructions. The Saviour himself alone had, to this time, performed the duties of preaching the gospel and working miracles, but now he invested the apostles with these powers.

Knowing the character of Herod the Tetrarch, who had put John the Baptist to death, Jesus felt it would not be safe to remain in his jurisdiction, therefore he conducted his disciples privately to a desert place, belonging to the city of Bethsaida, in Galilee, but the multitude from whom his movements could not be concealed followed him, and moved with pity, he did not check their curiosity but received them kindly, and preached to them, and healed the sick, and cared for their physical wants.

The Lake Cities. — The Saviour was in Galilee when he delivered his fearful judgment against the cities of

Chorazin, Bethsaida, and Capernaum, where he had performed a large number of his miracles, and delivered many of his parables, yet the inhabitants, to a great extent, rejected the gospel. He said it would be more tolerable for Tyre and Sidon — heathen cities — in the day of judgment, than for them, for Tyre and Sidon would have repented in sackcloth and ashes, had the gospel been preached to them. Sackcloth was a coarse fabric worn by the poor, and on occasions of mourning. The Jews also were accustomed to put ashes on their heads, as an expression of grief. Capernaum had been highly favored, as Jesus spent a great part of his public life there, and taught the people. He said, "Though it was exalted to heaven, it should be brought down to hell," or Hades. The city had been peculiarly favored in regard to worldly advantages, as well as religious privileges. It was wealthy and prosperous, and had been specially distinguished by the preaching and miracles of Christ; but because the people rejected him, it should be reduced to the lowest place among cities. The prediction of Christ in relation to this city, as well as to Chorazin and Bethsaida, has been literally fulfilled. In the war between the Jews and the Romans, they were destroyed.

Discourse at Jerusalem. — The circumstances which led to this discourse were briefly as follows: Jesus went from Galilee to Jerusalem to attend one of the great festivals, as the law required, and while there he cured a man on the Sabbath, as related in a previous chapter.

The Jews wished to take his life because he had performed this miracle on the Sabbath, but the Saviour vindicated his conduct by affirming that his Father worked on that day, that is, He did not suspend his labors, but continued to provide for all his creatures just the same, "Therefore," said Jesus, "I work." This was another cause why they wished to kill him, for he had not only violated the Sabbath, but had made himself equal with God, by calling him Father. Jesus then addressed them in a discourse of some length, affirming his authority and its source, and the intimate relation between the Father and Son, and that the latter was entitled to the same honor as the former. If the Saviour was to be equally honored with the Father, was it not a proof of his Divinity? The Jews so understood it.

The discourses of Jesus in the Temple during the Feast of Tabernacles were desultory, as he was frequently interrupted by questions and angry debates. He had retired to Galilee on account of the danger of assassination by the leaders in Judea, but when the feast was about to be celebrated at Jerusalem, his brethren, who did not believe in him as the Messiah, said in derision, "Do you go to Judea, that the disciples now there may see your works, for all men seek notoriety, and if you *do* work miracles, let it be known to the world."

Jesus replied, "The time for me to go has not come, but it makes no difference when you go, as you do nothing in opposition to the rulers, therefore, they do not hate you as they do me, because I bear witness against them."

The Saviour then tarried in Galilee until his brethren had gone to the feast, when he departed secretly,

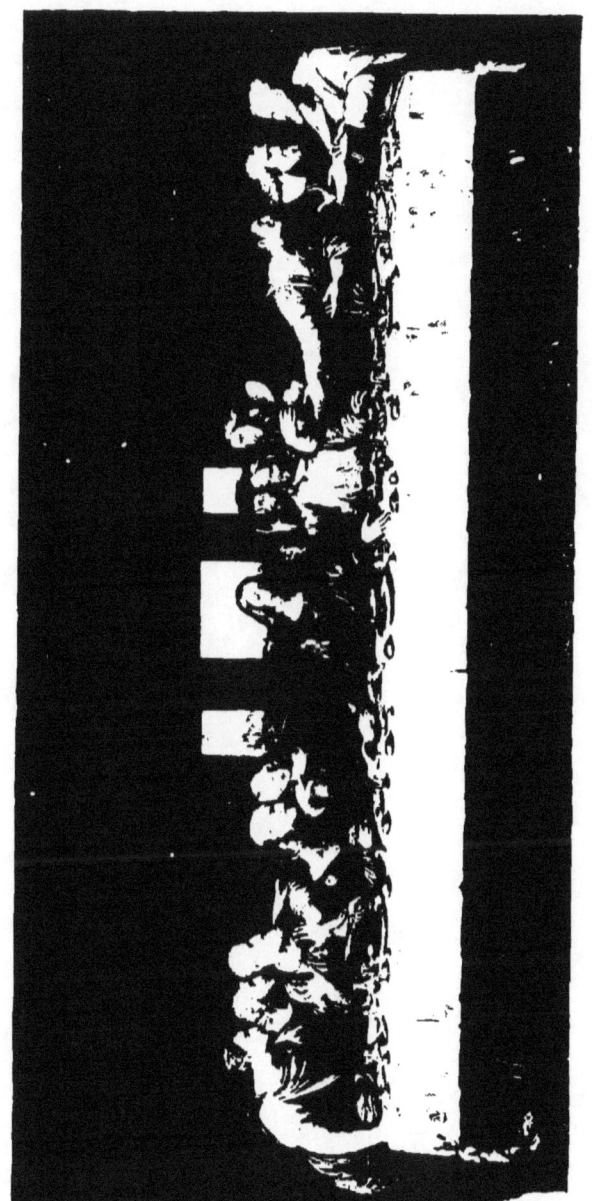

THE LAST SUPPER.

that he might avoid danger. The Jews were expecting him at the festival, and were discussing the subject, since there was a difference of opinion about him, some affirming that he was a good man, others, that he was an impostor, yet no one spoke openly of him for fear of the rulers. About the middle of the feast, or four days after it began, Jesus came to the Temple to instruct the people, when he aroused the curiosity and surprise of his listeners. "How is it," said they, "that this man understands the Scriptures and the traditions of our nation, seeing he has never been instructed in our schools of learning?"

Jesus understanding their doubts said, "My teaching and doctrine are what my Father sent me to proclaim, and if any one is willing to accept them, he shall know whether they are from Him, or only my own. Did not Moses, whom you all respect, give you the law, yet none of you keep it? Why do you seek to kill me?" Some one replied, "Who attempts to kill you? Thou art possessed of the devil, and art mad." This man may not have been aware of the design of the rulers to take his life, therefore he considered the Saviour insane. He referred to his miracle of healing a man on the Sabbath at which the Pharisees were greatly offended, yet they performed one of their rites on the Sabbath, therefore they were charged with passing unrighteous judgment.

Some one in the company said, "Is not this the one whom the rulers seek to kill? Yet they do not arrest him. Do they believe he is the Messiah? We know whence *he* is, but when Christ appears, no one can tell from what place he comes." The Jews understood he would be born in Bethlehem, but after his birth, they believed he would be concealed in a mysterious way, and then suddenly appear from some unexpected quarter.

Jesus raised his voice so that all could hear and said, "You know me and know whence I am," meaning, you should understand, since you have clear evidence of my Divine mission, and then added, "I come not of myself, but my Father sent me." After this his enemies sought an opportunity to arrest him, yet they did not carry out their plans. Many of his hearers believed on him and said, "When Christ comes, will he do more miracles than he has performed?"

When the chief priests and Pharisees heard what the people said, they sent officers to arrest him, and when they returned without their prisoner, they inquired why they had not brought him. Their reply was, "Never man spake like this man." The Pharisees said, "Are ye also deceived? Have any of the rulers believed on him? The multitude who have never been taught in the schools are of no account and are cursed." Nicodemus, one of the Council, said, "Does our law judge a man without a trial?" To express their contempt they said, "Are you from Galilee? Out of Galilee ariseth no prophet." There was so much disorder in the Great Council that it broke up in confusion, and every member returned to his own home.

Jesus told his audience that, "Only a little while am I with you, and then I shall go to Him who sent me, but where I go ye cannot come." It was supposed this was said about six months before his death. The expression, "Ye shall seek me and shall not find me," has been explained as follows: You shall seek the Messiah to deliver you from the Romans, during the siege of Jerusalem, as you expect him to appear as a conqueror. His listeners did not understand him, and conversed among themselves about his assertion that they could not follow him. "Where will he go that we cannot follow him? Will he go to the Gentiles and teach them?"

During the last and most important day of the feast, Jesus said, "If any man thirst, let him come to me and drink, and from him that believeth on me shall flow rivers of water," a figure of speech that means his piety would be like a running stream, carrying blessings to others. The gospel would be a constant and life-giving source of spiritual favors. The discourse made an impression on his audience, yet there was a difference of opinion, some affirming that he was the prophet to appear before the Messiah, others thought he was the Christ, while others probably doubted and inquired, "Will Christ come from Galilee? Hath not the Scriptures said that he will descend from the family of David, and his birthplace will be Bethlehem, the city of David?" These doubters, it appears, were ignorant of the Saviour's native place.

The Ears of Corn. — When travelling with his disciples during a missionary tour in Judea, they passed, on the Sabbath, a field of grain consisting of wheat or barley called corn. The disciples being hungry gathered some of the stalks of grain and rubbing them in their hands, to separate the kernels from the stems, they began to eat them. When the Pharisees saw them doing this they asked their Master why he allowed them to do what was not lawful on the Sabbath? Moses had given a law making it right to gather the ears of corn or grain on the Sabbath, to relieve present necessities, and Jesus asserted that it was not unlawful, according to the teachings of their great lawgiver.

He then strengthens his argument by referring to an incident in the life of David, whom all the Jews venerated, which was as follows: When hiding from the deadly hatred of Saul, faint and hungry, he went to the priest for some of the shew-bread, which none but priests were allowed to eat, but David, in opposition to this law, partook of it to satisfy his pressing wants, and was justified in doing so. The Saviour then refers to the custom of sacrificing animals on the Sabbath in the performance of religious ceremonies, which required labor, and closes his discourse by defending his conduct for allowing his disciples to gather the ears of wheat on the Lord's Day, saying that he was "Lord of the Sabbath," and that "it was made for man and not man for the Sabbath," meaning that it was intended for his welfare, and that his real wants must be considered, but he does not teach that it is not a violation of the Sacred Day to attend to unnecessary business, or indulge in worldly pleasures.

Sabbath Work. — This discourse was given at Capernaum, and the occasion was the miracle of curing a man whose hand was paralyzed; this was done in a synagogue, on the Sabbath. For this act the Pharisees held a council to devise some plan to murder the Saviour, but, understanding their plot, he withdrew from that vicinity, followed by a great crowd, whom he charged not to make known to the rulers his place of retreat. The time had not come for him to be delivered to his enemies, therefore he would be prudent and not expose himself unnecessarily to danger. The Herodians, a political party adopting the views of Herod the Great, who had sought to take the life of the infant Saviour, joined the would-be murderers of Jesus. When the Jewish leaders heard that he had cured a man blind, dumb and possessed with an evil spirit they said to themselves, he performed his miracle by the power of Beelzebub, the prince of devils. They could not deny that a miracle had been wrought, but they were determined to counteract its influence by ascribing it to the power of demons. Jesus reading their thoughts preached a sermon, based upon arguments they could not answer. First, "A kingdom or a house (family) divided against itself cannot stand. Second, If I cast out devils by Beelzebub, by whom do *your* disciples cast them out, a power they claim to possess? Third, If I cast them out by the Spirit of God, then His kingdom has come." Another illustration was the method a burglar would pursue when breaking into a house. He would first bind the strong master of the house, and then proceed to plunder it. The Saviour then states the general principle that there can be only two parties in the world, — one in sympathy and acting with him, and the other against him. He states the awful nature of the sin the Jews were committing against the Holy Spirit, and if they continued in this sin they could never be forgiven, for it was blasphemy against God. A word against the Son of Man might be pardoned, but one spoken against the Holy Spirit, meaning, probably, the Divine nature of Christ, cannot be forgiven, and the one guilty of the offence is in danger of eternal condemnation. Jesus further illustrates his subject by saying "A tree is known by its fruits," that is, one's character is known by his works. If he, the Saviour, was in league with Satan, he was wicked, but if not, their charges were blasphemous. He then compares his enemies to vipers or poisonous serpents, emblems of malignity and mischief. This metaphor signifies the exceeding wickedness of some of the Jewish nation in his day. Jesus closes his discourse with the solemn declaration that for every idle word, that is, vain, thoughtless word, or more especially wicked, malicious word, men shall give an account in the Day of Judgment, for they are the indications of the true state of the heart.

The Bread of Life. — The discourse on this subject was, to some extent, colloquial, since Jesus was interrupted by questions and dissents from his hearers. He had performed the miracle of the loaves, and as a result those who witnessed it professed their belief that he was the Messiah whom they supposed was to be a temporal prince, therefore they wished to proclaim him king and *compel* him to assume the title and dignity of one, since he was not disposed to assume the office which belonged to him. To avoid this forced recognition, Jesus withdrew from the multitude and retired to a mountain alone, doubtless to hold communion with his Father in heaven. Then followed the tempest and miracle of walking on the sea.

The people were not disposed to abandon their purpose, therefore they crossed the Sea of Tiberias and came to Capernaum seeking Jesus, and when they found him said, " Rabbi, when didst thou come hither ? " The Saviour improved this opportunity to preach a

PETER DENYING CHRIST.

sermon, in which he showed them that selfishness was the motive which governed their actions. He said, "Ye seek me, not on account of the miracle, but because ye were fed by the loaves. Labor not for temporal blessings," that is, be not over-anxious about them, "but strive for those which are enduring, such as the Son of Man will give, for Him hath God the Father sealed," that is, approved. His miracles were proofs that his doctrines were true, just as a seal confirms a deed or a compact.

The people interrupted the speaker by inquiring what they ought to do in order to obtain the blessings of salvation. They requested him to give a sign or some evidence apparent to the senses, such, perhaps, as a comet, thunder and lightning, sudden darkness or an earthquake, a remarkable request after the miracles they had witnessed or heard of. They referred to the manna with which their ancestors were fed in the wilderness and which they said Moses gave them. He replied that it was not Moses that gave them the manna, implying it was Jehovah who gave it, and then adds that his Father gives them the real bread for the nourishment of the soul, and that the bread from heaven sent for the life of the world was himself, and those who come to him shall never hunger, and those who believe in him shall never thirst. "All that the Father giveth me shall come to me, and him that cometh to me I will in no wise cast out." Jesus continued his discourse by asserting that no one would be lost of those whom the Father had given him, but he would raise him at the last day, and he should have eternal life.

The Jews murmured among themselves because the Saviour said, "I am the bread that came down from heaven." "Is not this Jesus, the son of Joseph? how then did he come down from heaven? Is he greater than Moses?" Knowing their thoughts, he said, "Do not murmur among yourselves, for no one can come to me and accept my doctrines unless he is drawn by the Father who sent me, and all such I will raise up in the last day." He then alludes to the teaching of the prophets who affirmed that the saints shall all be taught of God, and to guard against any delusion, he said "No one has seen the Father except the One who is of God," referring to himself. The preacher then reaffirms the doctrine that he was the Bread of Life, "Your fathers are dead who partook of the manna, but I am the Living Bread of which if one eats he shall live forever. The bread I will give is my body, that is given as an atonement for sin."

These sentiments aroused opposition from his hearers who had a controversy among themselves, saying, "How can this man give us his flesh to eat?" Jesus understanding their doubts affirmed with great emphasis, that unless they partook of his flesh and blood, they had no life in themselves, but those who did should participate in the resurrection of the just, and then repeated what he had previously said about his being the Bread of Life that came down from heaven.

At this stage of his discourse, many of his followers said it was a doctrine too difficult to believe, when Jesus knowing their thoughts, said, "If this offends you, what will you think when you see the Son of Man ascend to heaven?" He closed his discourse by saying there were some of his hearers who did not believe, and from that time many of his professed disciples left him. When he asked the apostles whether they would forsake him, Simon Peter replied, "To whom shall we go? Thou hast the words of eternal life, and we believe and art sure thou art the Christ, the Son of God." To put them on their guard against temptation and the deceitfulness of their own hearts, the Saviour said, "I have chosen from the great multitude of my followers only twelve apostles, and yet of this small number one is a devil."

CHAPTER XVIII.

DISCOURSES OF CHRIST — CONTINUED.

Traditions. — While Jesus was laboring in the towns and villages, some of the scribes and Pharisees from Jerusalem came to him, not for instruction, but to find fault with his teaching, doubtless. During their visit they were probably entertained at the same house with him and his disciples, when they observed that the traditions of the elders about washing the hands before eating had not been respected by the followers of Jesus.

The Jews attached great importance not only to the frequent washing of the hands, but also of cups or drinking-vessels, pots or measures for liquids, vessels of brass used for cooking, and tables, or more properly couches, on which they reclined at meals. Cleanliness, it is admitted, is a very important habit, conducive to health and pleasure, but the error of the Jews was they placed the ceremonial above the moral law. They believed that Moses on Mount Sinai received two different kinds of laws — one was revealed in their Scriptures; the other comprised such as were transmitted verbally from one generation to another, and that Moses delivered them to Joshua, that *he* taught them to the judges and *they*, to the prophets.

These traditions were numerous, and some were trifling, but the Jews regarded them of more importance than the teachings of Moses or the prophets as recorded in the Scriptures; they were contained in the Talmuds, the great depositories of the doctrines and opinions of their nation.

When they noticed the disciples did not wash their hands before eating, the scribes and Pharisees complained to their Master, who, in his answer, implied that no one was under obligation to obey their traditions, since they were not given by Divine authority, and then mentions a special case in which tradition made void the law commanding all persons to honor their parents, and shows them how they had violated this command. They were in the practice of dedicating to the service of God, any of their possessions they chose, by saying it was *corban*, that is, a gift, and when this decision was made, it must be observed, without respecting the claims of needy parents, while the Mosaic law required that a son should provide for his parents when they were feeble and unable to care for themselves.

The Saviour did not intend to condemn the practice of giving for religious and charitable objects, for both in the law and in the gospel this was required, but he meant it was wrong to withhold from parents and other relatives that assistance they needed, under the pretence of religion. He told them plainly they were hypocrites, and applied to them the language of Isaiah who condemned the Israelites of his time for teaching the doctrines of men instead of the Lord. Jesus taught that the heart was the source of pollution, not what one eats.

The scribes and Pharisees were, of course, offended at his doctrines, since he set aside their traditions, and when the disciples told their Master about it, he replied, "Every plant or doctrine not given by my Father will be uprooted. Do not be troubled, they"—that is, his enemies—"are blind leaders of the blind, therefore both will fall into the ditch." The disciples, not understanding their Teacher's meaning, asked for an explanation. As if surprised at their ignorance and dulness of apprehension, he said, "Are ye also without understanding? Do you not know the food eaten does not affect the soul? The doctrine of the Pharisees about washing the hands is absurd; it is the heart that must be cleansed." Jesus then states what does constitute sin: First, evil or wicked thoughts; Second, murder; Third, adultery; Fourth, theft; Fifth, false witness or lying; Sixth, blasphemy; Seventh, covetousness; Eighth, wickedness, that is, malice or the desire to injure others; Ninth, deception; Tenth, lasciviousness, lust or unbridled passion; Eleventh, an evil eye, or a malignant, proud, injurious disposition; Twelfth, pride or self-exaltation; Thirteenth, foolishness or choosing wrong methods for gaining a purpose. These are what defile the man, and all have their origin in the heart.

Forgiving Injuries. — This topic has been referred to on another page, to which may be added further remarks. According to Luke, the Saviour said in substance, "If a person does you an injury, go and tell him of his fault and ask an explanation, and if he repents, forgive him, not once only, but seven times a day, if he asks it." He illustrated his subject, as before stated, by the parable of the king and his servants. Jesus declared that "Unless ye forgive men their trespasses, your Heavenly Father will not forgive your trespasses." The duty of forgiving those who injure us seemed so difficult, that the apostles said, "Lord, increase our faith."

The Feast of Tabernacles. — This festival was celebrated at Jerusalem, as previously stated, from the fifteenth to the twenty-third of the seventh month, that is, October, to commemorate the journey of the Israelites through the desert of Arabia on their way from Egypt to Canaan. The eighth day of the feast was especially important, and during the festival the people dwelt in booths or tents. It was also a feast of thanks for the vintage and gathering of fruits, therefore called also the "Feast of Gathering," and was a joyful occasion when many sacrifices were offered and special ceremonies were observed, briefly as follows: The priests drew water from the fountain Siloam near the eastern walls of Jerusalem, carried it through the water-gate to the Temple, and poured it on the ground near the altar, the Levites, meanwhile, playing upon musical instruments and singing Psalms cxiii, cxiv, cxv, cxvi, cxvii and cxviii.

Lights were kept burning in the Court of the Women, during the festival, in four golden candlesticks of great height, while the priests and Levites standing on the steps of the Inner Court sang the Psalms from the cxx to the cxxxiv, called the "Song of Degrees," accompanied by music and dancing; the performers bearing lighted torches in their hands. Every day of the feast the people carried branches of the palm, willow and myrtle trees in procession around the altar, shouting "Hosannah," and on the seventh day the ceremony was repeated seven times.

The great festivals of the Jews comprised the Passover, which continued seven days, the Pentecost, one day, and the Tabernacles, eight days, at which all adults able to attend were required to do so. Besides these some other national feasts were observed.

While present at one of the festivals in Jerusalem, Jesus passed the night at the Mount of Olives, about one mile east of the city. The Garden of Gethsemane was on the western side of the mount, and the town or village of Bethany on the eastern side. Early in the morning he left Bethany, walked to the capital, entered the Temple and sat down, ready to instruct the great company assembled from all parts of Palestine and other regions where Jews lived, to celebrate the Feast of Tabernacles. During his discourse the scribes and Pharisees imagined they had found an opportunity to entrap the Saviour, by compelling him to adopt one of two alternatives that might bring him into trouble, either with the Romans or his own countrymen.

They brought to him a woman arrested for violating the seventh commandment, and stating the circumstances, said, "Master, the law of Moses requires that one guilty of such a crime shall be stoned, what dost thou say?" They did not state the case exactly, for though the punishment for such an offence was death, the particular manner of the execution is not specified, though the Jews, at a later period, decided it should be by stoning. Different modes of execution had been adopted for a violation of the Mosaic laws, such as strangling, death by burning, by the sword, and by stoning. If Jesus decided that the criminal ought to die, his enemies might accuse him of claiming power which belonged exclusively to the Romans, their conquerers, while if he gave an opinion that the accused ought to be pardoned, they could say he denied the authority of Moses.

Their plan was artfully laid and they undoubtedly felt sure they had entrapped him so that he could not escape, yet the question was met with marvellous wisdom, and his enemies retreated in disgrace. Apparently, the Saviour gave no attention at first to the subject, and stooping down wrote with his finger on the ground or the dust of the pavement, in the Court of the Temple. What he wrote is not revealed, but it may have been a denunciation of the hypocrisy of the accusers. However that may have been, it is evident they did not understand the character of the writing, and as Jesus seemed to take no heed of their question, they continued to ask him for a decision, when at length he stood and said, "Let him that is without sin among you," that is, who is guiltless of the same offence, "cast the first stone," then he resumed his writing. Under the Jewish law, in the punishment by stoning, one of the witnesses cast the first stone, that he might feel his responsibility in giving evidence. Jesus well understood the moral character of the woman's accusers, therefore he knew that no one would dare to cast a stone.

When the scribes and Pharisees heard the command of Jesus, conscious of their guilt, they left his presence one by one, beginning with the eldest, until no one was left but the accused. The Saviour rising and seeing her alone, said, "Where are thine accusers? Hath no man condemned thee?" She replied, "No man, Lord." "Neither do I condemn thee, go and sin no more." By this acquittal he meant that he did not pass sentence as a magistrate, for this was what the Jews desired, that they might accuse him of assuming illegal powers under the Roman Government, but it is not implied that he did not consider her offence a crime, only that he had no authority to pass a judicial sentence.

Shepherds and Sheep. — The patriarchal shepherds, as Abraham, Isaac and Jacob, were wealthy nomads, attended by a numerous train of servants. They exercised the rights of sovereign princes, such as making war upon their enemies, forming treaties, alliances, etc., yet they were free from the courtly ceremonies of royal potentates. They did not live in palaces, but in tents, and removed from one place to another at will, in search of pasture for their flocks, including sheep, hence their leaders were styled shepherds.

Many rhetorical figures are borrowed from the habits of a pastoral life, with which the Jews were very familiar, therefore the Saviour often alludes to the relation existing between the shepherd and his sheep, an office he claimed to sustain in regard to his followers. In his discourse on the subject, he presents a clear and interesting account of the office of a shepherd, or what he should be to his flock. Here is a description of the sheepfold, an enclosure for the sheep at night, to protect them from wild beasts and robbers. It was surrounded by walls and guarded by watchmen, and entered by a door or gate opened and closed by a porter, so when the shepherd appeared, it was opened to him.

CHRIST LEAVING THE PRÆTORIUM.

No thief or robber would come to the gate if he intended to steal from the flock, but he would gain access to the fold by climbing over the wall.

The Pharisees professed to be the guides or shepherds of the people, but Jesus charged them with spiritual blindness, consequently, they were unfit for the office. The prophets referred to the Messiah under the image of a shepherd, therefore the Jews asked Jesus when he called himself the Good Shepherd, whether he was the Christ.

The discourse about the Good Shepherd was delivered during the festival called the Feast of Dedication, which occurred about the middle of December, when Jesus was walking in Solomon's Porch, or covered way on the east side of the Temple. This feast was instituted by Judas Maccabeus, between one and two centuries before the present era, to commemorate the purification of the Temple, after it had been profaned by Antiochus Epiphanes, when he captured Jerusalem, slaughtered forty thousand of its inhabitants and sold as many more for slaves. The festival continued eight days and was celebrated by singing hymns and psalms, and offering costly sacrifices, and during the time the Temple was decorated with gold crowns and shields, the city was illuminated, and other demonstrations of joy occurred.

In early times the method of controlling flocks was by leading instead of driving them. The shepherd went before them and the sheep, recognizing his person and voice, followed him; the relation between them was similar to that of a father and his children, one of great tenderness, especially when the shepherd is represented as carrying the young lambs in his arms. He feels an anxious solicitude for any wanderer from his flock, and does not abandon his search until he finds it. He also gives special names to individual sheep.

This animal is one of the most timid and harmless, as well as one of the most helpless against an enemy. It cannot defend itself, and conscious of this it becomes strongly attached to its leader, and will follow him wherever he leads. The shepherd has a strong attachment for, and a wonderful influence over his flock, which he guides by day and watches by night. The Psalmist says, "The Lord is my Shepherd. He maketh me to lie down in green pastures. He leadeth me beside the still waters."

Jesus is the loving Shepherd of his flock who gave his life for them He said one who is hired to care for the flock, and is not the owner, will forsake it in time of danger, but he gave his life to save his sheep. He yielded to his enemies when the time came for him to die, but until then he avoided danger. Self-perservation is a duty, though sometimes life must be surrendered in defence of a just cause. The discourse of Jesus about the Good Shepherd is full of Divine love, tenderness and encouragement.

The Rulers Denounced. — Certain of the scribes and Pharisees came to the Saviour and requested him to give them a sign, that he was sent of God, entirely ignoring the fact that he had performed a large number of miracles, some of which they probably had witnessed, and of others they had heard from reliable authority. The request was not made in sincerity, but to tempt him, and in the discourse that followed, the

Saviour severely denounced the hypocrisy and wickedness of the Jewish rulers, or the scribes and Pharisees.

He said an evil and wicked generation seeks for signs, but he would give one, however, and then referred to the prophet Jonah who was three days and nights in the stomach of a sea-monster, and by a miracle was preserved and restored to land; so the Son of Man would be raised to life after lying in the tomb for the same length of time. He then told his hearers that the people of Nineveh would appear in judgment against them, for they repented at the preaching of Jonah, and here was one — Christ himself — greater than Jonah. He illustrated his subject by another example: The Queen of Sheba came from the distant parts of the earth to be instructed by the wisdom of Solomon and there was One among them greater than Solomon. Jesus employed, as a figure, to teach them an important lesson, their custom of cleansing their cups and platters, done with scrupulous care, while at the same time they were given to vicious habits, and were not careful to keep their hearts pure. He reproaches them for not understanding that God who made the body created the soul also. "You, Pharisees," said he, "are very careful to keep the body clean in order to please Him, but did not He create the mind or soul that is of vastly greater importance?"

He advised these self-righteous, hypocritical Jews to give alms to the poor, from their possessions acquired unjustly, and then pronounced a woe upon them, for giving tithes of their garden plants, such as mint, anise, and cummin, herbs of little value, while they neglected the more important subjects of the law, such as justice, mercy and faith. He told them they committed the grossest sins under the guise of religion, saying, they neither entered into the kingdom of heaven themselves, nor allowed others to enter. They were very zealous to make proselytes, and when they were won, they were greater sinners than before; they taught false doctrines, and rendered void the obligations of an oath; they were superstitious, exact in small things, but indifferent about those of great importance. They were anxious to *appear* righteous, at the same time they were deceitful and false at heart; they professed great veneration for the pious dead, while they practically approved the murder of the prophets. Jesus compared the scribes and Pharisees to " whited sepulchres " which outwardly appeared beautiful, yet within were the decaying bodies of the dead. Tombs, among the Jews, were annually whitewashed to make them conspicuous, so that no one might come in contact with them, for, according to their law, such persons would be considered unclean. The scribes and Pharisees were represented as adorning the tombs of the prophets, yet cherishing the same spirit that influenced their murderers. "Fill up the measure of your fathers," said the Saviour, in reference to their putting him to death. He called them a generation of vipers, and then asks, "How can ye escape the punishment of hell? The judgments due for shedding the blood of the saints from Abel to Zacharias, whom they slew between the Temple and the altar, shall come upon this generation, and you will fill up the measure of your iniquity by killing the Son of Man."

Jesus accuses them of laying heavy burdens upon

the people, while they would not render the least aid. They occupied Moses' seat, that is, as expounders of the law in the synagogues; and made broad their phylacteries. These were strips of parchment or vellum on which were written certain passages of Scripture and were worn as amulets or charms. The practice was derived from a literal interpretation of the Divine command to the Israelites, to have the law on their foreheads and between the eyes. The frontlet, so called, was composed of parchment with inscriptions bound on the forehead with a thong or ribbon, and worn when they went to the synagogue. The Pharisees enlarged them to signify they had a peculiar reverence for the law. A symbol to be worn upon the hand was made of two rolls of parchment, written with ink of a special kind, and these were also enlarged for the same purpose. The Pharisees made the borders of their garments, that is, the hem or fringe, conspicuous to attract notice, and chose the highest seats and chief places in the synagogues; they sought to win the salutations or greetings of their countrymen in the market places where multitudes were accustomed to assemble, and to be addressed by the title "Rabbi," meaning great or master, given to eminent teachers. These rabbis officiated at marriages, announced divorces and taught in the synagogues and schools of learning. Their chief studies were the Talmud which contained the text of the law, and the Cabala or record of traditions. The Saviour forbade his disciples to be called Rabbi, neither should they call any man "Father" in the sense of a religious teacher, "for one is your Father, even God who is in heaven."

When Jesus was denouncing the sins of the scribes and Pharisees, one of the lawyers, a class learned in the teachings of the Mosaic law, interrupted him by saying, "Master, you reproach us." He was self-accused, knowing he had done the same things. The Saviour then denounces the lawyers for offences similar to those of the scribes and Pharisees.

The Jews were greatly exasperated at the charges brought against them, for they knew they were true, but instead of repenting of their sins, they became violent in their hatred of the Saviour, and tried to provoke him to say something that would bring him into trouble and danger. They sought to entangle him in a snare, as birds are often taken, that they might accuse him before the Sanhedrim, and have him condemned.

Humility, Prudence and Other Topics. — When Jesus was in Galilee, on a certain occasion he was invited by a member of the Great Council to dine with him on the Sabbath. His host had also invited some of his own friends as guests. The hospitality offered the Saviour may have been to lead him to perform some act, or make some remarks which might afford sufficient ground for accusing him before the Sanhedrim.

There was an individual present afflicted with the dropsy, a distressing and almost incurable disease. He may have been a servant or a member of the Pharisee's household, brought into the room to see whether Jesus would heal him on the Sabbath, that they might say he had not observed the day as enjoined by the law. They closely watched him, to find some cause for accusing him, but Jesus, understanding their thoughts and

THE CROWN OF THORNS.

motives, asked the Pharisees and lawyers whether it was lawful to heal on the Sabbath. They were silent, knowing the law did not forbid it. Having cured the man, he inquired "Who among them, would not rescue one of his dumb animals, that might have fallen into a pit on the Sabbath; how much more valuable is a man than a beast, and if it was right to save the animal, how could it be wrong to cure a human being?" No reply could be made to such an argument.

Jesus noticing that some of the guests were anxious to secure the most honorable seats at the table, or those nearest the host, gave them a lesson in humility, saying, "When you are invited to a feast," naming especially a wedding entertainment, "do not take the seat nearest the head of the table, lest the master of the ceremonies should request you to give place to a guest whom he considers more honorable than yourself, and with mortification you are compelled to take a more humble position; but take the lowest seat, showing you are not seeking distinction, then, should the host say to you, 'Friend, take a higher seat,' you will be regarded with respect by the guests when they witness the honor conferred upon you. Whoever exalteth himself shall be abased, and whoever humbleth himself shall be exalted." This is a general maxim both in relation to the dealings of God and man.

The design of the Saviour seems to have been to teach the lesson that one should not make a practice of inviting to an entertainment only wealthy friends and neighbors to prove his intimacy with them, for they could return the compliment, but when a feast was given, the poor, the lame, the blind, the friendless, who could not make any recompense, should be invited. Those who pursued such a course would receive their reward at the resurrection of the just. One of the guests at the table said, "Blessed is he that shall eat bread in the kingdom of God," referring to the kingdom of the Messiah who the Jews were expecting would soon appear as a temporal prince. The Saviour corrected these false ideas by relating the parable of the Great Supper. The illustration selected by the Saviour was taken from the customs observed by the Jews when giving a supper or entertainment on other occasions, and is similar to the parable related by Matthew about the king's supper. In this instance, it was given by a wealthy man, who invited many guests, but instead of appreciating the honor, they excused themselves from attending on trifling grounds. One had bought a piece of ground and he must go and see it. If the purchase had been made, why could he not defer his visit, at least one day? Another had bought five yoke of oxen and he must test them, perhaps by ploughing a little, to see whether he had made a profitable bargain, while a third offered the excuse that he had just married, and could not come. In each instance, the deed had been accomplished, and attending the feast could have made no change.

The servants bearing the invitations returned and informed their lord of the result, when he ordered them to go quickly, as the feast was ready, into the streets and lanes of the city, where the poor, the blind, cripples and other vagrants were accustomed to assemble, and invite them to come. The servants, having obeyed their master's orders, returned and said they had done what was commanded, and yet the seats at the table were not filled. Their lord told them to "go into the highways and hedges and compel them to come," that is, to urge them persistently. Those in the "hedges" were poor laborers, engaged in making them to enclose fields and vineyards. The master said, "None of the guests first bidden shall taste of my supper."

The first guests invited were intended to represent the wealthy and prosperous Jews; and by the later ones, or the poor, lame and blind, were meant the Gentiles.

Having concluded his remarks, Jesus left the house of the Pharisee who had entertained him as a guest, and was followed by a great crowd eagerly waiting for him to appear, when turning about, he resumed his discourse, and told them the conditions required for discipleship. They must bear the cross and follow him, alluding to the demand that a condemned person should carry his own cross to the place of execution; a disciple must love him, the Master, more than he loved his parents, brothers, sisters, wife or children, and even his own life. If he was not willing to forsake all things, suffer all things, if necessary, and persevere to the end in his service, he could not be a disciple. He illustrated his theme by the judicious forethought of a husbandman who wished to build a tower, as a place of observation from which intruders into his vineyard could be watched. The owner would carefully estimate the cost of such an undertaking and his means to carry it through for fear of beginning a work and not being able to complete it, when the tower must remain unfinished or fall into the hands of his creditors. In either case it would bring upon himself the contempt of his acquaintances.

He gives another example to make clear his subject: A king, whose dominions are threatened by a hostile invasion, learns that the enemy's forces comprise twenty thousand men, while his own number only ten thousand. He calls a council of war to ascertain the opinion of his generals, and they decide it would be assuming too great a risk to meet him in open conflict, therefore he sends an embassy to treat with his enemy, and offer terms of peace.

Jesus closed his discourse with a metaphor derived from the properties of salt, a substance of remarkable perservative qualities which render it very useful. He calls his true disciples the salt of the earth, and says if it loses its savor or saltness, it is not useful for any purpose and is thrown away. The salt used in the Saviour's time was different in composition from that now used, which, if it lost its saltness, would have nothing left, but the salt of the ancients, being mixed with other substances, could lose its valuable quality and still retain a considerable quantity of earthy matter which by exposure to sun and rain lost its flavor entirely.

The lessons taught by this discourse were, that every one who becomes a follower of Christ should be prepared to assume responsibilities, act with prudence, and resolve, aided by the grace of God, to perform all duties faithfully, but must expect difficulties and practise self-denial; that every Christian must have conflicts with evil which will require constant vigilance and implicit trust in God to overcome.

CHAPTER XIX.

DISCOURSES OF CHRIST — CONTINUED.

The Sufferings of Christ. — The time was drawing near for the accomplishment of the most important, solemn and tragical events in the life of Christ. He was going from Galilee to Jerusalem to attend, for the last time, the Festival of the Passover, an occasion for large companies of Jews to repair to the capital.

As he was soon to be taken away from the apostles, he gave them some private instructions he did not wish others to hear. Jesus had previously informed them that he would be delivered into the hands of his enemies by one of his professed friends, but he now repeated 'the declaration with more emphasis, saying the Son of Man would be delivered to the chief priests and scribes, they would condemn him to death, the Gentiles would mock, scourge and crucify him, and that on the third day after his death he would rise from the grave.

The Saviour was interrupted in his discourse by Salome, the wife of Zebedee, and mother of the Apostles James and John. She came to ask a favor for her sons, perhaps at their suggestion, which was, that when he had established his kingdom, and had assumed the office and dignity of a prince, he would confer upon her sons the honor of positions near him, one on his right hand, and the other on his left. The disciples were still deluded by the expectation that he would establish a temporal kingdom, and reign with great pomp and glory, and they wished to be distinguished in the event of their Master's triumph.

Jesus rebuked James and John for their worldly ambition, and for not understanding better the character of his mission. He said, "Ye know not what ye ask. Can ye drink of my cup and be baptised with my baptism?" that is, suffer with him. The Saviour employed figures of speech frequently used to denote suffering, that is, *cup* and *baptism*. These apostles replied, "We can." "Ye shall indeed drink of this cup, but to sit on my right and left are favors bestowed only on those for whom they were designed by my Father from the beginning."

When the other apostles heard the request of Salome, they were offended that her sons, James and John, wished to be honored above their brethren. To give them a lesson in humility, Jesus gathered them about him and said that, "Kings and princes have their favorites whom they appoint to places of honor and power, and they give to some authority over others," but he then added that his kingdom was established on a different base. There were no distinctions of rank but all, rich and poor, learned and ignorant, bond and free, were to be on an equality. Whoever would be great among them, let him be a servant, since their Master came not to be ministered unto, but to minister to others.

About the Destruction of Jerusalem and the Second Coming of Christ. — This was the most solemn and impressive discourse uttered by the Saviour that has been recorded. He had come to the capital for the last time, and was aware that the close of his earthly labors was near, and that he must soon endure the fearful sufferings that would finish his life on earth. He loved his nation, his country and the remarkable city so dear to the heart of every Jew, therefore it was no wonder that with his tender affectionate heart, he should have wept on account of the terrible judgments that would visit his people before many years.

As he was about leaving the Temple to go to the Mount of Olives, his disciples called his attention to the beauty and grandeur of this remarkable building, including the surrounding courts, porches and walls, mentioning in particular the stones of white marble, employed in the construction of the building. Some of these were more than seventy feet in length, ten in width, and eight in height. Jesus was, of course, familiar both with the Temple and the city, having made annual visits to them at the festivals, but the disciples, being Jews, felt a national pride in pointing out the exceeding beauty, richness and magnificence of the Temple where their ancestors, for many generations, had worshipped. "Do these things please you?" inquired the Saviour. "I tell you there shall not be left one stone upon another that shall not be thrown down." They were doubtless greatly astonished at such a prediction, for at that time nothing seemed more improbable, yet little less than forty years later it was literally fulfilled. The Romans under Titus, 70 A. D., after one of the most terrible sieges on record, captured the city and destroyed the Temple, so that nothing of the sacred edifice remained. The Roman general wished to save the Temple, and sent Josephus, the Jewish historian, to persuade his countrymen to surrender and thus preserve the city from utter destruction, but the Jews themselves, in their mad fury, set fire to the porticos of the Temple where one of the Roman soldiers threw a fire-brand into a window, which set the building on fire, and all efforts to extinguish the flames were unavailing. On account of their hatred of the Jews, the soldiers could not be restrained by their commander, and the work of destruction went on until the city was in ruins.

When Jesus came to the Mount of Olives commanding a fine view of Jerusalem, Peter, Andrew, James and John came and asked him privately when these things should happen, and what would be the sign of his coming and of the end of the world. The prediction about the destruction of the Temple had been made in the presence of all the apostles, but only the four just mentioned sought private instruction. There were three distinct questions asked, as previously mentioned: First, when will the calamities predicted of Jerusalem come to pass? Second, what will be the signs of the coming of Christ? Third, what will be the signs of the approaching end of the world?

The answers to these questions occupy much space, as recorded in the Scriptures. Jesus did not answer them separately but intermingled the descriptions about the capture of Jerusalem and the end of the world, as both events could be expressed in the same language. A similar use of words is employed by the prophet Isaiah in describing the return from the Babylonish captivity, and the deliverance by the Messiah.

Jesus then proceeds to caution his disciples against deceivers who would claim to be the Messiah, which actually occurred before the Roman conquest. Some of these impostors led the multitudes to the deserts, and promised to work miracles and give other signs of their pretended Divine mission. These false Messiahs continued to appear at times for many succeeding centuries. The Saviour told the apostles there would be wars and warlike demonstrations between nations and kingdoms, which actually occurred before the destruction of Jerusalem. In the short period of eighteen months, four Roman emperors suffered violent deaths, namely, Nero, Galba, Otho and Vitellius, which caused civil strife throughout the Empire. The Jews and Syrians were engaged in conflicts, and Judea and Italy were the scenes of civil commotions. Famines prevailed in Palestine, Rome and Greece, and a pestilence raged in Babylonia, 40 A. D., and in Italy, 60 A. D. Earthquakes visited several places, and destroyed partially or entirely several cities, including Laodicea, Hieropolis, Colosse, Pompeii, Herculaneum, Smyrna, Miletus, Chios and Samos.

Christ predicted that fearful sights and great signs from heaven would appear. Josephus has recorded that an appearance resembling a sword seemed suspended over Jerusalem, and a comet was observed for a whole year. The appearance of what seemed a sword may have been a meteor. It is, moreover, recorded that during the night at one of the festivals a bright light was seen about the Temple and altar for half an hour, and the eastern gate of solid brass, requiring the strength of twenty men to close it, opened in the night without human aid. A few days after the feast, chariots and troops of soldiers in armor were seen in the clouds, while the sound as of a multitude was heard in the Temple, saying, "Let us remove hence." Some years before the war with the Romans began, a husbandman named Jesus, son of Ananias, came to the Feast of Tabernacles, during a time of peace, and began to shout, "A voice from the east, the west, and the four winds; a voice against Jerusalem and the Holy House, a voice against the bridegroom and the bride, and a voice against the whole people." Doubtless he was a maniac, but his ravings seemed to have been fulfilled. He was scourged, and at every stroke he cried, "Woe, woe, to Jerusalem!" He continued this every day for several years, it is said, until he was killed in the siege when exclaiming, "Woe, woe, to myself also."

After predicting the fearful calamities that would befall the nation, Jesus declared they were the beginning of sorrows. He said of his disciples that the Jews would deliver them to the Sanhedrim to be scourged, imprisoned, and killed, and that they would be hated by all nations for his sake. This prediction was fulfilled in the martyrdom of nearly all the apostles, and the millions of Christians who have suffered almost every conceivable torture from the death of Stephen to the present day. Many, said Jesus, who were accounted believers would become apostates, and even

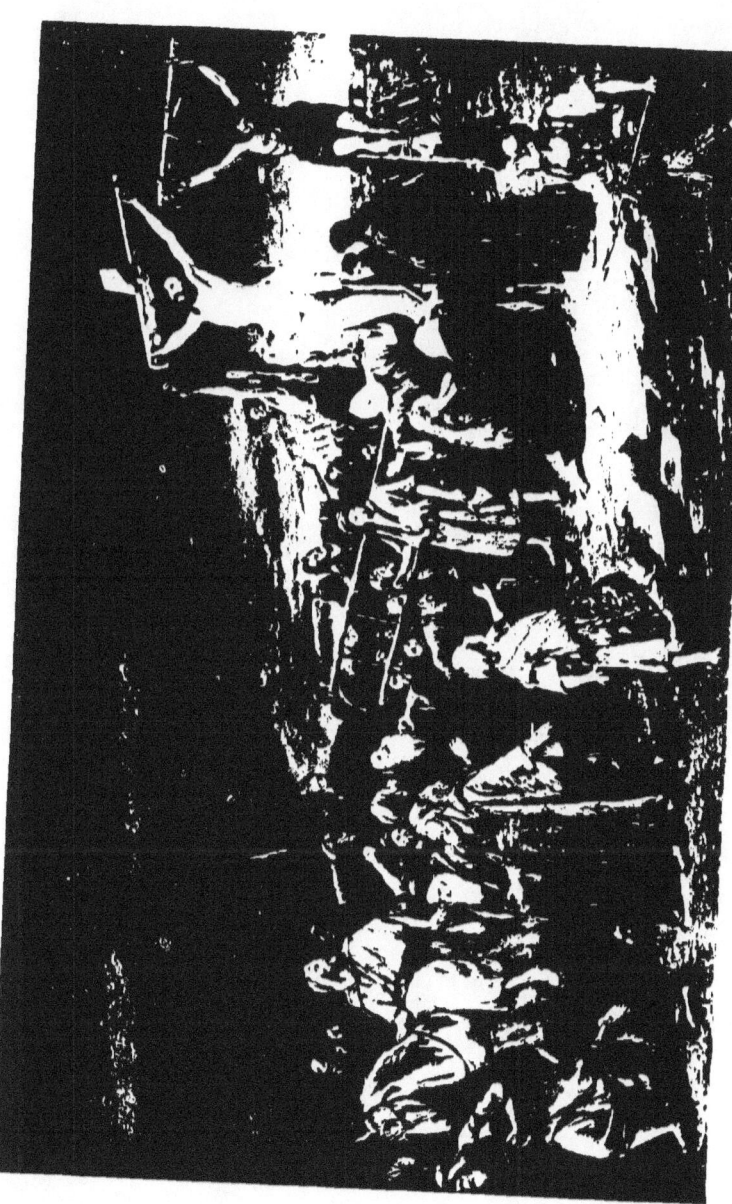

CHRIST ON CALVARY.

parents, brothers, kindred and friends would betray and persecute one another, but those who were faithful to their Divine Master would be safe in his care, that is, they might trust all to him.

Jesus declared the gospel should be preached to all nations, including Gentiles. Paul said it had been proclaimed among all the people of his day, that is, so far as he knew. He travelled for this purpose through distant countries, and the other apostles carried the gospel to many nations.

"When you see," said the Saviour, "these emblems in the holy city or about the Temple, it is time for you to escape." When it became apparent what the result of the war with the Romans would be, the Christians escaped to the mountains and found a safe retreat in the caverns. They had been warned that the danger would be so imminent, that those on the housetops or in the field must not tarry to collect their goods, not even an outer garment which may have been put off. These injunctions of the Saviour were so implicitly obeyed, that not a single Christian, it is said, perished in Jerusalem during the siege, but they all escaped to Pella and other places beyond the Jordan. "The destruction is certainly coming," said Jesus, "but pray that your flight," that is, of the Christians living at the time, "may not be on the Sabbath or in the winter," since in either case it would increase their sufferings. He predicted there would be great tribulation, such as never occurred before even from the beginning of the world, and would never happen again.

What a fearful picture, considering the horrors of war before and since that time, yet these predictions were strictly fulfilled. What dreadful crime had the Jewish nation committed, to bring upon themselves such fearful punishment? They had rejected and put to death their Messiah. If the calamities of the siege should be prolonged, the Saviour declared, none of the Jews would be left alive, for the war, famine and pestilence would utterly exterminate them, but for the sake of the Christians, the contest would not be long.

According to history, Titus planned at first to reduce the city by famine, therefore he built fortifications around it to prevent any one from escaping, or any provisions from being carried into it, but the Jews outside the walls engaged the Romans in battle, when the latter, having the advantage, entered the city and took it by storm, contrary to their original plan. As the Jews were expecting their Messiah would appear to deliver them from the Romans, it was natural that impostors would appear, claiming that power, therefore the Saviour warned his followers against the danger, as before stated, and added, "If any one should say, behold he is in the desert, or concealed in some house, or retired part of the city, believe him not, for as the lightning," using an expressive metaphor, "appears in one part of the heavens, and is seen in another part, so will be the coming of the Son of Man."

There has been some doubt expressed whether the phrase " coming of the Son of Man " in this place refers to the destruction of Jerusalem, or the Day of Judgment. There are two events in which our Lord is represented as coming, namely, at the overthrow of the Jewish capital, and the end of the world, and the same language can properly describe both. He illustrated his subject by the habits of birds of prey. Jerusalem was like a putrid corpse, ready to be devoured by vultures; so the Roman army will be attracted thither as birds of prey are by a dead carcass. The Son of Man would come to destroy the city through the power of a conquering army, and then he emphasizes his prediction by a striking figure, as follows: "The sun shall be darkened, the moon shall not give light, the stars of heaven shall fall, and the powers of heaven shall be shaken." These figures of speech are used to denote any great catastrophe, such as the overthrow of kingdoms, the destruction of cities, the overwhelming defeat of armies; for example, the destruction of Babylon and Tyre, the slaughter in Bozrah and Idumea are expressed in similar language. There shall also be great distress and strange natural phenomena, as the roaring of the sea, and the fear of men will be so overpowering as to deprive them of strength and courage. Then shall appear the sign or evidence of the coming of Christ. At the end of the world he will appear in the glory of his Father, attended by a company of angels, and with power. The living will be changed, the dead will be raised, the world will be consumed by fire, the wicked will be consigned to everlasting punishment, and the righteous will be rewarded by eternal life.

Before the end, but preparatory for it, Christ will send his angels to collect, by the sound of the trumpet, his elect or the saints from all parts of the world. This figure is borrowed from the custom of the Jews, to sound the trumpet for assembling the people on special occasions, and also in time of war. Jesus then recalls the attention of his hearers to the destruction of Jerusalem, saying, "When you see these signs, you may know the calamities are near, even at your doors. Indeed this generation shall not pass away until these predictions are fulfilled. You may sooner expect that heaven and earth will pass away, than that my words should fail. But of the precise time they will come to pass," that is, Christ's coming to judgment, "neither men nor angels know; that is a secret of my Heavenly Father."

The coming of the Son of Man would be sudden and unexpected. It would be like the flood when the people were attending to their usual occupations and enjoying their customary pleasures. He further illustrated the subject by men laboring together in the field and women grinding at the same mill, that one of the two in each case would be taken and the other left. He closed his solemn and impressive discourse by an earnest exhortation to be ready and watchful, and emphasizes his teaching by the conduct of a wise and faithful servant who performed his duties in the absence of his master, and by another who neglected them.

The Day of Judgment. — The general opinions on the subject, founded on the declarations of the sacred writers, are substantially as follows: This solemn event will end the present dispensation, and settle eternally the destiny of every human being; that it is necessary to vindicate the justice of God who will judge the world by his Son Jesus Christ, when he will appear in his glorified human form visible to every one, and attended by a great company of holy angels, when the living will be assembled, and the dead of all nations will be raised from their graves, to be judged according to their deeds. Not only the human race but the "fallen angels," with Satan their leader, will receive their final doom. When the last trumpet is sounded, the righteous dead will first be raised, and the bodies of those living will be changed from mortal to immortal, when they will go to meet the Lord in the clouds. The earth with all it contains will be destroyed, and "the heavens will pass away with a great noise" when the Judge — the Saviour — will be revealed to every one, as he descends with his glorious escort.

Then will the great court be opened, and the books brought forth in which the record had been kept, using a figure of speech. These books comprised various kinds, as the Book of Remembrance, of Conscience, of Providence, and others besides the Book of Life in which were enrolled the names of the righteous, who will be justified and presented by Christ to his Father, when they will be admitted to the honor and happiness of dwelling in the presence of God forever, while those who are condemned will be excluded from the heavenly paradise. It is believed that the human soul, at death, immediately passes to a state of either happiness or misery, but it does not receive its full reward until the day of final judgment, which is inevitable, and every one must meet the Judge, though some are represented as calling upon the hills and mountains to hide them from his presence. According to the testimony of Jude as expressed in his Epistle, Enoch prophesied of his coming, saying, "Behold the Lord cometh with ten thousand of his saints, to execute judgment upon all, and convince all that are ungodly of their deeds," etc., and the Apostle John said, "Behold he cometh with clouds, and every eye shall see him, and all kindreds and nations of the earth shall wail because of him. Mark, in his Gospel, adds, "The sun shall be darkened, the moon shall not give her light, and the stars of heaven shall fall, and the powers shall be shaken. Then shall they see the Son of Man coming in the clouds with great power and glory, and he shall send his angels to gather his elect from the utmost parts of the earth, to the utmost part of heaven."

The last judgment previously referred to, but now repeated, as described by Christ himself, is briefly as follows: The disciples had inquired of him about the end of the world, and in reply he said, "When the Son of Man shall come in his glory," that is, as supreme King and Judge, "he will sit upon his throne and all nations will be gathered before him, that is, to receive their final sentence. He then employs the figure of a shepherd separating the sheep from the goats. The sheep or saints he places on the right hand, as the position of honor, and the goats or the wicked on the left hand, the place of dishonor, signifying condemnation. The Judge first addresses those on his right hand, saying, "Come, ye blessed of my Father, inherit the kingdom prepared for you from the foundation of the world." He gives as a reason for this favor, that when he was hungry, thirsty, naked, sick or in prison, they had ministered unto him. They replied, "When did we see thee in distress and relieved thy wants?" "Inasmuch as ye did it to one of the least of these," that is, the poorest, most neglected, or most despised, "ye did it unto me."

To those on his left hand he will say, "Depart from

THE CRUCIFIXION.

me, ye cursed, into everlasting fire, prepared for the devil and his angels," and then gives as his reason, that they had not performed any of the deeds of mercy and kindness ascribed to the righteous. They wished to know when they had neglected to minister to him. "Inasmuch as ye did it not to one of the least of these, ye did it not to me," was the answer. According to the final decision, the wicked were banished to everlasting punishment, but the righteous were rewarded by eternal life. No human mind can possibly comprehend the solemnity of this scene, nor its momentous consequences. Its certainty is affirmed, but the time is concealed from all, no one but the Supreme Being knows when it will occur, hence the Saviour's injunction, "Watch, for ye know neither the day nor the hour when the Son of Man cometh."

CHAPTER XX.

DISCOURSES OF CHRIST — CONCLUDED.

Discourses of Consolation. — The most tender and affecting of all the instructions of the Saviour to his apostles were those given just before his death. It was during the Feast of the Passover at Jerusalem, when seated at the table on the night in which the Lord's Supper was instituted, that he addressed them on various subjects of vital importance, in language so tender that it must have stirred their hearts deeply, and moved them to tears; yet one of the number was, even at this touching scene, planning to betray his Master to his enemies. Before giving his last instructions, however, he taught them a practical lesson in humility, by performing the duty of a servant. He arose from the table and laying aside his mantle or outer garment, took a towel and a basin of water, and began to bathe the feet of the apostles. When he came to Simon Peter, he said, "Lord, you must not wash my feet, I am not worthy of such an act of condescension." The reply of the Saviour was, "If I do not wash thy feet, thou hast no part with me," that is, of possessing my spirit or participating in my glory. Peter, with characteristic ardor, said, "Not my feet only, but also my hands and my head." Jesus informed him that was not essential, and then again intimates that one of them was false.

The disciples were greatly distressed about their Master's leaving them, as he had told them he would, and aware of their anxiety, he tried to console them. They were still seated at the table, when he began by saying, "Let not your heart be troubled, neither be afraid. You have confidence in God, believe also in me. In my Father's house" — comprising the entire universe — "are many mansions," or splendid palaces for the abode of the righteous after they leave this world. "I am going to prepare a place for you in these mansions, and then I will return for you, that you may dwell where I am. You understand where I am going and know the way that leads to them." Thomas said, "We do not know whither thou goest. How then can we know the way?" Though Jesus had often told his disciples about his death and resurrection, they did not understand him, but still cherished the common opinion of their nation about his temporal kingdom. Jesus replied "I am the way, the truth, and the life; no man cometh to the Father except by me. Had you understood me, you would have comprehended the designs of my Father concerning me."

Philip said, "Give us some visible manifestations of the Father, and we shall be satisfied." It was a strange request to make, since Jesus had been with them three years working miracles, and giving other evidences of his Divine mission. There was a gentle rebuke in the Saviour's reply to Philip, "Have I been so long with you and yet do you not know me? He that hath seen me hath seen the Father." By this was meant some manifestation of the Father had been given, in the character and scenes of the life of Christ, especially his transfiguration, his miracles, and labors.

The Saviour told the apostles they would perform even a greater number of miracles than their Master had done. The miracles of Christ were almost entirely confined to his own country and nation, but those of the apostles were witnessed both by Jews and Gentiles. He promised to give them whatever they should ask in his name, that is, for the work of spreading the gospel. "If you love me," said Jesus, "you will keep my commandments, and I will pray to my Father that He may send you another Comforter, the Holy Spirit, to abide with you." This refers to Christ's intercession for his followers after his ascension to heaven, where he appears as their High Priest at the right hand of God.

The word "Comforter" is used five times in the New Testament; in four instances it refers to the Holy Spirit, and in the other to the Lord Jesus, who is called an Advocate or Comforter. The word is used by Greek and Jewish writers to denote an advocate in court; one who intercedes for others, a teacher, assistant or helper. The Spirit was sent to comfort, teach and assist the apostles in their special work. By his influence they were enabled to plead their cause before kings and magistrates, and by his influence sinners are brought to Christ.

Jesus very tenderly encourages his desponding disciples by saying he would care for them, and never forget them. "It will be only a short time before I leave you "—this was the day before his death—" but as I shall arise from the grave, you also will be raised up to live with me." Judas, called Lebbeus and also Thaddeus, said, "Master, how can you appear to us and not to the world?" This referred to his promised appearance after his resurrection. His reply was that they should have the presence both of the Father and the Son, and then renewed his promise that the Comforter should be sent, and pronounced the benediction "Peace, I leave with you," and encouraged them to be fearless. He added, "The time of my death draws near, and I will not say more to you, for the prince of this world" — Satan — "cometh, but he will not prevail." Satan is supposed to have appeared to the Saviour in the Garden of Gethsemane and tempted him a second time, but of course, failed in his diabolical purpose. Christ was subjected to this ordeal to prove that his integrity had been tried, but he passed safely through every form of temptation. It is said he was tempted in all points as we are, yet without sin, that is, he had no inclination to yield.

Here ended Christ's discourse at the Passover when he instituted the Lord's Supper, and after singing a hymn, he said to the apostles, "Arise, let us go hence," that is, to the Mount of Olives.

The walk to the Garden of Gethsemane was the most memorable on record. It has been supposed by some, that Jesus gave his discourse on the way, as recorded in the John's Gospel, Chapters xv and xvi, and offered his prayer as recorded in Chapter xvii, while others have thought it was in the upper chamber where the Lord's Supper was instituted. The time was towards midnight, and there was a full moon. Jesus was about to be removed from his little flock, and during the solitary walk in the stillness of the night, he gives them his last counsel, and invokes the blessing of his Father to attend them in their labors, discouragements and persecutions. The occasion was unsurpassed for interest, tenderness and pathos. The company consisted of their Lord, and eleven apostles, Judas Iscariot having withdrawn from their number. Perhaps they were grouped in companies of two, the same as when they were sent out on their missionary tour. However that may have been, they were so near their Leader they could hear his words. He began his discourse by alluding to the grapevine, probably they passed one on the way,—saying, "I am the true vine and my Father is the husbandman." He then notices the manner of cultivating the vine in order to secure the most fruit. The dead branches must be removed, while those left must be pruned.

Continuing the figure of the vine, Jesus said, "Abide in me, that is, be united to me by a living faith, and I will remain with you as your teacher, guide and comforter, but if you do not abide in me, you will be like the withered branch which is removed from the vine, and is used for fuel. But if ye abide in me, ye shall have what you ask in faith, and according to the will of my Heavenly Father, and if you bear much fruit He will be glorified." The Saviour not only exhorted them to abide in his love, but also to love one another, and the highest proof one could afford that he loved his friend, was to give his life for him, "I call you not servants who are not given a reason for the duties required of

DESCENT FROM THE CROSS.

them by their master, but I call you friends, and have made known to you my Father's will." They, the apostles, as they had been selected for a special purpose, should abound in good works, and should love one another, a duty enjoined upon all Christians. "You will be hated by the world," said he, "for it hated me, your Lord. Remember what I said to you about the servant, that he is not greater than his master, therefore, if they have persecuted me, they will treat you in the same manner, but they have no excuse for their sins, since I have taught them the truth. By rejecting me, the world shows its hatred for my Father. The Comforter or Holy Spirit, whom I will send from the Father, will testify of me, and you shall bear witness that I am the Messiah, as you have been with me from the beginning of my public ministry. I have given you these instructions and warnings, that you may not be led astray, for you will be persecuted both by Jews and Gentiles. You will be excluded from the synagogues, and whoever kills you will think he is doing God service. These things will happen to you, therefore be prepared for them." Jesus continued his discourse, which in substance was as follows: "Now I am about to leave you, yet none of you inquire why I go, but you seem to be overwhelmed with grief. It is necessary that I should leave you, that the Comforter may come and guide you into the truth," that is, pertaining to their mission as preachers of the gospel, when the innocence of Jesus, who was to suffer death as a malefactor, but would rise from the dead, thus proving his claim to be the Messiah, would be vindicated, and the prince of this world or Satan would be judged.

The Saviour repeated what he had said before, though in different words, namely, "A little while and ye shall not see me, and again a little while and ye shall see me, because I go to the Father." His death occurred the next day, and for a short time he was concealed in the tomb. Some of the apostles said among themselves, "What does he mean? We cannot understand him." Jesus knowing their perplexity said, "Ye shall weep on account of my sufferings and death, while the world will rejoice, but your sorrow will be changed to joy at my resurrection, and after that, your prayers in my name will be granted." Their petitions were to be offered to the Father in his name as their High Priest and Intercessor. Hitherto they had not offered prayer in the name of Christ, because he was with them in person. After his resurrection he would teach them more plainly by the Holy Spirit; while with them, he had given his instructions largely by parables, which they did not always understand. He said that he came from the Father, who loved them because they loved him, their Master, and believed he came from God. The apostles now understood him better and were more confirmed in the belief that he knew all things and came from God. They had expressed their doubts only among themselves, but the answer he gave them, revealed the fact that he knew their hearts, therefore he must come from God, or possess Divine attributes.

"Do you truly believe?" said their Master. He wished them to examine their hearts, for their faith was soon to be tried. "The hour is at hand when every one of you will be scattered, and will leave me alone. I have told you these things to comfort and sustain you, for trials and tribulations await you, but be of good cheer, for I have overcome the world."

The Prayer of Jesus. — The preceding instructions having been given, the Saviour, when on the way to the Garden of Gethsemane in the middle of the night, accompanied by the eleven apostles, on the eve of the most solemn and important occasion that ever occurred, offered his remarkable prayer, one of the longest recorded in the Scriptures. In this prayer several different petitions are expressed. Jesus first invoked the blessing of the Father upon himself, saying, " Glorify Thy Son," which will be honoring the Father also. He then prayed that his Father would honor him in his death, resurrection and ascension, and thus afford positive evidence that he was the Son of God. He acknowledged the power conferred upon the Son to give eternal life to the elect. He said he had finished the work his Father had given him to do, that is, to preach the gospel, and now he was about to go to Him, and participate in the glory he had with Him before the creation of the world. He offered a petition for his disciples that they might be kept safe in a world of trials and temptations. While he was with them, he kept them from yielding to sin and becoming apostates, except one whom he denominated the "son of perdition." He prayed for their sanctification through the truth, and also for all who should become his disciples through the preaching of the gospel, that they might be one in aim and purpose, and that his followers might be with him and behold his glory, after they left this world.

Perhaps there is nothing in the teachings of Christ more tender, loving and encouraging to the Christian, than this prayer of his dear Lord just as he was about to give his life for him. Neither has this love and care been withdrawn, for he still appears as the Advocate of his disciples before the throne of God, and will continue to intercede for them.

Jesus, having given his last instructions to the apostles and offered his remarkable prayer on the way to Gethsemane, crossed the small stream Kedron and entered the Garden with his followers, and it was here that he was arrested by the chief priests and Pharisees, having been guided by Judas Iscariot. A more particular account is given of the closing scenes in another chapter.

CHAPTER XXI.

CLOSING SCENES.

The Arrest and the Trial. — Jesus had previously told the apostles that he would be delivered to his enemies by one of their number, and be crucified, in order to prepare them for the tragical event, and now the time had come for the fulfilment of his prediction. The chief priests, scribes and elders assembled at the palace of the high priest, who, at that time, was Caiaphas, and held a council to decide how they might arrest Jesus by artifice, and kill him, but it must not be attempted during the Passover for fear of an uprising of the people, with whom he was very popular.

Judas Iscariot, one of the apostles, had been planning in his own mind to betray his Master, with the hope of receiving a bribe, as the love of money was his strongest passion. He went to the chief priests and inquired what they would give him to deliver Jesus into their hands. They promised to give him thirty pieces of silver, a sum equal to about fifteen dollars, the common price of a slave. They did not pay Judas then, fearing, perhaps, the traitor might deceive them, but they deferred the payment until he was in their power. From that time Judas sought an opportunity to accomplish his purpose.

As the time for the celebration of the Passover had arrived, the disciples inquired of their Lord where they should make preparations for the feast. None of them had homes in Jerusalem, therefore they did not know where to go. He told them, as they entered the city, they would meet a certain man bearing a pitcher of water. "Tell him the Master saith, my time is at hand; I will keep the Passover with my disciples at thy house." They went as directed, and meeting the man they delivered the Lord's message, when they were conducted to an upper room, already prepared for the occasion. It is probable that this man was a friend of the Saviour.

When the evening came, Jesus and his disciples, forming a company of thirteen, sat down to the table to eat the pascal lamb which had been prepared for them. During the feast, Jesus made the startling announcement that one of their number would betray him. They were greatly surprised and distressed about it, and each one asked, "Lord, is it I?" He replied, "It is one of you who is eating with me," and then added the fearful words, "Woe to the man by whom the Son of Man is betrayed. It had been better for him had he never been born." Judas had kept silence, but fearing, perhaps, he might be suspected, inquired, "Master, is it I?" Jesus replied, "It is." This was, doubtless, said in a tone the others did not hear. Judas, of course, knew who the traitor was, for he had already formed his plans to betray the Saviour. The traitor then withdrew from the company, when the Lord's Supper was instituted, as previously mentioned. After singing a hymn they all went to the Mount of Olives.

DESCENT FROM THE CROSS.

Jesus told the eleven disciples that they would be offended, or severely tried, on his account, for it was written, "I will smite the Shepherd and the sheep of the flock shall be scattered abroad. But after I rise from the grave, I will go before you into Galilee." Peter said, " Though all the other disciples should be offended because of thee, yet I will never be offended." The word offended in this connection means to become a stumbling-block, or the means of leading one to fall. Jesus replied, " This night, before the cock crows, thou wilt deny me thrice." Peter and all the other disciples affirmed that though they might die on his account, yet they would never deny him, neither would they have admitted that they would have forsaken him. At length they came to Gethsemane. The word signifies " valley of fatness " or fertile valley, and also a " winepress." The place is called a garden by John the Evangelist, though it was not properly a garden for vegetables, but was planted with trees and, perhaps, supplied with a fountain of water, groves and walks, affording an agreeable retreat from the crowded streets of the city. It was situated on the side of the Mount of Olives, a short distance east of Jerusalem. The Saviour often made this garden a place of retirement, meditation and prayer, for, according to Luke, he was accustomed to withdraw to the Mount of Olives to avoid the crowd.

The Feast of the Passover was celebrated in April, therefore it was the month when Jesus died.

After the Lord's Supper, the Saviour, accompanied by the eleven apostles, crossed the Kedron or Cedron, a small stream, and came to Gethsemane, when he told them to remain where they were, while he would go farther and pray, but he requested Peter, James and John to attend him. These three disciples had, on two other occasions, been selected as special witnesses of certain events in the history of their Lord,— that of raising to life the daughter of Jairus, and his Transfiguration.

Jesus became so overwhelmed with anguish, he said, " My soul is exceedingly sorrowful, even unto death." He was so distressed in view of his approaching sufferings for the salvation of the race, that he was in danger of dying before he came to the cross. " Tarry here, and watch with me," that is, by seeking Divine support, and preparing themselves for the fearful trials and dangers they would soon meet.

The Saviour then retired a short distance and kneeled down, but in his extreme agony, he fell prostrate with his face to the ground and prayed, saying, " O my Father, if it be possible, let this cup pass from me; nevertheless, not as I will, but as Thou wilt." Drinking the cup is a figure of speech to denote suffering, derived probably from the ancient practice of compelling persons condemned to death to drink deadly poison as a means of execution. After his prayer, Jesus returned to the three disciples and found them asleep. He said to them, and to Peter especially, perhaps on account of his ardent professions, " Could ye not watch with me one hour? " This implies that the Saviour had been wrestling in prayer that length of time. He then exhorted them to watch and pray that they might not be overcome by the calamities about to overtake them. Jesus again left them and offered the same petition, but it is probable his prayers in the Garden were much longer than what are recorded in the gospels. His mental anguish was so intense that blood issued from the pores of his flesh, and mingling with his sweat, fell to the ground. Such an effect of extreme mental suffering has been known to happen to others when enduring inexpressible agony. As Jesus returned a second time to the apostles, Peter, James and John, and found them asleep, he withdrew the third time for the same purpose, and coming back, discovered them still asleep. At first thought, this seems heartless, but it cannot be possible they were indifferent to their Lord's sufferings; they were doubtless overcome with sorrow and sympathy for their Master, as excessive grief not unfrequently induces sleep. While Jesus was suffering in the Garden, an angel appeared to comfort and sustain him.

It was the will of the Father that his beloved Son should suffer, since it was necessary for the salvation of men, and the Saviour himself was fully aware of this, therefore, it was not possible he prayed to be saved from the sufferings of the cross, as he knew what he must endure before he undertook the work of redemption, but he may have felt that his mental agony on this occasion, unless subdued, would unfit him for his approaching trial, condemnation and crucifixion, therefore he prayed for relief. The causes of his inexpressible anguish may have been various, but no human mind can fully comprehend the nature or depth of his mental sufferings which he endured, not for himself, but for others.

As Jesus returned to his disciples the third time, he

said, "Rise, behold he is at hand that doth betray me." Judas was familiar with the Garden, as he had, on former occasions, accompanied the Saviour to this place, and he supposed his Master had retired to this favored spot after the Passover, or he may have been informed of the fact.

During the great festivals at Jerusalem, the Romans were accustomed, after the conquest, to station a band or guard of soldiers at different places, to maintain order and these were at the disposal of the chief priests. Judas, having been furnished with one of these bands of Roman soldiers, armed with swords, and accompanied by a crowd of people who had seized any weapon at hand, such as clubs, or staves, as they are called, proceeded to Gethsemane, where he expected to find Jesus. He was to give the soldiers a sign which person to arrest, as they did not know the Saviour by sight; this signal was to be a kiss, and when given, they were to arrest Jesus, and place a guard over him, lest the multitude should rescue him.

When Judas came to the Saviour, he said, "Hail!" and kissed him. Jesus said to him, "Betrayest thou the Son of Man by a kiss?" The word "hail" used as a salutation meant "rejoice" and denoted joy at meeting a friend. When the soldiers approached him the Saviour inquired whom they sought? They replied, "Jesus of Nazareth." "I am he," was the reply. They were so awed by his presence, they went backward and fell to the ground. He asked them again whom they wanted, when they made the same answer. Jesus said, "If ye seek only me, allow the disciples who are with me to go in peace." The chief priests, elders, and

THE WOMEN AND THEIR DEPARTED LORD.

officers of the Temple had joined the crowd, when the Saviour inquired whether they regarded him as a thief, since they came to arrest him with swords and clubs. He told them he had taught in the Temple and in their synagogues, yet they had not arrested him on such occasions.

Peter in his rash zeal drew his sword and cut off the ear of Malchus, one of the servants of the high priest. Jesus rebuked the apostle for his imprudence, and told him to put his sword into its sheath, for by this act he had endangered his own life, and perhaps the lives of the other apostles. Jesus said if his Heavenly Father desired him to be rescued he would send more than twelve legions of angels for this purpose, that is, more than 72,000, a Roman legion being more than 600 men; but "how then can the Scriptures be fulfilled?" that is, the passages which foretold that Christ would die for the world. Jesus then restored the servant's ear by a miracle. Did the apostles stand by their Master when they saw him in the power of his enemies? Not one of them, but on the contrary, they all forsook him and fled. As the crowd passed a certain house on the way from the Garden to the city a young man was aroused from sleep by the noise, and, arising hastily, he seized an article from the bed and wrapping it about his body, rushed into the street to ascertain the cause of the tumult, when he was caught by the soldiers, who supposed he was one of the disciples, but he threw off the linen cloth with which he had covered himself, and fled. It is not known who this young man was, but he may have been the owner of the Garden and the friend of Jesus.

After his arrest Jesus was bound and conducted to

the city, first to Annas who had held the office of high priest, and was the father-in-law of Caiaphas, then occupying that position. The Saviour was detained at the palace of the high priest until the Sanhedrim or Great Council of the nation could be assembled. This tribunal was instituted by the Maccabees, a prominent Jewish family who lived about 170 B. C. and later. It comprised seventy-two members, including chief priests, elders or princes of tribes and heads of families, while the high priest was generally the president of the Council. Appeals and other weighty matters, comprising a claim to the prophetic office, were brought before this tribunal for settlement. After the Roman conquest the power of the Sanhedrim was limited so that, in the time of Christ, it could not inflict the sentence of death, though it had the right to try persons for offences and condemn them. The time for holding this court was in the morning, and it was not lawful to try capital cases in the night, or pass sentence and execute it on the same day, but these conditions were set aside in the trial of the Saviour, hence it was illegal according to the Jewish laws. The members of the court were seated during the trial, and the accused stood before them. Two witnesses, at least, were necessary, who were sworn and examined separately, but the accused had the liberty to be present when the testimony was given.

Though Peter fled with the other apostles when their Master was arrested, yet he followed him at a distance to the palace of the high priest, which he entered, and stood with the servants to see how the case would be decided. The weather was cold, the time was in the night, and the place where the trial was held was open to the sky, therefore a fire had been made on the pavement, and Peter stood and warmed himself before the fire. The Council sought witnesses against Jesus, but found it difficult to obtain such testimony as would convict him. Two witnesses at least were required by their law, therefore they did not venture to condemn their prisoner without them. Finally, they succeeded in obtaining the testimony of two men, which was as follows: "This fellow said, 'I am able to destroy this Temple of God, and build it in three days.'" They had perverted the words of the Saviour who, on one occasion, said, "Destroy this temple," meaning his own body, "and after three days, I will raise it up." These witnesses stated neither the facts nor the language correctly.

The high priest arose and demanded of Jesus why he did not reply to the testimony of these witnesses, but he remained silent, for the evidence was unsatisfactory, and the councillors were aware of it. Something more definite must be brought against him, therefore the high priest put the Saviour under oath, saying, "I adjure thee by the living God, that thou tell us whether thou art the Christ, the Son of God." This was the usual form of an oath among the Jews. Had he been silent now, his judges would have considered it a denial of his claim of being the Christ, hence he replied, "Thou hast said the truth," and after he acknowledged himself to be the Messiah, he said, "You will not believe me nor set me free, and if I refer you to the evidences of my mission, you will not accept them. I tell you that hereafter you shall see the Son of Man sitting on the right hand of power, coming in the clouds of heaven."

When Jesus made this declaration, the high priest

rent his garment as an expression of horror. The Jews were accustomed to wear a kind of mantle expressly for this purpose, when they wished to denote grief, indignation or disappointment, but it was not lawful for the high priest to rend his clothes when officiating in that capacity, but on this occasion he may have worn the garments used as president of the Sanhedrim. The high priest declared that Jesus had spoken blasphemy, as he had, under oath, assumed what only belonged to God, for in asserting that he was the Son of God he claimed to be equal with the Father, and entitled to the same honor, and sitting at His right hand was a favor that belonged to no man. If Jesus had not been the Christ, the charge would have been true, but the real question was, had he not given them sufficient proof that he was the Messiah, the Son of God? The high priest then said, "You have heard his blasphemy, why do we need further witnesses? What do you think?" The members of the Council replied, "He is guilty, and deserves death."

The punishment for blasphemy among the Jews was death by stoning, but the chief priests would not have ventured to put him to death in that manner, even if they had the power to inflict capital punishment, for fear of exciting a popular tumult, therefore they decided to deliver him to the Romans, who inflicted death by crucifixion. As the Roman law did not recognize blasphemy a crime punishable by death, the Sanhedrim resolved to deliver the Saviour to the Romans on a charge of a civil nature, which was that of corrupting the people by forbidding them to pay tribute to Cæsar, or the Roman Government, which would be regarded as rebellion.

Before surrendering the Saviour to Pilate, the Roman governor, the soldiers, assisted by the mob and the servants of the high priest, insulted him for their amusement, spit in his face, struck him with their hands or fists, smote him on the mouth, blindfolded him and said, "Prophesy, and tell us who smote thee." When Jesus was arrested in the Garden, he was bound, and afterwards was conducted to Annas, the former high priest, who, to make his escape impossible, had his hands and ankles bound with chains, when he was led to Caiaphas, the high priest, and by him was sent in this condition to Pilate. The Saviour was then conducted to the Hall of Judgment, or Prætorium, the place where the Roman prætor, or governor, heard and decided cases, but the Jews who accompanied him would not enter, lest they be defiled and prohibited from eating the Passover. The Roman governor of Judea resided at Cesarea, but he came to Jerusalem on the occasion of the great festivals of the Jews, as before mentioned, to prevent any disorders or uprising of the people.

CHAPTER XXII.

CLOSING SCENES — CONCLUDED.

PETER had followed the crowd when his Master was brought to the palace of the high priest, and stood with the servants near the fire in the lower part of the hall, when a damsel who kept the door, or served in the capacity of a porter, recognizing him as one of the disciples of Jesus, inquired, "Art not thou one of this man's disciples? Thou wast with him in Galilee." She may have suspected he was on account of his being in company with John, who was known by the high priest. Peter denied before them all that he knew anything about Jesus. This was in the early part of the trial. Doubtless he was greatly troubled by the question, and to avoid attracting attention, he left the hall and went into the porch where he encountered another person who knew him and repeated the charge. Peter then denied his Lord a second time, and confirmed it by an oath. This was about midnight, and when Peter was in the porch the cock crew.

About an hour later he returned to the hall and stood by the fire, when another person who knew him said, "Surely thou also art one of them," meaning the apostles, "for your language is proof that you belong to his company," that is, he spoke the dialect of Galilee, somewhat different from that of Judea, and this charge was supported by a kinsman of Malchus, the servant of the high priest, whose ear Peter cut off in the Garden. He could no longer resist the evidence that he was known, for his language and the testimony of three witnesses had decided it, therefore he would use still more emphatic expressions, and to the sin of denying his Master, he added that of cursing and swearing, when immediately the cock crew the second time, which was about three o'clock in the morning.

Jesus turned and looked upon Peter, doubtless with a reproachful yet tender expression, as if he would say, "How could you do this after I had given you warning?" They were in the same room, Jesus being in the upper end of the hall, which was elevated for holding courts, hence the Saviour could look down upon him while he was standing by the fire on the pavement. By a single glance from his Master, all the promises of the erring apostle, and all the warnings that had been given him, were brought to his remembrance, and he was overwhelmed with a sense of his guilt, so that he hastily left the palace, retired to a solitary place, and there wept bitterly and confessed his sin with deep repentance.

The fall of Peter is a melancholy instance of human weakness, perhaps one of the saddest in the history of the Christian church. A short time before, he was zealous in the cause of his Master, ardent and confident in his avowal of attachment to him, and had been, moreover, distinguished throughout Christ's ministry by peculiar favors. He was one of the three disciples who witnessed the Transfiguration, and on other occasions he had been honored by special confidence, yet sad to say, he profanely called upon God to witness what he knew was false. Some useful lessons may be learned from the conduct of Peter on this occasion; as for instance, too great self-confidence is dangerous; the highest favors and most exalted privileges will not keep one from sinning; when one sin is committed the next step is easy; a look from the Saviour may bring the sinner to confess; true repentance is deep and thorough; while sometimes genuine Christians may, for a time, go astray, yet they will eventually return to the fold; but Peter's repentance and forgiveness should not be an excuse for wrongdoing, though they may encourage the wanderer to return. That the fall of Peter is recorded by the four evangelists is proof of their honesty. Mark is very explicit in his account, yet it is believed that his gospel was written under the direction of Peter, and was submitted to him for examination.

As Judas Iscariot, one of the chosen apostles, was the chief actor in the arrest of Jesus, it may be well to give a brief sketch of him at this stage of the tragedy, and of the fearful ending of his career. He was, probably, induced to follow the Saviour from wordly motives, as a love of money was his leading passion, and he seemed the best adapted to attend to the financial affairs of the company of apostles since he was their treasurer, or carried the purse or "bag," as it is expressed. Like many others of his contemporaries, he may have expected that Jesus, as the Messiah, would assume his position as prince, and reward his followers by worldly riches and honors, but when he saw his Master refuse to be crowned King of the Galileans, after the miracle of

A SHEPHERD AT THE CROSS.

feeding the multitude, he may have been disappointed. Perhaps Judas thought if he delivered Jesus to the Sanhedrim, he would openly confess that he was the Messiah, and if acknowledged as such by the nation, he would be able to reward his followers by earthly favors. It is possible, if not probable, that the detection of his treachery stimulated Judas to betray his Lord from a feeling of revenge, or he may have supposed that Jesus would deliver himself from the hands of the chief priests, and by doing so, the Saviour would be secure, and he, the traitor, would gain a small sum of money; but when he saw that his Master was condemned to be crucified he was seized with remorse and returned the thirty pieces of silver, saying, "I have sinned in betraying the innocent." The priests brutally replied, "What is that to us? see thou to that."

Judas then went into the Temple and placed the money in the treasury or place for receiving the offerings of the people, but the officers at the Temple would not use it for such a purpose, because it was the price of blood, therefore they bought with it the potter's field to be used as a burial place for strangers. Judas withdrew to some lonely place and hanged himself, but while he was suspended, he fell headlong and burst asunder. He may have been hanging on a tree near a precipice, it has been suggested, when either the cord or the branch gave way, and he was precipitated to the bottom and dashed to pieces.

Had the repentance of Judas been genuine, he would not have committed suicide. He has been called the "son of perdition," and it was said that it would have been better for him, had he never been born, and that he went to his own place, implying it was to the region of the lost. His history is a fearful illustration of the danger of making the acquisition of wealth the supreme object of life.

The potter's field was afterwards called "Aceldama," meaning field of blood, and was outside the walls of Jerusalem, south of Mt. Zion. Thus the prophecy was fulfilled that says, "they took the thirty pieces of silver, and gave them for a potter's field." It was the price at which the Saviour was estimated by his countrymen.

Pontius Pilate forms so conspicuous a figure in the trial, condemnation and death of the Saviour, a brief account of this Roman governor is important. It is supposed he was a native of Rome, or at least of Italy, though nothing is known of his family. He was sent governor, or more properly procurator, to Judea, as a successor to Grotius, about 26 or 27 A. D., during the reign of the Emperor Tiberius. He presided over the province of Judea during ten years, and is represented by the historians Philo and Josephus as a man of an impetuous and obstinate disposition, and one who could be bribed to pronounce any sentence desired. The latter historian relates that he was guilty of rapine, murder and other crimes, inflicted tortures upon the innocent, and put to death persons accused, without trial, when it suited his pleasure. It is stated by Luke that he caused the death of certain Galileans, while they were offering sacrifices in the Temple, at Jerusalem. No reason is given for this act, but probably he suspected them of conspiracy, or some other crime against the government. On account of his mismanagement of public affairs, Pilate was deposed by Vitellius, proconsul of Syria, 36

A. D., and sent to Rome to answer the charges brought against him before the Emperor Caligula, who banished him to Gaul, where, being reduced to great extremity, he committed suicide.

Annas, called by Jewish historians Ananus, whose name occurs in the trial of Christ, was high priest eleven years, or from 13 to 24 A. D., when he was succeeded by Caiaphas, his son-in-law, though he still bore the title of high priest, and exercised an influence in public affairs. Annas was regarded as one of the most honored men of his nation, and five of his sons held that office, a dignity no other priest ever attained. When Jesus was arrested he was first brought before Annas.

Joseph, surnamed Caiaphas, held the office of high priest nine years, or from 26 to 35 A. D., when he was deposed by Vitellius two years after the sentence pronounced against the Saviour. When the priests were discussing the question what should be done with Christ, Caiaphas said there was no occasion for debate, as it was expedient that one man should die, rather than the whole nation perish, referring probably to its overthrow by the Romans. As Jesus had been condemned by the president of the Sanhedrim, there was little prospect of his being acquitted by this body of councillors.

When Jesus was brought before the high priest, he was questioned about his disciples and doctrines for the purpose of ascertaining the number and power of his followers, that some cause might be found to arraign him on the charge of sedition or rebellion against the Roman Government, and to make the charge plausible, it was important there should have been so large a following as to constitute a strong and dangerous faction, but as there was no proof that Jesus had a large and well-armed force at his command, the high priest attempted to ensnare the prisoner, by inquiring what doctrines he taught. The answer of Jesus was that if he had intended to excite the people to rebel, with the object of overthrowing the government, he should have formed his plans and trained his followers in secret, but instead of pursuing such a course, he had proclaimed his doctrines openly and had publicly taught in the Temple and the synagogues, places to which Jews resort. Jesus said, "Why do you ask me? Inquire of those who heard me."

In these questions, the Saviour asserted his innocence and his rights when on trial. It was proper for him to demand justice, since laws were made to protect the innocent, as well as to punish the guilty. When he answered the high priest, one of the officers who stood by struck him, in violation of law and justice, saying, "Do you answer the high priest in this manner?" Jesus replied, "If I have spoken evil, or shown any disrespect to him then administer punishment according to the law which says, 'Thou shall not curse the ruler of my people,' but if I have said only what was right and proper, why do you smite me?"

After the Saviour had been condemned by the Great Council, he was conducted to Pilate's house early in the morning, to undergo another trial. During the preceding night, he had passed through varied and distressing experiences, beyond the power of the human mind to comprehend. He had celebrated the Passover with his disciples, had instituted the Lord's Supper, had been betrayed by one of the apostles, had given his dying in-

THE RESURRECTION.

structions to his followers, and offered his memorable prayer for them and others, had suffered intense agony in the Garden of Gethsemane, had been arrested there by a band of soldiers guided by Judas, had been bound twice, brought before Annas, and then before Calaphas, where the Sanhedrim assembled to examine him, was condemned for blasphemy, and then sent to the Roman governor to be tried for high treason. He had been denied three times by Peter, and deserted by all the apostles, and had been insulted and smitten for claiming that justice should be shown him, and at last came his trial before Pilate.

When Jesus was brought before him the governor made some attempts to release him, for Pilate knew the Jews had delivered him through envy and hatred. The governor's wife, alarmed by a dream, sent a request to her husband not to condemn that just person. He tried to avoid the responsibility of pronouncing judgment by sending the prisoner to Herod King of Galilee. This was Herod Antipas, son of Herod the Great, and the one who put John the Baptist to death. He was at this time in Jerusalem, and Pilate, learning that Jesus was from Galilee, sent him to Herod since he belonged to his jurisdiction. The king was very glad of the opportunity for seeing one who had excited so much public attention, and he hoped to see him perform some miracles. Herod asked Jesus many questions, but he made no reply. The chief priests and scribes, his accusers, violently charged him with stirring up sedition in Herod's province. The king's soldiers or guard, incited by their master, treated him with contempt and ridicule, dressing him in a gorgeous robe, that is, a white garment, such as Jewish kings wore; this was done in mockery because he claimed to be a king. The royal color of the Romans was purple, therefore when Pilate made the Saviour a subject for ridicule, he had him dressed in a purple robe, so that the Saviour wore the royal colors of both nations. After Herod had offered these indignities to the Son of God, he sent him back to Pilate, which was regarded as a mark of respect to himself, and after this the king and the governor became friends, for there had previously been enmity between them.

It was the custom for the Jews, at the Feast of the Passover, to ask the Roman governor to release one prisoner whom they might prefer. At this time there was a noted criminal in custody, named Barabbas, who had been engaged in an insurrection, and had committed murder. These facts were well known to the Jews, yet when Pilate proposed to release Jesus there was a tumultuous cry from the mob, "Not this man, but Barabbas." They had been told to do this by the rulers. Pilate then inquired, "What shall I do with Jesus?" They shouted, "Let him be crucified." They said if he set Jesus at liberty he would not be the friend of Cæsar, that is, the emperor. As the Saviour's accusers would not go into the palace of the Roman governor for fear of becoming defiled, Pilate went out and asked them what accusation they brought against this man, that is, of what crime was he guilty. They said, "If he was not a malefactor, we should not have delivered him to you." He told them to judge him themselves, according to their law, and they replied, "The Romans had deprived them of the power to inflict the death penalty."

It appears the Jews did not deliver Jesus to Pilate for trial, but for him to pronounce the sentence of death at once, as they had tried and condemned him before the Sanhedrim, but the governor proceeded to give him another trial.

After the Jews had accused the Saviour of perverting the nation by forbidding them to pay tribute to Cæsar, that is, of high treason, Pilate returned to the Judgment Hall, and calling Jesus before him, said, "Art thou the King of the Jews?" He replied, "Do you make this inquiry from anything you have seen or heard about my plotting against the Roman Government?" Pilate said, "Am I a Jew?" That is, "Am I, being a Roman, likely to be influenced by Jewish prejudices? Your own nation and the chief priests have delivered thee to me, what hast thou done?" The governor implied that it was not from anything that *he* had known that Jesus was arraigned, but from charges brought against him from his own countrymen. Two specific charges had been preferred, namely, for blasphemy and for treason. Jesus declared before Pilate that his kingdom was not of this world, for had it been, his servants or followers would have fought for him, as was the custom among earthly sovereigns, defended by large armies. Had the object of the Saviour been to establish an earthly empire, he would have aroused the multitude that always followed him to prepare for war. He would have been attended by an armed host wherever he went, and they would not have allowed him to be arrested in the Garden. Christ's kingdom was of a spiritual nature, and he rules the hearts and consciences of his subjects. Pilate, who did not fully understand him, inquired,

"Are you a king then? Do you lay claim to a kingdom of any kind?" Jesus replied, "I am a king," and then adds that his object in coming into the world was to bear witness to the truth. This was the nature of his kingdom, not to assume power, organize armies to maintain it, and subdue nations by war, but to preach the truth and save sinners.

"What is truth?" inquired Pilate, probably in contempt, therefore the Saviour made him no reply. The governor, perhaps, considered Jesus a deluded fanatic, but innocent of any crime, therefore not dangerous. The question, "What is truth?" had long been agitated by philosophers who maintained different opinions, and had Pilate been sincere and waited for an answer, perhaps the Saviour would have expressed his view of truth. The Roman judge went again into the porch and said to the Jews, "I find no fault in this man, therefore as it is the custom to release one prisoner on this occasion, shall I not release the King of the Jews?" but they all clamored for the pardon of Barabbas, when Pilate inquired, "What shall I do with Jesus who is called Christ?" They all said, "Let him be crucified." "Why, what evil hath he done?" This question was asked three times, when in a loud voice came the response, "Let him be crucified." Eager to spare the innocent prisoner, Pilate told them he would chastise him, that is, scourge him, and then release him, for he could find no cause for his execution. He may have supposed that if Jesus was publicly whipped it might satisfy his enemies, but he was mistaken. When he saw the mob was excited and uncontrollable, he washed his hands before them, as a sign that he was free from

EASTER MORNING.

any responsibility for his death. The Jews answered to this act of the governor by saying, "His blood be upon us and our children," a fearful imprecation for which they have suffered ever since.

Among the Romans, it was customary to scourge a slave condemned to be crucified, which added to the fearful sufferings attending this mode of death, and as Jesus was to die the death of a slave, he was scourged. According to the declaration of the prophet, " he endured the cross, despising the shame." Having pronounced the sentence from the tribunal, and written the inscription to be placed upon the cross, which was "Jesus of Nazareth, King of the Jews," Pilate surrendered him to the Roman soldiers to be crucified. Some of the Jews went to the governor and asked him to change the inscription, which was written in Hebrew, Greek and Latin, to " He said I am King of the Jews," but Pilate very curtly replied, "What I have written, I have written," that is, he would not change it to please them.

CHAPTER XXIII.

AT THE CROSS.

Before Jesus was conducted to the place of execution, the soldiers, to express their contempt of him, and ridicule his claim to royalty, took him to the Common Hall, or the governor's dwelling, and gathered the whole band to join in the sport. A band or cohort was the tenth part of a Roman legion, and comprised from four hundred to six hundred men. They removed the Saviour's upper garment, and dressed him in a scarlet or purple robe, such as was worn by distinguished officers of the Roman army, and was probably one that had been cast aside as useless. Purple was the royal color, and this circumstance would be a taunt on account of the Sufferer's claim to being a king. It was necessary that a king should wear a crown, therefore they made a wreath of the branches of a thorn-bush growing near, and placed it on his head. Kings usually carried a sceptre, as the emblem of royalty, hence the Saviour must be supplied with one, and for this purpose, they took a staff from some one present, which consisted of a reed or shrub growing on the banks of the Jordan, and placed it in his right hand for a sceptre, when they bowed the knee before him in mockery, saying, "Hail,

King of the Jews." Besides these indignities, they spit upon him as a token of the greatest contempt and insult, and taking the reed from his hand, they struck him on the head. This not only inflicted pain from the force of the blow, but it also caused suffering by pressing the thorns of his crown into his flesh.

After the soldiers had mocked and insulted the Saviour as long as they pleased, they removed the purple robe and clothing him in his own garments, led him away to the place of execution. It was a part of the punishment of a condemned person to bear his own cross, therefore, they at first laid it upon Jesus, but he was so weak and exhausted from his previous sufferings, that his strength failed, when they compelled a man named Simon, from Cyrene, a city in Libya, Africa, to assist him by bearing one end of it after the Sufferer. Simon, being a Jewish name, suggests the idea that he may have been of that race who came to Jerusalem to celebrate the Passover.

At length they came to Golgotha, meaning " the place of a skull," or Calvary, a Latin name signifying the same; both words indicate it was a place of execution. It was without the walls of the city on the northwest, only a short distance off. Capital punishments were not allowed within the walls, neither by the Jews nor the Romans. The bodies of animals slain for sacrifices were burned outside the gates, hence Jesus, the antitype, must also suffer beyond the walls. While on the way to Calvary, a large company followed, including many women who expressed their grief in tears and loud lamentations, when Jesus turning around, said, "Daughters of Jerusalem, do not weep for me, but weep for yourselves and your children, for the time is coming when such calamities will come upon the nation, they will call upon the hills and mountains to fall upon and hide them." He referred to the destruction of Jerusalem by the Romans, a little more than thirty years after.

When the soldiers arrived at Calvary, they fastened the Saviour to the cross, by driving nails or spikes through his hands and feet. The usual way of making a cross was by two pieces of wood, one upright and so high that the feet of the victim were about a yard from the ground. It had a projecting seat to support the sufferer, since his hands were not strong enough to sustain the body, which was sometimes left upon the cross, until consumed by vultures, or wasted by decay. The hands were fastened to another piece of timber, placed at right angles with the upright post. Sometimes a cross was made in the form of the letter X, and sometimes the sufferer was tied to the cross, when his life was prolonged until death gradually released him. When nailed to it, the sufferer's agony must have been intense. A mixture of wine, called vinegar, containing wormwood, supposed to stupefy the senses, was often given to the victim to render him insensible to pain. When this was offered to the Saviour, he refused to drink it, saying, the cup which his Father had given him, he would drink, meaning that his sufferings were necessary in the work of atonement. The agony endured naturally produced a feeling of thirst, and when Jesus said, "I thirst," some one ran, and dipping a sponge in vinegar, which in this case was a mixture of wine and water, the common drink of the Roman soldiers, placed the sponge on a reed, and offered it to him. He did not refuse it, since it contained no opiates, and would not render him insensible to pain.

Death by crucifixion was attended by the most intense suffering, besides the degredation connected with it, being regarded as proper only for the lowest criminals. The circumstances attending this mode of execution were the following: The condemned must carry his own cross to the place of execution, amidst the insults and uproar of the mob. A cavity having been made in the ground for the cross, it was laid upon the earth, when the victim was disrobed and extended on it, and his hands and feet were fastened by nails. It was then raised and violently dropped into the place prepared for it; this performance greatly increasing the sufferer's agony. He was generally left in that condition, until pain, exhaustion, hunger and thirst combined to end his life that sometimes lasted for days, and his body was left to be consumed by birds of prey. Death by crucifixion was not only the most painful, but was also considered by Greeks and Romans, the most ignominious, and was inflicted only upon the worst criminals, therefore those who proclaimed the gospel were exposed to shame and contempt because its Founder suffered on the cross. Some of the natural causes of the physical agony attending this mode of death are the following: The unnatural position of the body; the nails driven through the hands and feet which contain numerous tendons and nerves; exposure to the air causing violent inflammation, a free circulation of the blood interrupted, more being carried to the arteries than could be returned by the veins, causing great pressure and violent pains.

The sufferer did not usually survive beyond the third day, but the Saviour expired after a few hours, probably on account of his previous exhaustion and mental distress.

It was customary to remove most of the garments of those to be crucified, to be divided among the executioners, therefore they disposed of the Saviour's in the same manner, dividing them into four parts, giving to the four soldiers who were the executioners, one part each, but his tunic, called a coat, they did not divide, but cast lots for it. This tunic was similar to the one worn by the priests, and consisted of a long vestment without seam, but with openings for the head and hands. It appears that the garment of Jesus, our great High Priest, was similar to that of the Jewish high priest. The Psalmist, referring to this subject, says, "They part my garments among them, and cast lots upon my vesture."

The inscription, signifying the name and offence of the sufferer, being written in three different languages, as before stated, could be read by every one present, even by those who came from different countries to attend the great festival. Two robbers or thieves who had been condemned to die were crucified at the same time, one on the right and the other on the left of the Saviour. When Pilate, who did not reside at Jerusalem, came to the capital on the occasion of the annual festivals he held courts for the trial of criminals, and it is probable these robbers had been tried and condemned at that time. To show contempt for Jesus, he was crucified with them. The four soldiers who had charge of the execution watched him to prevent his friends removing him from the cross.

SUPPER AT EMMAUS.

Some of those who witnessed the execution, tossed their heads in derision, saying: "Thou that destroyest the Temple and buildest it in three days, save thyself. If thou art the Son of God, come down from the cross." The chief priests, scribes and elders who were present said, "He saved others but he cannot save himself," that is, he pretended to save others; they were speaking ironically, "If he is the King of Israel, let him descend from the cross and we will believe him. If he is the Son of God," they said with a sneer, "God will deliver him."

One of the thieves reviled him, saying, "If thou be the Christ, save thyself and us," but the other rebuked him thus: "Do you not fear God, seeing you are condemned? We are justly punished, for we are guilty, but this man has done nothing wrong." He then turned to the Saviour and said, "Lord, remember me when thou comest into thy kingdon." This petition implied that the penitent thief believed that Jesus was the Messiah, and though he was dying, he would eventually set up his kingdom. It is possible the robber had heard the Saviour preach. Jesus replied, "Today thou shalt be with me in paradise," an answer that must have given inexpressible joy to the penitent criminal. It teaches the doctrine that the soul will exist separate from the body, and also the penitent or righteous will be happy immediately after death.

Among the friends of Jesus at his death were the Apostle John, Mary, the mother of the Saviour, Mary, the wife of Cleopas, Mary Magdalene, Mary, the mother of James the Less, and Joses and Salome, besides other women who had accompanied him from Galilee. Most of the women stood at some distance from the cross, perhaps on account of the crowd, though his mother was near. The Saviour seeing her, said to John, "Behold thy mother," and addressing her, said, "Behold thy son," meaning John. This apostle took her to his home and cared for her as if she were his own mother.

Remarkable phenomena were witnessed while Jesus was on the cross. There was darkness over all the land, that is, Judea and perhaps some adjacent countries, from the sixth hour — twelve o'clock, noon — until the ninth hour — three o'clock, afternoon — when the Saviour expired. The darkness could not have been caused by an eclipse of the sun, since the Passover was always celebrated at the time of the full moon when that planet is always opposite the sun. Perhaps the vapor and clouds preceding the earthquake that followed, caused the darkness which could not have been complete since persons at the cross could distinguish one another; it was, however, a remarkable phenomenon, and one of the proofs that Jesus was the Messiah. It is said that a Roman astronomer, named Phlegon, has recorded that in the fourteenth year of the reign of Tiberias, the geatest eclipse of the sun ever known occurred, when on account of the darkness, the stars appeared.

Just before the Saviour expired, he exclaimed, "Eli, Eli," or "Eloi, lama sabachthani?" This was in the Syro-Chaldaic language understood at the time, meaning, "My God, my God, why hast thou forsaken me?" Eli or Eloi was one of the names of Jehovah. This mournful cry of Jesus indicates the most intense suffering, but no created being can fully comprehend the cause for this sense of desertion. His agony was beyond

THE ASCENSION OF CHRIST.

the power of human or even angelic beings to understand. Never was there an exclamation more pathetic, and it is not in the power of language to express the depth of suffering that called forth such a cry. The perfect acquiescence of the Saviour's will with that of his Father, the tender relation between them, the character of the Son, being perfect, the infinite love, mercy and compassion of the Father, all render it incomprehensible that Jesus should have died under a cloud. Most Christians are sustained in the hour of death by a sense of the Divine presence, but it was different with our Lord. In what sense was he forsaken by his Father? It is certain He approved the work of Jesus who had always been an obedient Son, and never, in a single instance, had he been unfilial or indifferent in his devotion to his Father. The only reason for his suffering understood by man is that it was necessary as an atonement for the sins of the human race. Jesus said this was the time for the "power of darkness," when his enemies — Satan and the Jews — were allowed to do their utmost. When Christ was tempted in the wilderness, it was said that Satan departed from him for a season, as if he would make another attempt. Was it possible that he appeared again to incite the enemies of the Saviour at the cross to increase his agony by insults and injuries which led him to feel he was deserted by his Father?

When Jesus cried "Eli," some of the crowd did not understand his language, or pretended they did not, and said, "This man calleth for Elias," that is, Elijah. "Let us see whether Elias will come to save him." This was said in derision. It was the belief among the

Jews, and a doctrine taught by Christ, that Elijah would appear before the coming of the Messiah, which did occur in the person of John the Baptist, his antitype. The Saviour, when on the cross, offered the prayer, "Father, forgive them, for they know not what they do," referring to those who put him to death. The Roman soldiers were only obeying the command of their rulers, and did not know that he was the Son of God, while the Jews knew he was innocent and they had ample proof that he was the Messiah, but they did not know what judgment they were bringing upon their nation.

When the Saviour expired, the vail of the Temple was rent into two parts by a miracle. This vail or curtain separated the Holy from the Most Holy Place, thus dividing the sacred building into two apartments. The Most Holy Place was regarded as a type of heaven, therefore the rending of the vail from top to bottom signified that the way to heaven was open to all who chose to enter, since the Lord Jesus, the Great High Priest, had just entered, where he would appear as the Intercessor for his people. Another remarkable phenomenon occurred when the Saviour died — an earthquake which opened the graves and some of the departed saints arose, and after the resurrection of Christ appeared to others in Jerusalem, and perhaps ascended to heaven to be with their risen Lord.

When the Roman centurion present at the crucifixion witnessed these wonderful scenes, he was surprised and terrified, and declared, "This was the Son of God," or a god, "and he was innocent." The soldiers had heard that Jesus claimed to be the Son of God before Pilate, and seeing these wonders they thought his claim was just. The centurion being a heathen had no distinct idea what the expression "Son of God" implied. He might have thought he was like pagan heroes who had been deified. The original expression, "son of a god," would coincide with polytheistic ideas.

It was a law among the Jews that the bodies of executed criminals should not remain suspended during the night, therefore they requested Pilate to give orders to have their limbs broken in order to hasten their deaths, that they might be removed from the cross before the Sabbath. This was Friday and their Sabbath occurred on Saturday or the seventh day of the week. Pilate having given the order, the soldiers, finding the two thieves alive, executed the governor's command, and broke their legs, but when they came to Jesus, and discovered that he was already dead, they did not attempt it, and thus the Scripture was fulfilled, that "not a bone of his shall be broken"; this primarily referred to the pascal lamb, a symbol of Christ. To make sure that he was dead, however, one of the soldiers pierced the Saviour's side with his spear, which penetrated his heart, whence there issued blood and water. Had he not been already dead, he must have died from this wound. The membrane surrounding the heart contains a fluid resembling water, and this being mingled with the blood from this organ gave rise to the expression, "blood and water." By this act of the Roman soldiers, that prophecy was fulfilled which declares, "They shall look on him whom they pierced."

What shall be done with the body of Christ? The question was settled by Joseph of Arimathea, an honorable man and a Jewish councillor, who believed that Jesus was the Son of God, and was one of his disciples, though secretly from fear of the Jews. He no longer concealed his sentiments, but went boldly to Pilate and asked for the Saviour's remains still on the cross. The apostles had fled through fear, but had any of them asked this favor of the Roman governor, they would probably have been denied, since they had no influence at his court, and their Master would have been buried in the common grave of malefactors. It required great courage in Joseph to ask the favor, and when he presented his request Pilate was surprised that Jesus was so soon dead and called the centurion, and inquired whether it had been any length of time since he died, for generally one suffering on the cross lived several days, from two to seven, not infrequently. When Pilate was satisfied that the Saviour was actually dead, he gave permission to Joseph to take the body, who, after removing it from the cross, wrapped it in fine linen and laid it in a sepulchre designed for himself, hewn out of a rock, but had never been occupied by the remains of any deceased person; this sepulchre was in a garden near Golgotha or Calvary. Before the corpse was entombed, Nicodemus, a member of the Great Council, who came to Jesus to be instructed as previously mentioned, brought a mixture of myrrh and aloes, weighing about one hundred pounds, and placed it about the Saviour's body, a method of embalming among the Jews. After he was placed in the tomb, a large stone was laid at the entrance to close it securely.

The chief priests and Pharisees went to Pilate, saying, "We remember how that Deceiver said while he was alive, 'After three days, I will rise again.' Command, therefore, that the sepulchre be made secure until the third day, lest his disciples come by night and steal him away, and then say to the people, 'He is risen from the dead,' so the last error will be worse than the first." Pilate said, "Ye have a watch, go and make the sepulchre as safe as you can." The Jews were allowed a guard of Roman soldiers, who kept watch in the Tower of Antonia, northwest of the Temple, and there was also a guard that attended the crucifixion. The Pharisees made the sepulchre secure by sealing the stone at the opening, and setting a watch. By impressing it with a seal, they would know whether any one had attempted to roll away the stone, therefore they were sure it was safe.

CHAPTER XXIV.

THE RESURRECTION AND ASCENSION.

On the first day after the close of the Jewish Sabbath, it was discovered by the disciples of the Crucified One that a remarkable phenomenon had occurred. There had been a concussion resembling an earthquake, and an angel had descended from heaven and rolled away the sealed stone from the entrance to the tomb where the body of Christ had lain, and sat upon it. The countenance of this celestial being was "like lightning," using a forcible metaphor, "and his raiment was as white as snow." The guards were so terrified at the sight that they "became as dead men," that is, they fainted or were unconscious. It was then Jesus rose from the grave, consequently was not seen by the soldiers.

The first to visit the tomb of their risen Lord were women, and it was to a woman he first revealed himself after his resurrection. Mary Magdalene came first to the sepulchre, before daylight, when she found the stone taken away from the entrance. She was joined by other women who came to pay respect to their departed Lord, including Mary, the mother of James and Joses, Salome, the mother of the Apostles James and

John, and Joanna, the wife of Herod's steward. They had bought sweet spices the evening before the Sabbath, but waited until the close of the sacred day, when they added more spices to their collection, and at the dawn of the first day of the week started for the sepulchre on their errand of love. It required no little courage to do this, since they were aware the tomb was guarded by armed Roman soldiers, and had been closed by a sealed stone. They conversed about it while on their way, and wondered who would remove it for them to enter, but, to their surprise, when they arrived there they found the stone had been removed, and entering into the sepulchre they were astonished to see two beings, clothed in radiant garments, sitting where the body of Jesus had been laid. They arose, and as the women bowed their faces to the earth, one of the angels said, "Why seek ye the living among the dead? He is not here, but is risen, as he declared he should rise. Come and see the place where he lay, and go quickly and tell his disciples," that is, the apostles, "that he will go before them into Galilee, where they will see him."

The women departed quickly with fear and joy, and ran to carry the news to the disciples. As they were going, Jesus himself met them and said, "All hail!" They came near and, falling down, worshipped him. He said, "Be not afraid, but go and tell my brethren," — he does not say disciples, but addresses them as if they were still dear to him, though they had deserted him in his hour of danger — "that I will meet them in Galilee," — and mentions Peter in particular, as if he wished him to know that he had been forgiven the sin of denying his Master.

When the women, with their unguents prepared to anoint the bandages wrapt about the body of their Lord, came to the sepulchre, it was just as the day began to dawn, therefore objects were seen indistinctly. Not finding him whom they sought, Mary Magdalene was alarmed, supposing he had been stolen, therefore she left the other women and started in haste to go to the city, half a mile distant, to inform the apostles. She found Peter and John, and said to them, "They have taken away my Lord and I know not where they have lain him." By *they* she probably meant some of the friends of Jesus. After she had gone, the other women immediately returned to the city, but by a different road, therefore they did not meet her. When Peter and John heard what Mary told them, they started in haste for the sepulchre, but John, being the swifter runner, left Peter behind and came first to the tomb, but he did not enter, yet stooping down and looking into the sepulchre, he saw the grave-clothes of the Saviour. When Peter arrived, he went in and saw the napkin that had been wrapped about his head folded and laid by itself, indicating there had been no haste. When Mary found the apostles, they were mourning and weeping, but they did not believe their Master had risen from the dead, notwithstanding what he had told them about it. They returned to the city, but Mary Magdalene, whose attachment to her Lord was ardent, remained weeping at his tomb. It was then he appeared to her before he was seen by the other women. She did not at first recognize him, but, supposing him to be the gardener, said, "If he would tell her where the body was, she would take it away." By one word — "Mary" —

gently and tenderly spoken, she knew his voice and said, "Rabboni," signifying Master, and falling at his feet worshipped him.

After the Roman guards recovered from the effect of their terror, some of them returned to the city and informed the chief priests what had occurred. The Sanhedrim immediately assembled, and passed a resolution intended, they supposed, to prevent the people from accepting the report as true, that Christ had risen from the grave. Their plan was to bribe the soldiers "to declare that the disciples of Jesus came and stole his body while they slept, and if the governor should hear of it," said they, "we will conciliate him and save you." The penalty of sleeping when on guard was death. The soldiers accepted the money, and did as they were requested, therefore this falsehood was circulated among the Jews who believed or pretended to believe the rumor. The inconsistency of the statement is apparent, for if the soldiers were asleep, how could they know the disciples had removed the body of their Lord?

Some of the proofs that Jesus rose from the grave have been given as follows: First, He had often foretold his death and resurrection. Second, There was no doubt that he really died; the disciples, the Jews, and the Romans believed it. Third, Every precaution was taken to prevent his body from being removed by stealth; a guard of, perhaps, sixty Roman soldiers had been set to protect the tomb. Fourth, On the third day the body was missing. The high priest did not dare to question that, therefore he attempted to account for it, but there were difficulties to be met. The Roman guard was large, and the penalty for sleeping at their post was death. The disciples were few in number, unarmed and timid. They had just fled before those who came to arrest Jesus in the Garden, besides, how could they know the guard was asleep, even had they planned to steal the body? The order in which the grave-clothes were arranged does not show haste. Jesus appeared many times to his disciples after his resurrection, and under different circumstances. On one occasion, two disciples, one of whom was Cleopas, and the other is supposed to have been Luke, who recorded the event, were walking to Emmaus, a village about seven or eight miles west of Jerusalem. They were conversing about the remarkable events that had just occurred and, perhaps, expressed their disappointment and doubts about Jesus being the Messiah, or that he had risen from the grave. They were joined during their walk by another traveller, whom they supposed a stranger, who inquired what was the subject of their conversation, for they seemed to be sad. Cleopas said, "Are you only a stranger in Jerusalem, and do you not know what has happened lately?" "What things?" the stranger inquired. "Those concerning Jesus of Nazareth, a remarkable prophet, but the chief priests and rulers condemned him to death; he was crucified, and this is the third day since he died. We trusted that he would have redeemed Israel," meaning that he was the Messiah. "Besides, certain women of our company astonished us by saying, that when they came to the sepulchre, they did not find his body, but were told by angels that he was alive and some of the disciples confirmed their testimony."

Still appearing as a stranger, he said, "How slow to

understand what the prophets have said about the Messiah." Then beginning with Moses he expounded the Scriptures that referred to him.

When they arrived at Emmaus, the traveller was going on farther, but they urged him to remain with them, as it was late in the day, and he accepted their invitation. They had been so delighted and instructed by his conversation they wished to hear more of his discourses. As he sat at the table with them he took bread, and after asking a blessing, gave it to them, when "their eyes were opened," speaking in a figure, and they recognized in the stranger their Lord, when he suddenly disappeared before they had recovered from their surprise. They said to each other, " Did not our hearts burn within us as he talked to us by the way?"

Though it was late in the evening, they immediately returned to Jerusalem and informed the apostles, who had gathered in a room by themselves, that the Lord had indeed arisen, and then related what had happened on the way to Emmaus. While they were speaking, Jesus appeared in their midst, though they had closed and barred the door for fear of the Jews. They were frightened when the Saviour appeared, supposing they had seen a spirit. He said, " Why are you afraid and troubled? Behold the wounds in my hands and feet; a spirit hath not flesh and bones, as you see that I have." He then proceeded to give them another proof that he was the same person who had been crucified and had arisen from the grave, by eating with them. He expounded more clearly the prophecies concerning his death and resurrection, and told them it was necessary that Christ should suffer and rise from the grave, and that the doctrine of repentance should be preached among all nations. He said they were witnesses of his life and teachings, and that he would fulfil the promise to aid them by the Holy Spirit, but they must remain at Jerusalem until they were endowed with power from on high. Thomas, one of the apostles, was not present when Jesus appeared to them, but they told him they had seen the Lord. He replied, "Except I see the wounds in his hands and side, I will not believe that he is alive." Eight days after, the apostles had again assembled and Thomas was with them, the doors being closed as before, when Jesus appeared and said, "Peace be with you." Then addressing Thomas, he told him to look at his hands, feet and side, and see the print of the nails and the wounds inflicted by the soldiers, and be not faithless, but believing. The doubting apostle exclaimed, "My Lord and my God!" "Because you have seen, you believe," said Jesus, "blessed are they who, though not seeing, yet believe."

The Saviour had promised to meet the apostles in Galilee, which occurred on this wise: Many of them had been fishermen, and they decided to resume their former occupation, as they must labor for a support. While waiting in Galilee for the appearance of their Master, Peter said, "I am going a fishing." Thomas, Nathaniel, James and John, with two others, said, "We will go with you," therefore they entered a boat which was anchored on the bank of the Sea of Tiberias, and rowed from the shore. This was early in the evening, and though they toiled all night, they did not succeed in catching any fish. When morning dawned they saw in the dim light a man standing on the bank, whom

THE RESURRECTION AND ASCENSION.

they did not recognize at first, but soon after, John exclaimed, "It is the Lord!" They hastily started for the shore. Peter departed by swimming, and the others in their boat, to meet their Master, who gave them bread and fish to eat, when he asked Peter the question, "Lovest thou me?" three times, and told him what his future would be. This interview is related in one of the chapters on the Miracles of Christ.

On another occasion when Jesus appeared to his disciples, they inquired whether he would restore again the kingdom to Israel. He replied that was not a subject for them to know, but they should receive power from heaven, and become his witnesses by preaching the gospel in Judea, Samaria and other parts of the world, beginning at Jerusalem. When he had uttered these words he led them to Bethany, and as they watched him he entered into a cloud and disappeared from their sight. While they were gazing with astonishment two celestial beings, clothed in white, appeared to them, and said, "Ye men of Galilee, why do you stand gazing into heaven? Jesus, who ascended thither, will return in like manner."

The Saviour, having fulfilled his mission on earth, and having given proof of his resurrection, was taken bodily to heaven forty days after his death, from the Mount of Olives, near Bethany, in the presence of eleven apostles, to appear as the High Priest of his people until his return to judge the nations at the end of the world. He had remained forty days after his resurrection to afford proof of that event, and to instruct more fully the apostles in regard to their mission and the declaration of the Scriptures concerning himself.

The proofs of his ascension were sufficient to establish the fact. The apostles witnessed it; multitudes of angels attended him with shouts of praise; the descent of the Holy Spirit confirmed it; Stephen, John and Paul saw him after he ascended. By this act Christ appears as King and Priest of his redeemed, has opened the way to heaven more clearly, and has proved more definitely that after their resurrection the bodies of the saints would ascend to heaven. The phrase "spiritual body" has been defined, as applied to the saints in glory, one of material elements, but perfectly adjusted to the use of the spirit: such was the body of our Lord after his resurrection, and with which he ascended. The redeemed after death, it has been supposed, are not disembodied spirits until after the resurrection, but they have a temporary body until that event, and with such they sometimes appeared to persons on earth. Jesus, as the incarnate Son of God, our Intercessor, is still the same as when on earth, in every essential quality. His ascension was an entrance upon a new sphere of activity for the salvation of men, and his work will continue until the kingdoms of the earth become, in a spiritual sense, his kingdoms.

As recorded in the Scriptures, Christ appeared after his resurrection on the following occasions: First, To Mary Magdalene. Second, To other women, namely, Mary, the mother of James and Joses, to Salome and Joanna. Third, To Peter. Fourth, Two disciples on the way to Emmaus. Fifth, The apostles when Thomas was absent. Sixth, The apostles when Thomas was present. Seventh, The apostles Peter, Thomas, Nathaniel, James and two others, at the Sea of Tiberias.

Eighth, The apostles on a mountain in Galilee. Ninth, The apostles at his ascension from Bethany. As stated by Paul, he appeared to him and to more than five hundred disciples on a certain occasion.

Some of the names and titles applied to the Saviour in the Sacred Scriptures are the following:

Jesus, same as Joshua, or one who sees; Christ, or the Annointed One, a Greek word; Messiah, a Hebrew name meaning king, prophet, priest; Emmanuel, or God with us; Son of God; Son of Man; God; Jehovah; King; Branch of Righteousness; The Lord our Righteousness; The Creator; The Beginning; The Life; The Word; The Man; The Child; The Prophet; The Saviour; The Lamb; The Shepherd; The Bridegroom; The Tree of Life; The Branch; The Vine; The Bread of Life; The Light of the World; The Sun; The Day Star; The Servant; The Rock; The Hope of Glory; The Beloved; The Elect; The Truth; Faithful Witness; Holy One; First Born; Redeemer; The Resurrection; Captain; Prince of Peace; Judge; Refuge; Strength, and others.

The prophecies concerning Christ were proofs that he was the Messiah. The condition of the world at the time of his advent confirmed it, and prepared the way for such an event. The Jews were subject to a powerful nation, though, to a considerable extent, they were governed by their own laws, administered by the Great Council. The other tribes were dispersed, but "the scepter had not departed from Judah," and the Temple was then in its glory. The predictions concerning the family of Jesus, the place of his birth, and his home at Nazareth had been quite definite. A census ordered by Cæsar made it necessary for Joseph and Mary to go to Bethlehem to be registered, hence the prediction about the native place of the Saviour was fulfilled. The tragical events connected with his death had been foretold, such as his betrayal for thirty pieces of silver, his scourging and insults, his pierced hands and side, the vinegar and the gall, the division of his raiment and casting lots for his vesture, the manner of his death, his burial, resurrection and ascension to heaven.

The Saviour's poverty and humble condition in life, his public career, teaching and miracles were positive evidences that he was the Messiah.

The proofs of the Divinity of Christ are positive. The same names and titles are applied to him that are given the Father, which, had he been only human, would have been profanely preposterous. The Jews understood that Jesus claimed to be Divine, therefore they called him a blasphemer, and on this ground condemned him to death. The perfection of his character, and his miraculous powers were such as only belong to the Supreme Being. All things were created by Christ and "he upheld all things by his power"; he is the Saviour of sinners, therefore has the power to forgive sins, he will raise the dead and judge the world, and the angels of God are commanded to worship him. Baptism is performed in his name jointly with those of the Father and the Spirit. The soul is committed to him in death, as in the case of Stephen the Martyr, while most Christians worship him as a Divine Being, hence, if he is not, they are idolators. Though Jesus is Divine, he was also human, otherwise he could not have suffered death for the redemption of the human race.

THE RESURRECTION AND ASCENSION.

Jesus in his earthly life was pre-eminent for his devotional habits. When in the wilderness forty days, he doubtless spent most of the time in meditation and prayer and on other occasions he withdrew from the multitude to desert places, for the purpose of prayer and communion with his Father. During his walk to Gethsemane, he offered his memorable prayer and he sought relief during his inexpressible anguish in the Garden by prayer. His last prayer was for his enemies, when he was on the cross. Our Lord often enjoined upon his followers the duty of prayer and watchfulness.

Christ, it has truthfully been affirmed, "was not only a preacher of the gospel, a teacher and a performer of miracles, but he was also a poet." "True poetry," it is said, "consists of great, forceful and beautiful thoughts expressed either in verse or prose," and some of the most genuine poetry is in the form of the latter. Much of the power of the Scriptures depends upon their poetry. It has been said of Jesus, that he may be called the "Infinite Poet in the grandeur of his conceptions, the sublime heights of his moral scope, and the profound depths of his expression. He became the Divine Mystery, the Wonder of the Universe, the one Eternal Poet of Heaven and Earth. His greatness is seen in his imagery." He employed many different objects and scenes for illustration, such as are found in Nature, including the animal kingdom, and sometimes he even refers to angelic beings for the same purpose.

All the moral aims and objects of poetry are fully exhibited by the Saviour. Some of the examples of his poetical nature are the following, as related by a writer on the subject: "'Consider the lilies of the field, how they grow. They toil not, neither do they spin and yet even Solomon was not arrayed like one of these.' The imagination is guided to the Saviour's early home, when his mother, perhaps, was engaged in spinning, and thence to the glory and luxury of Israel's sumptuous king who lived many centuries before. The immortal Bard refers to the servants ploughing and feeding cattle, to the sower scattering seed, the cockles and darnel mixed with wheat, the angel reaper, the hen gathering her brood, the fox with his hole in the thicket, the birds building their nests, the shepherd seeking the lost lamb, the toiling fishermen casting their nets, the travelling merchant seeking pearls, the costly robes of the wealthy, and the ravens without store-house or barn fed by the Creator's hand.

"Love for children was a prominent trait in his character, and also reverence for woman, whom he treated with a respect and tenderness she had never known before. Sympathy for the suffering and compassion for the erring were very conspicuous traits in his character, while his love of Nature was unsurpassed. For him the winds were voices, the skies frowned, the flowers and waves of the sea afforded emblems, and even beggars by the wayside and highway robbers were employed as figures of speech to enforce his teaching. He uses some isolated word and gives it a poetical dress: as, for example, grain signifies grace; the moon, blood; the stars, ripe figs; anguish, a worm that gnaws; and fire denotes great suffering. Men are compared to sheep, disciples are stewards and branches, conversion is a marriage, the world is a vineyard, the church a fold, heaven, our Father's home."

There was a shade of sadness pervading the teachings of the Saviour, especially when he refers to the destruction of Jerusalem, and on other occasions, which led him to weep. The condition of the masses who were like sheep without a shepherd, and the hardness and unbelief of his countrymen, often moved him to tears. It is not in the power of the human mind to comprehend fully a character so comprehensive, complete and exalted, yet so meek, tender, loving, sympathetic and forgiving, so instructive in his teachings, and attractive in manner. No one of his biographers has ever been able to do this, for the reason he was Divine as well as human.